FAR AND WIDE

BRING THAT HORIZON TO ME!

NEIL PEART

ECW Press

Cover design: Hugh Syme
Text design: Tania Craan
Editorial assistance by Danny Peart and Mike Heppner
Editor for the press: Jennifer Knoch
Producer: Jack David
Photographic supervision: Craig M. Renwick
All unattributed photos courtesy Neil Peart.
Proofreader: Crissy Calhoun
Type: Troy Cunningham

Maps on pages 208 and 237 used with permission of Rand McNally.

All Rush lyrics reproduced and reprinted courtesy of ole.

Published by ECW Press
665 Gerrard Street East
Toronto, Ontario, Canada M4M 1Y2
416-694-3348 | info@ecwpress.com

Library and Archives Canada
Cataloguing in Publication

Peart, Neil, author
Far and wide : bring that horizon to me! / Neil Peart.

Issued in print and electronic formats.
ISBN 978-1-77041-441-9 (paperback)
978-1-77041-348-1 (hardback)
978-1-77041-366-5 (special edition)
978-1-77090-894-9 (PDF)
978-1-77090-893-2 (ePUB)

1. Peart, Neil–Travel. 2. Motorcycling–North America. 3. Drummers (Musicians)–Canada–Biography. 4. Lyricists–Canada–Biography. 5. Rush (Musical group).

I. Title.

ML419.P362A3 2018   786.9'166092
C2017-906606-4

Every effort has been made to trace copyright holders and obtain their permission for use of copyright material. The publisher would be grateful if notified of any errors or omissions.

The publication of *Far and Wide* has been generously supported by the Canada Council for the Arts, which last year invested $153 million to bring the arts to Canadians throughout the country, and by the Government of Canada through the Canada Book Fund. *Nous remercions le Conseil des arts du Canada de son soutien. L'an dernier, le Conseil a investi 153 millions de dollars pour mettre de l'art dans la vie des Canadiennes et des Canadiens de tout le pays. Ce livre est financé en partie par le gouvernement du Canada.* We also acknowledge the support of the Ontario Arts Council (OAC), an agency of the Government of Ontario, which last year funded 1,737 individual artists and 1,095 organizations in 223 communities across Ontario for a total of $52.1 million, and the contribution of the Government of Ontario through the Ontario Media Development Corporation.

Canadä

PRINTED AND BOUND IN CHINA

Casebound: 5 4
Paperback: 5 4 3

To All the Listeners and Readers
Who Have Made This Book,
and This Life,
Possible

And to the Guys at Work—
Ditto . . .

PHOTO BY CRAIG M. RENWICK

Table of Contents

"*The truth is of course that there is no journey.*
We are arriving and departing all at the same time."

David Bowie (1947-2016)

"*You gotta be true to your sixteen-year-old self.*"

Lesley Gore (1946-2015)

THIRTY-FIVE CONCERTS. 17,000 MOTORCYCLE MILES. THREE MONTHS. ONE LIFETIME.

"Begin as you mean to go on" is an old English expression that comments amusingly on this photograph. I am poised to go onstage to start the second set of a show on the Rush fortieth anniversary tour, R40, in the summer of 2015. The glowing lights at my waist are the radio pack that drives my in-ear monitors, which will fill my head with musical information and consume my "interior world" for the next ninety minutes or so. The blazing lights ahead of me are an arena filled with something like ten thousand people. The heat and light of their joyous excitement is an utter contrast to my cold fire of determination and will—as it should be. It is my job to reward their anticipation—to be all they expect and more.

Beginning as I would go on, my energy is tightly coiled in anticipation of that challenge before me. Even the first song in that second set,

"Tom Sawyer," remained a mental and physical ordeal after thirty-five years and thousands of performances. In the reverse-chronology setlist we followed for that tour, each song led back in time, album to album, year to year. Thus I would have to replicate drum parts conceived and executed when I was a *child*—barely into my twenties. As a harsh-but-fair critic (like myself) might describe how I played the drums back then: "More energy than skill; more ideas than technique; more influences than originality; more enthusiasm than accuracy." Since then, with the benefit of many years of practice, dedication, and the guidance of three phenomenal teachers—Don George, Freddie Gruber, and Peter Erskine—I have balanced those scales a little, at least.

And at almost sixty-three years of age, I was glad I could still *do* all that—bring the energy and enthusiasm of my twenties to the somewhat improved technique and accuracy of maturity. But . . . it was a battle—a battle against *time*, in more than one sense.

Another edge to that waiting-offstage mindset was a visceral awareness that so much can go wrong, human and technical, in one's immediate future. And in front of a *lot* of people. Performers of every kind might define their audience as "strangers with expectations." During the uncertain heat of live performance, I fear human errors, and I fear electronic letdowns. As much as ever in my life, I want every show to be *good*, but can never be sure, or even confident, that it will be. In that pre-show mindset, I almost sympathize with athletes who pray before a game, or Grammy winners who thank "the Creator" for giving them a trophy. (A friend's Jewish grandmother once said, "What do you get when you get old? A *trophy*!" She meant "atrophy.")

So when the houselights go down and I dash through that curtain and up the stairs to the stage, I am tense with focus and uncertainty—though equally focused on not *displaying* tension or uncertainty.

People sometimes say things like, "You look so relaxed when

Bubba Ponders
PHOTO BY CRAIG M. RENWICK

you're playing the drums—so in command." I can only laugh and say, "Well, I sure wish it *felt* that way!"

"Begin as you mean to go on" can also refer to my intention to take a cue from the *R40* tour's reverse-chronology setlist, and open this story with the final show. If I am going to try to tell something about a forty-one-year relationship with Alex and Geddy, and a separate relationship with the music we have made together over those decades, it will be necessary to do some leaping about in time. So why not start at the Los Angeles Forum on August 1, 2015, the final show of the *R40* tour . . .

We had played in that building many times (twenty-four, according to a plaque on the wall there—so now twenty-five), but the last time had been two nights on the *Test for Echo* tour, in late 1996. After that the building's ownership had fluctuated for a while: it was one of the first to bear a corporate name (such shall be nameless here—fight the power, fight the branding), then was owned by a church for several years. For complicated and tragic reasons, we did not return to perform again in Los Angeles until 2002, and that time we tried playing at the new mega-arena, named after a chain of business-supply stores. We didn't like that cavernous space, but later enjoyed playing the Hollywood Bowl and Universal Amphitheater (now demolished for a Harry Potter–themed ride at the adjacent amusement park) a few times, and last tour at the Finnish Telecommunications Company Theater downtown.

Before the *Time Machine* tour in 2010 we had planned to do our production rehearsals and first show at the Forum, but there were worrisome rumors of imminent bankruptcy—and the possibility of our equipment being impounded inside. So we set up our production and rehearsed in a film studio soundstage instead, the old Paramount Studios (now Sony) in Culver City.

On the next page we see double-nought spy Bubba (my longtime nickname among many friends, first applied by Andrew MacNaughtan, our late photographer, assistant, and friend, who also introduced me to my wife, Carrie, in 1999) and my Aston Martin DB5 in front of the Garbo Building. (Greta Garbo is mentioned in one of the Bond books, maybe *From Russia, With Love*, when the face of one of the "Bond girls" is compared to Garbo's.)

The Los Angeles Forum was developed by a Canadian entrepreneur, Jack Kent Cooke, who was born in Hamilton, Ontario, almost exactly forty years before I first drew breath in that same town. (The nearest hospital to our family dairy farm near Hagersville.)

Before Rehearsals
at Sony Studios, 2010
PHOTO BY CRAIG M. RENWICK

The Forum was built in Canada's centennial year, 1967, the same year the old Philadelphia Spectrum went up—two buildings that always felt alike to me in our early days. There was something about those two venues—I don't think we ever had a bad show in them. They were small enough (considered as *arenas*) to sound good when they were full of people; the audiences were energetic and enthusiastic, and we always seemed to play well.

Another connection—in the 1980s I rode my bicycle to both of those venues several times, and remembered the neighborhoods on the way. From Philly's venerable downtown through ritzy/quaint Rittenhouse Square, then through streets of tidy working-class row houses down into military housing farther south. In Los Angeles, pedaling downhill from West Hollywood on La Cienega past commercial districts, body shops, and bungalows with iron grilles over doors and

Soloing
PHOTO BY CRAIG M. RENWICK

windows. Then up and over a bleak hill with nodding oil wells—one of many oilfields under the city—and down to Inglewood, which was said to be "dangerous." That was never a problem on a bicycle—in Harlem; downtown Detroit; the East End of London; or Inglewood, California, I was always seen as a harmless crank.

This time (everything so different now that I *live* in Los Angeles) I took a car. With a driver. For there would be another party after this show, naturally enough—but it was the third party that week. That was about three years' worth of parties for this Bubba. But it had to be borne, obviously. Just added to the pressure I was under.

To me, first, twentieth, or last show, this was still "just a show." Or, more accurately, it was just *still a show*. Meaning I felt no sense of lightness, relief, or "doneness." Not yet. There was still a long, hard, and always uncertain job to do.

A few days earlier, friend Stewart Copeland had emailed me:

> You had better jam your hat on tight next Saturday because me and every other drummer in town will be coming down for a last chance to cop your licks at the Forum show.
>
> Can't wait! I know it will be legendary and the bards will sing of it for generations. I'm polishing up my air drumsticks even now . . .

That was very sweet of him—"the praise of the praiseworthy" from a man and drummer I had long admired. I wrote back to him:

> On the bus outta Phoenix, heading for a Château Walmart in Pasadena, where we'll park for the last hour or two, then have breakfast and unload the motorcycles and ride—
>
> Home!
>
> In regard to your message, all's I can say is, *Gulp.*
>
> You know—it's only the last show of the last tour, and with all the "Judges" in attendance.
>
> Well, I'll just do what I do every night—try not to suck!

Stewart's reply was classic:

> Laaaast show?! I had better get a Late Nite permit.
>
> And please do, for all the children, suck just a little bit.

Well, of course I *did* suck just a little bit, here and there—human after all—but mainly played pretty well. No egregious errors, all of us made it to the end of "Monkey Business" together (a part that had plagued us during that third run of shows), and I was pleased enough with the final statement of my solo's odyssey. Its improvised narrative had grown throughout the tour, but as with everything else, I could never be *sure* it was going to "work." Stewart, Chad Smith, Taylor Hawkins, Doane Perry, and probably a few other drummers were in the house—and many other friends and family, including wife Carrie and five-year-old daughter Olivia.

That night violinist Jonny Dinklage, veteran of the previous tour's Clockwork Angels String Ensemble, joined us once more for "Losing It," as he had for two shows in the New York area. Recorded in 1982 for our *Signals* album, it was performed live for the first time this tour, but only a handful of times—including with original violin soloist on the record, Ben Mink, in Toronto and Vancouver. (A young Jonathan

Dinklage, growing up in New Jersey, heard that recording and was inspired to play violin.)

After playing that song with Ben a couple of times at soundcheck in Toronto, he remarked to me that he never paid much attention to lyrics, but that this song really resonated for him now. I think all of us must have felt that, in our own ways.

In the song's two verses, an aging dancer and writer face their diminishing, twilight talents. The dancer was inspired by a character in the movie *The Turning Point*, while the writer was Ernest Hemingway. Just before his suicide in 1961 he spent days staring at a blank piece of paper in his typewriter. He was trying to compose a few lines, a simple "regretful decline" to an invitation to the Kennedy White House. When he couldn't even do that, he got out the shotgun. ("The sun will rise no more" comes from Hemingway's first big novel, *The Sun Also Rises*.)

> *The dancer slows her frantic pace*
> *In pain and desperation*
> *Her aching limbs and downcast face*
> *Aglow with perspiration*
> *Stiff as wire, her lungs on fire*
> *With just the briefest pause*
> *Then flooding through her memory*
> *The echoes of old applause*
>
> *She limps across the floor*
> *And closes her bedroom door*
>
> *The writer stares with glassy eyes*
> *Defies the empty page*
> *His beard is white, his face is lined*
> *And streaked with tears of rage*
> *Thirty years ago, how the words would flow*
> *With passion and precision*
> *But now his mind is dark and dulled*
> *By sickness and indecision*
>
> *And he stares out the kitchen door*
> *Where the sun will rise no more*

After fifty years of devotion to hitting things with sticks, I would rather avoid any sense of "losing it" by simply *setting it aside* and moving onto other interests. You have to know when you're at the top of your particular mountain, I guess. Maybe not the summit, but as high as *you* can go.

In relation to both summits and Ernest Hemingway's story "The Snows of Kilimanjaro," in September 1987, right around my thirty-fifth birthday, I joined a five-day hike up and down Africa's highest mountain, Kilimanjaro. At 19,341 feet, I stood at Uhuru (Freedom) Peak with two of the guides and a German university student, Dieter, while an English student, Domenick, took the photo. Domenick also

Uhuru Peak, September 1987
PHOTO BY DOMENICK

contributed the bottle of whisky in the foreground, with which we all toasted our achievement.

Since then I have climbed many other mountains, often more for the view than the physical challenge, but have never felt drawn to take on, say, Annapurna or Everest. Kilimanjaro was the highest summit I ever needed to reach.

One major reality is that my style of drumming is largely an athletic undertaking, and it does not pain me to realize that, like all athletes, there comes a time to . . . take yourself out of the game. I would much rather set it aside than face the fate described in "Losing It."

Because I am *keeping* it, baby! No regrets here; I feel proud, grateful, and satisfied with what I have accomplished with two lumps of wood. My late teacher Freddie Gruber was friends with Buddy Rich for decades, and told many tales about the famously acerbic master. (Other drummers have played certain styles better, naturally, but no one has ever matched Buddy's hands and feet.) Buddy once pointed to the drumsticks in Freddie's hands and said, "Just remember, dummy—those two lumps of wood have kept you out of the electric chair, and out of working at the corner gas station!"

Late in his life, Buddy Rich was asked if he considered himself the world's greatest drummer, and he gave an inspiring reply: "Let's put it this way: I have that ambition. You don't really attain greatness. You attain a certain amount of *goodness*, and if you're serious about your goodness, you'll keep trying to be great. I have never reached a point in my career where I was totally satisfied with anything I've ever done, but I keep trying."

Warm-up at the Forum
PHOTO BY CRAIG M. RENWICK

Among my reading on the *R40* tour, on the bus and in motel rooms, was a biography of Buddy Rich's one-time employer Artie Shaw. A celebrated clarinetist (he called Benny Goodman "the competition") and charismatic big-band leader, Artie Shaw famously gave up playing at age forty-four. The book by Tom Nolan is called *Three Chords for Beauty's Sake*—from one of Artie Shaw's favorite phrases: "Three chords for beauty's sake, and one chord to pay the rent." Another quote of Shaw's I heard years ago was enough to make me curious about him: "I could never understand why they had to *dance* to my music. I made it good enough to listen to." Late in life, he summed up the arc of his career like this: "Had to be better, better, better. It always could be better . . . When I quit, it was because I knew I couldn't do any better."

Of course I wouldn't rate my own decision, or my limited mastery of my instrument, in a class with a brilliant musician like Artie Shaw. (Even now I hear the poignant strains of "Begin the Beguine" in my inner radio—the way he could bend notes on that clarinet.) After he quit, what Artie Shaw wanted to do was . . . write prose. And like Buddy Rich, Shaw had a quick and cutting wit. Toward the end of his life, his caregiver once asked him, "Mr. Shaw—are you comfortable?" After a perfect beat, the old man gave a rueful shrug, "*Eh—I make a living.*"

Prose writing offers another profound insight from one of my idols in creative non-fiction, John McPhee. He wrote, "People often ask how I know when I'm done—not just when I've come to the end, but in

A "Bow"–for Jonny
PHOTO BY CRAIG M. RENWICK

all the drafts and revisions and substitutions of one word for another how do I know there is no more to do? When am I done? I just know. I'm lucky that way. What I know is that I can't do any better; someone else might do better, but that's all I can do; so I call it done."

All of which goes to explain that this show felt like a journey's end, at least to me, so when Alex, Geddy, Jonny, and I played "Losing It" at the Los Angeles Forum on August 1, 2015, the song carried just a little more meaning for me, and perhaps for many others. As Jonny walked offstage beside my drum riser, I stood and gave him a "bow."

That I could feel *good* about this occasion—well, I can only compare it to the way I feel at the end of a long motorcycle journey. I don't regret that the ride has to be over, but rather feel grateful for the miles I have traveled, for the sights along the way, and to be exactly where I am.

PHOTO BY MICHAEL MOSBACH

Urban Art Installation

NOW–AND WAY BACK WHEN

That phrase I opened this book with, "Begin as you mean to go on," echoes through my life and work, as I guess it does for most everybody. In childhood I began with curiosity and a restless yearning to wander, and so I have gone on—now into my seventh decade. And even here and now, beginning as I mean to go on, I will ramble around the scenery with curiosity and restless yearning and report what I see. (I was delighted to learn the French have a literary term for such an approach. Thus I am not just a wandering loafer, oh no—*je suis un flâneur*.)

The title of the Introduction, "Thirty-Five Concerts. 17,000 Motorcycle Miles. Three Months. One Lifetime," was inspired by billboards advertising new movies and TV shows—high and prominent scenic attractions around my urban writing retreat. Located in what my letterhead terms "The Mean Streets of Midtown Los Angeles," my sanctuary, the Hallowed Bubba Cave, is a small cinder-block commercial building. The interior is painted white and raftered in bare wood and skylights. A row of six sports cars from the 1960s gleams under the skylights across one side, a historical array spanning Aston Martin, Jaguar, Corvette, Maserati, and Lamborghini.

Talk about "begin as you mean to go on," this baby picture foreshadows a lifetime of adventures behind the wheel—and behind the handlebars.

PHOTO BY GLEN PEART

On a whim that grew over time, all of my old cars are silver, and I call them the Silver Surfers because most of their driving is on the Pacific Coast Highway. Cruising north or south, I glance west over the ocean, passing the wet-suited kahunas riding the waves, and sometimes dolphins and pelicans. Farther out, enormous container ships lumber darkly across the horizon like vast unmoored buildings.

Opposite the row of cars, my desk sits in a bright alcove, with a cozy sitting area for relaxed lunches with visiting friends. In the middle of a solitary writing day, a brief interval of brotherhood and laughter is welcome.

My building is delightfully situated on a narrow sidestreet in a gritty neighborhood of auto repair shops and "gentlemen's clubs." Famed twentieth-century journalist H.L. Mencken, "The Sage of Baltimore," named the performers in such establishments "ecdysiasts," after the ancient Greek word for a snake shedding its skin. Canadian males of a certain class used to call them "peelers," with more obvious derivation. When I drive home from the Cave in late afternoon I sometimes see the girls—tall, slender, elaborately maned—arriving for work, handing over their Range Rovers and BMWs to the bouncers. So I guess they do all right. A girl's gotta eat. Not much in career prospects maybe, but if it's all they have—the dancers *and* the gentlemen—then bless 'em.

Same with the street people, poor mad souls. Sometimes I see them sprawled on a cardboard bed on the shady side of the street, while others assemble more ambitious dwellings on the sidewalk under the freeway. Ramshackle arrangements of soiled cardboard, plastic tarps, and carpet scraps are draped over the inevitable grocery

The Creative Corner

carts and junk furniture. After a week or two I might see a pair of police officers gently confronting the squatter, and next morning the warped expression of natural instincts for home and possessions will be cleared away. When I pass one such abode and find the builder awake, I pass him a folded piece of paper with a dead president on it. If I see a poor mad-eyed female shuffling by, or living in a place like that, my chivalrous heart aches and I am even more eager to help them. Because who could mistake their illness and misfortune for "laziness"?

Late one afternoon as I was about to drive home, I encountered a bizarre trio hanging by the Dumpster outside my gate. Not menacing, I didn't think—they seemed at ease where they were, with nowhere better to be. An African-American woman's lined face and sagging figure contradicted her youthful getup of cutoff denim short-shorts,

1964 Jaguar E-Type,
Big Sur Lighthouse

leopard print sleeveless top, and an unfortunate attempt at "blonde-ness" on her wild hair, like a hacked-up ball of yarn.

One could guess her profession had once involved "gentlemen" in the earlier sense, but her chemical indulgences had compromised even that. She stood on the sidewalk with two scrawny little white guys, scruffy and threadbare, with vacant yet friendly smiles. As with the woman, their ages could not be guessed—anywhere from thirty to fifty. Their years had been hard.

All of them turned to smile at me with cracked and stained teeth, pointing at my sleek and shiny Jaguar (described in its day by Enzo Ferrari himself as "the most beautiful car in the world") with obvious admiration. As I opened the narrow door and climbed out to close the gate, the woman said something I couldn't hear, so I walked closer.

She repeated, "You wouldn't happen to have anything *snortable*, would you?" (With the inevitable finger upside her nose.) "Something to make the day a little more . . ." she beamed a yellow smile ". . . *beautiful?*"

I smiled back with my palms outstretched and said, "I *wish!*" and heard a chorus of laughter.

Then to my new friends, with a smile and a dismissive wave, I said, "I'm too *old* for that stuff!" After a beat, I added, "It's okay for you *young* people!"

They hooted at that. I gave the woman a folded note and said, "Maybe this will help." Next morning they were gone, and I saw an empty bottle of cheap vodka and an empty pack of Pall Malls near the Dumpster. So I guess they found *some* way to make their day a little more . . . beautiful.

Bless 'em all.

In a similar spirit of making my own day more beautiful, one blazing afternoon I set out for a walk. As perfect as the Hallowed Bubba Cave is, sometimes it is refreshing to get outdoors. As my mother used to say when I was a kid, "Just go outside—it'll blow the stink off ya!" I also wanted to reward myself with a cheeseburger and a milkshake from a local joint, because I had just finished the first draft of this book. It had been a fairly urgent effort to get down all the "forgettable" details before they slipped from memory. As legendary editor Maxwell Perkins (F. Scott Fitzgerald, Ernest Hemingway, Thomas Wolfe) advised, "Don't get it right, get it *down*."

Bride World ("Bride" on right)

The getting it "right," the smoothing out and orchestrating, would take another few months. But I enjoy that kind of carpentry day after day, mingled with the diversions of "real life." The care taken in that work always has a clear aim—to help the reader *follow along*, in every sense. "Hard writing makes easy reading," as Wallace Stegner put it.

That day I walked out into my "mean streets" wearing appropriate hiking boots for the cracked and heaved pavement. Low, rough-hewn structures of crude masonry and corrugated metal sheltered behind iron gates topped with slashes of barbed wire or the forbidding coils of fanged razor wire. Any exposed surfaces were tattooed with bold, colorful scrawls of graffiti, which also decorated the weathered sides of old campers parked at the curb—the "gypsy RVs," as I thought of them. Following some arcane knowledge of city codes (I like to think of secret signs, like the hobos had in the 1930s—a whole guidance system they shared with one another), these battered machines migrate among certain backstreets and park for a few days. Sometimes they even run a little gas generator on the sidewalk outside, but I almost never see the residents. One day they are mysteriously gone, presumably having circulated to another louche neighborhood.

Above all our mortal coils of graffiti and loucheness, towering billboards looked down on the gridlocked drivers on nearby commuter streets. The ads for new movies and TV shows were punched up with strong graphics and pithy blurbs, like, ONE HOT DUDE. ONE HOT BABE. SEXY CHASE SCENES. PASSIONATE EXPLOSIONS.

The photo collage below was created by Greg Russell, combining riding partner Michael's images of me riding my motorcycle through a snowy landscape, waiting to go onstage, and drawing a route for the following day's travels. Picturing this combination of images as a huge movie billboard (ah, sweet dream! If only such a movie could be made without cameras intruding like so many eyes of Heisenberg—a futuristic notion of a film made from pure *memory*!), I imagined my own blurb under it. It sounds nice, rhythmically, looks good typographically, and the truth of it—well, that lies ahead.

Begin as you mean to go on—from the very beginning . . .

Literary Graffiti

Misfit Gypsy
Motorcycle Drumhead
PHOTOGRAPHS BY
MICHAEL MOSBACH

At the age of twelve, in 1964, I decided to be a drummer, wanting to emulate Gene Krupa. The 1959 movie *The Gene Krupa Story* made being a drummer seem exciting, glamorous, and dangerous. "That's what I want," I thought—not yet even *considering* that I might someday "make several dollars just playing the drums," or even "dazzle the chicks!" For me, though, it was not going to happen "in NO TIME."

For my thirteenth birthday Mom and Dad gave me drum lessons, a pair of sticks, and a practice pad. They said if I stuck to the lessons and practiced for a year, they would think about buying me drums. (The advice I still give to parents whose children say they want drums.) Not having real drums that first year at least exercised my imagination, for I would array magazines across my bed in the layout of Gene Krupa's drums, or later Keith Moon's, and beat the covers off them. I sat on a stool in front of a mirror and waved my sticks around—like the maniac I dreamed of becoming . . .

The next year Mom and Dad got me a three-piece set of Stewarts ($150) in red sparkle. Bass drum, snare drum, one tom, and one small (clanky) cymbal. Soon a cheap high-hat joined the "trap set" (from "contraption," dating to the silent-movie days when the pit drummers would have a wide range of percussion for sound effects).

That first day my shiny red jewels were set up in the living room, and over and over thereafter, I proudly played my two songs, "Wipe Out" and "Land of a Thousand Dances" (a local band, the British Modbeats—their eight-by-ten glossy hangs on the wall in the color photo—played a cover of the latter with a cool drum part). Then I moved the drums piece by piece upstairs to my room, and every afternoon after school played along with the pink spackle AM radio on

Red Sparkle Stewarts, 1966
PHOTO BY BETTY PEART

the steam radiator beside me. Whatever song came on the Top 40 station, I tried to play along.

Next Mom and Dad got me a floor tom, and I saved up paper-route and lawn-mowing money for a pair of Ajax cymbals (still clanky, but bigger!) and stands. And still I played along with the radio, to the hits of 1965, '66, and—look out, big changes ahead!—1967.

A few things I notice now in this photo of my teenage self (I had been sick in bed, hence the pajama bottoms, which add nicely to the op-art striped theme): the tight, round wear-spot on the snare head's sweet spot—working on good accurate technique even then. Like my unruly bangs, the cymbals way up high were a style of the times. The even-cheaper non-matching bass drum was a foolish trade with a school friend, but it was the desirable eighteen-inch diameter. Again, style over substance, like a callow youth of fourteen-and-a-half.

Age Fourteen-and-a-half, 1967
PHOTO BY GLEN PEART

The old-car wallpaper and the Corvette poster (a project for school) signified a boyhood infatuation with cars that would be eclipsed by drums for a while. Later I came back around to cars, and today that 1963 Corvette Sting Ray "split-window coupe" I so admired is a prized trophy in my Silver Surfers collection. The Sting Ray also starred on the cover of the 2014 Bubba's Bar 'n' Grill calendar.

This beat-up relic was my "drum throne" in the early years. (What marketing genius dreamed up the name "throne" to bolster the fragile egos of the poor disrespected basher sitting at the back of the band? Like the lyrics to Gene Krupa's theme "Drummin' Man":

"See that man sittin' on that stool? He's a cowhide-kickin' fool."

Well, now that cowhide-kickin' fool is sittin' on a *throne*, baby!)

This psychedelic red barrel dates to about 1967, when I got my first good drums, a small set of gray ripple Rogers—now owned and restored by friend Brad, who recently returned this souvenir to me. All through my earliest bands in the late '60s, to my time in England in the early '70s, and right up until my first audition with Rush in July 1974, I used it to carry my stands and pedals for transport. (For that first audition, I drove my mom's Pinto, as the drums wouldn't fit in my Lotus Europa—and in earlier years the drums traveled in the back of Dad's International Harvester pickup, the same color as

Rogers Drums, 1968
PHOTO BY BETTY PEART

I sprayed this barrel, International Harvester Red.) When the drums were set up and the barrel was empty, I turned it over and sat on it to play—cushioned with a square green pillow I "liberated" from Mom.

My first band's name, "mumblin' sumpthin'" (oh all right, one last time—from a Li'l Abner comic), is psychedelically rendered (à la Moby Grape) in Magic Marker.

The barrel originally contained calcium carbide, which my dad's farm equipment dealership sold to power "bird scarers." These were megaphone-shaped little cannons that made a big noise at intervals to scare birds away from orchards and vineyards. My battered old red barrel is kind of a fitting symbol of where I started, fifty years ago—a milestone for the time and distance I have covered.

By the time I was sixteen, I had been playing for three years, and began lobbying Mom and Dad for some *good* drums. With influence from Mom, Dad agreed to sign for a loan to buy a little set of gray ripple Rogers—costing an astronomical $675. (You do not ever forget numbers like that. Drumsticks cost $2.50, drumheads around $10, and my first good cymbal was $75.) I made the loan payments of $32 a month by delivering morning newspapers, mowing lawns, working Saturdays and holidays at Dad's farm equipment dealership, and bringing home an occasional "several dollars" from gigs at the Y, the roller rink, or high schools around Southern Ontario.

And again I return to "begin as you mean to go on." Many times I have referred to my own "inner teenager" as the ultimate authority on artistic integrity—my conscience, in effect. I have always made decisions as if the guy in this photograph (with the Keith Moon pose, and a piece of his cymbal—smashed onstage during the *Tommy* show in Toronto—around my neck) was judging me. I felt a glow inside when I read a quote from singer Lesley Gore, "You gotta make your sixteen-year-old self proud." Oh yes. I have spent almost fifty years doing that. That kid judges me on *everything*.

My ideals were so pure back then I didn't even know they *were* ideals—I thought it was how the world worked. I believed that good work was rewarded by success, and that if I could just get good enough at playing the drums, all else would follow. I never dreamed of being famous—not at all. I dreamed of being *good*.

And I also had the illusion that music was only ever played for *love*, not for anything so crass as money. Wealth, like fame, was the *effect*, not the cause—if you were good, the money and celebrity just *came with*. My categories of music were simple. There were only three styles: old people's music, like on my dad's radio station, was irrelevant (the music I listen to *now*, of course); bubblegum pop on the Top 40 stations was despicable; and the only *real* thing was genuine, heartfelt rock.

That music entered my life in 1964, at age twelve, at a Saturday matinee of a still-astonishing movie, *The T.A.M.I. Show* (Teenage Awards Music International). In *Traveling Music* I wrote a lot about the history and significance of that film, and how life-changing it was for me. I had seen the Beatles on *The Ed Sullivan Show*, but this was a powerful big-screen exposure (in "Electronovision" black and white) to "everything else": the Rolling Stones, the Beach Boys, James Brown (his performance alone was mind-blowing to this twelve-year-old small-town boy), Chuck Berry, Marvin Gaye, Smokey Robinson, Gerry and the Pacemakers, and an eighteen-year-old Lesley Gore—her feminist manifesto, "You Don't Own Me," galvanized me. (And still—oh, that *key change*!)

(Irresistible sidebar: Lesley Gore's hits were also the first successes for producer Quincy Jones, though he never made much of it in later years.)

By 1968 I was able to expand the Rogers with a second bass drum and small tom ($275), set up to emulate Cream's Ginger Baker. A homemade extension elevated the high-hat cymbals nearly as high as my crashes, and my pant legs were rolled up to avoid the pedal beaters (hadn't discovered bicycle clips yet). As the rock became harder, so to speak, I started playing hard enough to break off the tips of my Slingerland Gene Krupa model drumsticks. I found it more economical to turn them around and use the butt end, which would remain part of my (ahem) "style" right up to the mid-'90s. While studying with Freddie Gruber I revised many of my playing techniques and got used to holding the sticks right-way-around again.

The sweatshirt was my own creation (you couldn't buy anything like that in St. Catharines in the 1960s—probably not even in *Toronto*), with Magic Marker and fluorescent paint. The Who still topped my charts, obviously, but there was a lot of other great stuff going on, mostly outside the Top 40 mainstream. I was in my second band, the Majority ("Join the Majority," see), growing out of our blue-eyed-soul tastes to emulate the more adventurous rock coming from Led Zeppelin, the Doors, Spooky Tooth, *Super Session*–influenced jams like "Season of the Witch," and Procol Harum's masterly *Shine On Brightly*.

A friend mentioned Procol Harum in a letter lately, how they had been eligible for the Hall of Shame since 1992 and hadn't been inducted. That got me thinking about the depth of their influence, and I wrote back:

> Now . . . Procol Harum. "Whiter Shade of Pale," of course, an all-time classic for sure—but it occurs to me now that possibly no band was more *influential* to a young me, in a conceptual way—as examplars of "what to do and how to do it."
>
> They were the first to have a dedicated "lyricist," for example, Keith Reid, and what great lyrics, to that song and so many more. Similarly King Crimson later with Pete Sinfield, another band of over-arching influence—sometimes musically, but more important, *on what could be achieved*! (Or at least, "attempted.")
>
> That side-long piece "In Held 'Twas in I" (the first word to the lyrics of each section) and the *Shine On Brightly* album came out in 1968—when I was fifteen or sixteen. The cover! The music, the

intelligence, the ambition—how could a young aspiring kid *not* be influenced and inspired?!

Then a couple years later the live album with the Edmonton Symphony—"Conquistador" and "A Salty Dog" backed by an orchestra! Again, that would be a lasting example of what could be achieved.

Those roots and fruits on my tree are pretty obvious, eh?

Saw them live, too, in the early '70s at Massey Hall—oh yeah, and we also opened for Robin Trower in Philly in '75 or '76!

So in 1968, us kids with our guitars and drums in basements and garages were thinking bigger. When I joined J.R. Flood in 1969, we even wrote our own songs—adventurous, rambling-yet-intricate arrangements influenced by all those same seismic shifts, plus new arrivals like Santana; Deep Purple; Jethro Tull; the Nice; and Blood, Sweat & Tears.

But ambition seemed to fire me more than it did my bandmates—an early appearance of a youthful drive that would mature into full-blown hyperthymia. (Humorously defined as "having so much energy, doing so many things, and getting so much done—that it annoys other people.")

With J.R. Flood, 1970

Owen Hardy in *Clockwork Angels* was certainly modeled after my sixteen-year-old self: "In a world where I feel so small, I can't stop thinking big." I nagged at my bandmates excitedly—"Let's move to Toronto—to New York—to London!" But they wouldn't even talk about it. So in 1971 I packed up those drums and that barrel and shipped them to England, then back again in late 1972. As described more fully in *Traveling Music*, that sojourn that began with hopeful naïveté and ended with poverty and disillusionment had an importance in my life out of all proportion to a mere eighteen months. When I look back at youthful periods and try to organize the memories, the years all seem so impossibly *full*. Like just one band I was in, the Majority, went through so many different guitarists, bass players, and singers, so many changes of style, that I can hardly believe it only lasted two years.

RUSH
L. to R.
Geddy Lee, Neil Peart,
Alex Lifeson

Recording Exclusively For

mercury

A product of Phonogram, Inc.

First Record Company Eight-
by-ten, Central Park, 1974
(Note they didn't know who
was who yet!)
PHOTOGRAPH BY RICHARD FEGLEY

In 1973 I went to work at my father's farm equipment dealership as parts manager. (In later years, when a colleague of Dad's would gush to him about my success, Dad would say with a laugh, "Well, I still think he would have made a good parts manager!") In short order, I rented an apartment in downtown St. Catharines, bought a 1969 MGB roadster and had it painted purple, and put together a band to play the bars at night—playing cover tunes, but only cover tunes we *liked*. (I recall that one set was devoted to the Who's *Quadrophenia*, which would have pleased me. I did not, however, like playing until 2 a.m. and having to get up at 7 a.m. for work.)

In the summer of 1974 I joined Rush and became a Full-time Musician—a big dream achieved right there. Since then Alex, Geddy, and I have been writing, recording, and touring together in a career that has far exceeded our wildest teenage dreams. Yet at the heart of it, we remain three fairly dissimilar characters who have forged a way to work together, year after year, for four decades. And have a pretty good time doing it.

In the early years we used to joke about how our dads or uncles would preface their stories and opinions with, "The guys at work were saying . . ." or tell a joke punctuated with "Those crazy guys at work!" Naturally enough, over the years *we* became a lot like that, and thus in my writings I started referring to my bandmates and our crew as the Guys at Work. Likewise, I gained two nicknames of my own over the years, "Bubba" and "the Professor" (see story under that title in *Far and Near*), which came to represent a certain duality of, oh, sensibility and sense, you might say. (Qualities I believe I inherited from my mother and father, respectively.)

Of course back then we never imagined it was the beginning of forty-one years together—in a typical youthful worldview, we really never thought about the future at all, except as a vast amorphous cosmos of infinite *possibility*. We were just three young guys who would grow up together in music and in life, going through everything music and life can throw at you. All the while, we were doing what we wanted, the way we wanted to do it.

That's the quality I'm most proud of, really—just that we can stand as an *example*, in the face of what often seems like (well, actually *is*) a corporate entertainment factory.

In the epigraph to *Roadshow* I used a quote attributed to Hunter S. Thompson: "The music business is a cruel and shallow money trench, a long plastic hallway where thieves and pimps run free, and good men die like dogs. There's also a negative side."

My bandmates and I showed by example that once upon a time it was possible to make a career in music without giving away—or *selling*—your soul. You just have to be determined. And of course, *lucky*.

And it is helpful to have a certain quality I call "The Gift." In the fall of 2014, I had an unlikely epiphany as I was driving from San Francisco to Los Angeles, a trip of six or seven hours. Carrie and Olivia had thought they wanted to drive with me that one time, but after the long ride up, they decided they would rather fly back (enough said!). That left me alone in the family Audi wagon, and it was still an enjoyable drive, but not as "engaging" as it is in my Aston Martin Vanquish, for example. Interesting to note that in the Aston I never listen to music on the open road, I just listen to the V12's easy hum, look around, and let my thoughts roam. If I am stuck in city traffic, then the Great American Songbook creates a pleasant cocoon. No need to sift hungrily through the dross on the public airwaves in search of occasional gems. Nothing *but* gems, the Songbook has the best songs, the best arrangers, musicians, and singers, such as Big Frank, Ella, Tony, Matt Monro, Judy Garland, Nat "King" Cole, Bobby Darin, Billie Holiday, and Lena Horne. Even the greatest all-time drummers are there, to feed that side of my musical sensibility, like Sam Woodyard (Duke Ellington), Sonny Payne (Count Basie), Irv Cottler (Frank Sinatra), and my early idols Gene Krupa and Buddy Rich on many big band and small group sessions.

The lyrical side of my musical appreciation was well nourished in that Songbook, too. The words of those enduring songs display equal artistry, craft, and elegance, and I am constantly looking up the lyrics to, say, "I'll Be Seeing You," to figure out how Irving Kahal made that line resonate differently through the song and twist upward at the powerful ending. Or "Moonlight in Vermont"—no rhymes! The lovely melody and the vocalist's skill have to give it shape and symmetry. It is a marvel how Peggy Lee (in a performance conducted by Frank Sinatra) could wring true emotional depth out of what seemed like a merely sentimental notion, like Jerome Kern and Oscar Hammerstein II's "The Folks Who Live on the Hill."

Urban Poetry

(A fun anecdote, true or not, is related about the widows of Jerome Kern and Oscar Hammerstein II. At a party, Mrs. Kern said, "My husband wrote 'Ol' Man River.'" Mrs. Hammerstein snorted and said, "Your husband wrote 'dum, dum, dum-dum'—*my* husband wrote 'Ol' Man River.'")

But back to the Audi, where, an hour out of San Francisco, I started bouncing around the radio frequencies.

I picked up a hip-hop station from Fresno, then smiled and thought, "You know what? I am going to *listen* to a hip-hop station from Fresno!" Just open-minded curiosity, really, plus I genuinely do appreciate many styles of music. It's more about quality, and *sincerity*—the fakers and poseurs might fool most of the people most of the time (and they do), but someone who has been making music for fifty years can simply tell if it's real.

For two hours I checked out the popular sounds and rhythms, words and vocalizations in that style, by people whose names I knew only from the entertainment pages—Drake, Wiz Khalifa, Iggy Azalea, Nicki Minaj, and so on.

I couldn't help thinking of when we released our song "Roll the Bones" in 1990, with a "rap" section. As a lyricist, I had been attracted by the wordplay of "busting rhymes," and thought it would be fun to try. (No fear of being accused of cultural appropriation in those days.) I was glad when the other Guys went along, and Geddy delivered it with a deep-voiced electronic vocal effect over synthesizer noodles and triggered drum samples. Though played by a real drummer—me—rather than the machines that drove the rhythm on *every* one of the songs I heard "Straight Outta Fresno." A few years ago, while rehearsing in Toronto, I listened to a Top 40 station every day on my commutes to and from work. After two weeks, I decided the style was pretty healthy—traditional R&B mixed with hip-hop influence—but that in all those dozens of songs, I had not heard *one* real drummer.

(One resource I had hoped to use in this book was a collection of comical online postings relating to the band and the tour—but problems arose with both print quality and permissions. One I wanted to place here showed Kanye West sitting at a recording console with the caption, "I make my own beats," then a photo of yours truly smirking while I played my drums, with the caption, "Aw . . . that's cute.")

"What's the difference if you don't know the difference?"

That is one of Freddie Gruber's deepest quotes—I've been thinking about it for twenty years, and still haven't exhausted its applications. In this instance, if modern-day listeners and dancers are satisfied with machine-made beats, then what's the difference if they don't *care* about the difference?

As far as "judgment" goes, I always stick to two simple questions I learned from art historian Professor Gombrich many years ago.

1) What are they trying to do?
2) How well do they do it?

Only thing is, obviously, to make those judgments, you have to know the difference. Long ago I ran across the quote "Taste is an acquired luxury," and believe it to be true. In *Tibetan Peach Pie*, novelist Tom Robbins's non-fiction "remembrance" (he insists it's not a memoir or autobiography), he tells how in his early career he was a fine-art critic for a Seattle newspaper. He makes a profound comment about that kind of *informed* opinion, pointing out that "taste" may choose between Matisse and Picasso, but not between either of them and Thomas Kinkade.

Here is the rap section from "Roll the Bones."

Jack—relax
Get busy with the facts
No zodiacs or almanacs,
No maniacs in polyester slacks
Just the facts
Gonna kick some gluteus max
It's a parallax—you dig?
You move around, the small gets big—it's a rig
It's action—reaction—random interaction
So who's afraid of a little abstraction?
Can't get no satisfaction from the facts?
You better run, homeboy—
A fact's a fact from Nome to Rome, boy

What's the deal? Spin the wheel
If the dice are hot—take a shot
Play your cards, show us what you got—
What you're holdin'
If the cards are cold, don't go foldin'
Lady Luck is golden; she favors the bold
That's cold
Stop throwing stones—
The night has a thousand saxophones
So get out there and rock,
And roll the bones
GET BUSY!

(The closing lines represent one of my "hidden agendas" in the lyrics for that *Roll the Bones* album. I was determined to sneak in all the rock-lyric clichés I usually avoided like poison—words like "baby" and "rock and roll.")

Twenty-five years ago, we released "Roll the Bones" as a "radio track" (couldn't really be called a single). At least one radio station, in Michigan, played the song but *edited out* that part—because they sniffed, "We don't play rap." So silly.

When we played that song on the R40 tour, the audience cheered loudly as the rear screen showed a series of "guest artists" lip-syncing to that rap (featuring the hilarious Paul Rudd and Jason Segel, with the Trailer Park Boys, Peter Dinklage, Chad Smith, Tom Morello, Jay Baruchel, and Les Claypool).

That album's lyrics were all on the theme of chance, and the chorus of the closing song, "You Bet Your Life," again offered some fun wordplay. It also carried a deeper reflection that whatever politics, religion, or art you marry yourself to, you are quite literally betting your life on it.

anarchist reactionary running-dog revisionist
hindu muslim catholic creation/evolutionist
rational romantic mystic cynical idealist
minimal expressionist post-modern neo-symbolist

armchair rocket scientist graffiti existentialist
deconstruction primitive performance photo-realist
be-bop or a one-drop or a hip-hop lite-pop-metallist
gold adult contemporary urban country capitalist

In those days, "adult contemporary," "urban," and "country" were radio formats ("urban" a euphemism for African-American), while "lite-pop-metallist" defined the one genre I could never tolerate, then or now—fakery. Pop music is fine, even great, but not when it adopts the "swagger" of rock or hip-hop without the convictions that drive those forms in their purest expression. In either genre—in *any* genre—most people cannot distinguish between real and fake, so . . . what's the difference?

Thinking about why those performers on Fresno's hip-hop station were so wildly successful in this era of pop culture, I hit upon the idea of the Gift. People who admire any art or entertainment—singing, rapping, playing violin, painting pictures, acting the hero, hitting a ball with a stick—celebrate those who do it better than they could. That is the Gift.

In ancient days, quarreling villages each chose one man to fight as their champion—like David against Goliath. Champion didn't mean "winner," just "chosen representative." (Or sacrificial lamb.) I used to think that's what Freddie Mercury was singing about in "We Are the

Shared Moment
PHOTO BY JOHN ARROWSMITH

Champions"—that as artists they fought on behalf of others—but in an interview he said he "was thinking of football." Oh.

As the Audi cruised steadily south through the grasslands, orchards, and distant ranges along the I-5, the hip-hop station faded away. I bounced to "Bakersfield's Only Classic Rock," and there it was again—the Gift. In both styles, distinctive voices are the main focus, as in almost all popular music in the past century (excepting perhaps big-band, surf instrumentals, and bebop!).

This is a good place to highlight that a crucial factor in Rush's longevity as a touring band has been Geddy's *voice*. That he has retained his range and power is somewhat of a miracle, and without it, we'd be finished. Stewart Copeland and I agree that drumming is the hardest job, but singing is the *worst* job. Hitting things with sticks and feet is physically punishing, but the intimacy and vulnerability of opening your mouth and hoping a good, strong *accurate* sound emerges—that's tough. Geddy warms up his voice carefully before every show, and on days off he tries not even to talk, to thoroughly rest that delicate instrument as much as he can. (I can't remember the last time we had to cancel a show because of Geddy's voice, so obviously his care pays off.)

At the start of the tour I told Geddy that when he holds those long notes in "Headlong Flight" early in the show, or later when he has to sing the super-high stuff from the old days, I am *with* him. He will usually turn to me after one of those "exertions" and express the strain with a comical face, while I respond with one of sympathy.

Many modern pop, rock, and soul singers have taken on the Great American Songbook later in their careers, from Rod Stewart to Gloria Estefan to Lou Rawls, but one who succeeded earliest and perhaps best was Linda Ronstadt. She had the power, dynamics, phrasing, and *depth* for it. Sadly, in 2012 she was diagnosed with Parkinson's disease and became unable to sing. At the time I heard an interviewer talking to her and making a bizarre denial of her condition. In a cajoling tone, he said, "Oh, now—I bet you can still sing great," and she responded with proper impatience, "I assure you—I couldn't sing 'Happy Birthday' right now."

Or Robert Plant, in his late sixties, constantly pestered about a Led Zeppelin reunion tour. His vocal range has clearly not endured as Geddy's has, but he fends it off with graceful humor, "Look, in a few years I'll be using a *walker*!" But still they insist—maybe because if there were still a Linda Ronstadt or a Led Zeppelin, they could still be seventeen.

If the Voice is king of every style, from the Great American Songbook to hip-hop to classic rock, at least in rock music we bow second not to programmers and DJs, but to guitarists and drummers (on their thrones).

By definition, every pop star is popular, and what they are popular for is always a Gift—something those who admire them couldn't do themselves. (Even if it's just "look good.") But a Gift can only take someone so far. A quote attributed to Ernest Hemingway, "There are no failures of talent; only failures of character." Plenty of those kind of failures in every field of human endeavor, obviously. Over the course of a life, and after, a person will be judged by what they *do* with that Gift. Like some talisman from an ancient myth, you can give it away, share it, but you must never sell it. Strangers who admire your Gift may shower you with riches and fame, but they can just as quickly take it all away—betrayed by the shallow tides of fashion, sometimes, or by losing the battle to protect that Gift from others who would profit by it. There is such a condition in life as "selling out," and the price is Faustian—no less than your soul. The battle against those devils never, ever ends, and verily, it doth grow tiresome.

When I talk about "retirement," I like the French word *retirer*—"to withdraw, as from battle." That was the only thing I wanted to "retire" from, the struggle.

As I walked the streets around the Hallowed Bubba Cave one day, a song began playing in my head, and that is frequently a clue to my subconscious machinery—and proof that no matter what I choose to do with the rest of my life, music will *always* have a central place. Perhaps the difference is that music would be a vehicle I would no longer be *driving*, but only enjoying during the ride. I didn't know if I would ever play the drums "in anger" again, but there was no doubt I would forever sit at traffic lights with my indicators on and tap counter-rhythms on the steering wheel.

The song playing in my head at that moment was one from that Great American Songbook, "This Is All I Ask," by Gordon Jenkins. It was Tony Bennett's 1963 version I "heard," and I reflected on the lyrics. Then I thought, "Hmm. That probably means something."

> *As I approach the prime of my life*
> *I find I have the time of my life*
> *Learning to enjoy at my leisure*
> *All the simple pleasures*
> *And so I happily concede*
> *This is all I ask*
> *This is all I need*

SCIENCE ISLAND

In August 2014, I found myself revisiting some history—my own and the band's—and the time and place help to paint a larger picture of both stories.

For thirty-four years, over half my life, I have spent time nearly every summer and winter in the Laurentian Mountains of Quebec. It is a region I call my "soulscape"—sapphire lakes set among emerald mountains in summer, diamond dust in winter. The thick second-growth woods are rooted in ancient, worn-down peaks, some of the oldest rocks on Earth. A series of massive glaciers scraped those once Himalayan-sized mountains down and gouged out the lakes and valleys, flooding them with meltwater.

In these more recent times—say the last twenty-four years—my northern sanctuary has been on Lac St. Brutus. The lake has four major islands, fringed with gray boulders and wooded in fir, spruce, and occasional tall white pines. Each island is about an acre in size, and because they are inaccessible for half the year during freeze-ups and thaws, none has been built upon. For fifteen years I owned one of them, l'Île Selena, but sold it with my previous house and land when I briefly contemplated moving my retreat to Ontario. (Until my then-new wife, Carrie, visited, loved the area, and said, "Are you *sure* you want to leave here?" Which makes a guy go, "Hmm . . .")

Rich memories endure of my early days on that lake, before I even started to build a house there. Owning a stretch of wooded shoreline and an island with no buildings means no responsibilities—no expenses, no problems, no worries. Just playtime—and a boyhood fantasy realized. For a couple of summers in the early 1990s I kept a battered old rowboat inverted onshore, so I could drive over from the old cabin on Lac Écho to have a row around. When I was up there on my own with our white Samoyed, Nikki (for Nikita), many times I filled the boat with a load of camping gear and and the two of us headed out in the morning for an overnight stay. Once our camp was set up in a clearing in the middle of the island, Nikki lounged contentedly on a shady pine-needle bed, sniffing the various aromas of lake and woods, while I cleared trails and burned deadfall in the big firepit.

Actually *owning* an island, however small, encouraged a boyish enthusiasm even in a man then in his forties. It felt like a kingdom in the untamed wilderness for a boy and his dog. Like a conquistador or voyageur, I named each land feature after a friend or family member, and cleared winding little paths to each side of the shoreline.

In the evening I poured a measure of the Macallan into my plastic cup and sat on a log by the fire, just staring into the flames and thinking. Eventually I rose to prepare a campstove dinner—some dreadful mix of dehydrated noodles, powdered sauce, and canned fish (known to backpackers as "tuna wiggle"). The humble repast was elevated nicely by a good red wine, and an old-school percolator of dark coffee. After such an active day, I soon crawled into my little tent. It had a screened "skylight" I could zip open to look up through the silhouetted trees to the night sky, and a covered portico that just fit a curled-up Nikki. Breezes sighed in the trees and rippled at the shore, and among the stars and loons and woodsmoke the boy and his dog were very happy.

Near those four islands, a few tiny islets of rock stand above the water here and there. One of them is large enough to land a boat on and has a steep cliff into deep water that was always fun for a gang of adults and children to jump from. Twenty-four years ago, when I first visited Lac St. Brutus, just one solitary fir tree grew on its crown, so it became known as l'Île de Noël (Christmas Island). One neighboring couple told me that in the early years, before there were any houses, a certain unnamed couple once made the beast with two backs there. So they called it l'Île d'Amour. A large granite stone, an "erratic block" (meaning dropped by a retreating glacier), on top of it suggested the

shape of an eagle's head to this bird-brain, so our family called it Eagle Rock. With a young boy's natural reductiveness, Sam, the son of my long-time friend and riding partner (and "discoverer" of the lake that bears his name) Brutus, called it Rock-on-Top-of-Rock.

Eagle Rock

That is a lot of names for a little bump of ancient granite, and in the summer of 2014 yet another was bestowed upon it: Science Island. For all of August—the heart of summer, just as February is the heart of winter—I was fortunate to be at the lake. Carrie and Olivia joined me for two weeks in the middle, leaving a solitary, precious "reading week" on each side.

Nearly every day, five-year-old Olivia and I liked to venture out on the lake in our small electric boat, or in my sleek rowboat, and we often stopped at that little island. While pulling the boat up on the rocky shore, I showed Olivia the parallel grooves in the rock's surface that had been gouged out by glaciers. I explained how the tremendous mass of ice had dragged stones along and carved those grooves, at a speed of maybe an inch a year. Then I pointed upward as I told her the ice was once about two miles high above us.

She looked at me with that wonderful guilelessness of childhood (when does that go? About eight, maybe?) and said with a wide-open smile, "Was that before you were born?"

I assured her it was.

She pointed down at the pale green patches on the rocks and asked me what they were. I told her they were lichen, a primitive plant similar to the moss that carpeted the ground between the exposed rocks.

"They live off the stone itself," I explained, "from its moisture and minerals."

I thought of the old generality about "the nature of things," and pointed around us at the wooded shores as I said, "Everything we see is either animal, vegetable, or mineral."

She thought about that, then fastened on a natural objection. She pointed to the lake and said, "What about water?"

Ah, she had me there for a moment—but then I realized (with a little relief), water is assuredly mineral.

Growing up in California, Olivia has been raised to be conscious of water use—she explains solemnly, "because of the drought." I told her that in Quebec we didn't have to worry about that, which led to explanations of the water cycle of evaporation and rainfall that kept our woods green and thriving, and our lake full of clean, cold water. We talked about clouds, winds, rain, snow, fog, and dew and rainbows and the little stream that runs through our land and swells after rainstorms.

While drawing and coloring one day, we talked about the proper order of colors in a rainbow. I had always used a sequence that seemed good to me, while Olivia had her own preference. We decided to see what Science said. Olivia has great respect for science, especially the natural branches, and is proud when her mother calls her "my little scientist." (That will be helpful for her adult ambitions: to be a doctor, an astronaut, *and* a construction worker.) An internet search taught us the mnemonic ROY G BIV for the correct order. Red, orange, yellow, green, blue, indigo, violet. Lovely.

One of the oft-celebrated delights of northern lakes are the calls of loons. In our area, each lake has a resident pair that returns year after year. Their songs are eerie, unearthly, and endlessly haunting, especially on moonlit nights, when they can fish and move around the lake, calling to each other. Olivia and I had been seeing "our" pair of loons often, with their new baby chick. That is always an exciting event on the lake, because loon nests often fail due to a rising or falling waterline, or predators.

While rowing around the lake one day, Olivia and I heard the adults call to each other across the lake with their "I'm over here!" three-note yodel. We saw the baby loon swimming beside one of its parents, then dive under and come up in a different spot. I told Olivia

I thought it was the first day the baby loon had ever done that, and she called out, "Congratulations, baby loon!"

(Obviously a triumph another child would relate to!)

One time we saw a family of ducks called mergansers swim by, a mother and four youngsters hugging the rocks and trees of the shoreline. Not wanting to romanticize the natural world, I tried to tell Olivia delicately that they usually stayed safely close to shore like that because given the chance the loons would kill the babies. I offered the explanation that this seemingly murderous impulse was actually for "love"—intended to protect the loons' own babies from other fish-eating competitors.

I explained how both the male and female loons care for the eggs and young, unlike the mergansers—I have never even *seen* a male merganser. The flamboyantly colored males only hang around for mating season in early spring, then after the ten to twelve ducklings are hatched, they take off farther north to moult. (So they claim . . . the females probably think, "How *convenient*.") The female mergansers make up for being single parents by helping each other—I have often seen as many as thirty youngsters trailing after one mother who is baby-sitting for the others.

Loon and Chick
PHOTO BY CRAIG M. RENWICK

So, with all that talk about geology, meteorology, and biology, one day when we were rowing home, Olivia said, "We should call that place Science Island."

I said, "Yes. I like it! From now on that is its name."

Olivia turned five on August 12, and that spring her mother had signed her up for biweekly swimming lessons, so she was now a strong swimmer. No more life jacket or water wings for her—just foam noodles for fun. Swimming "free" like that opened a whole new world of enjoying life at the lake, for both of us. (Second time around for me, of course. It's becoming ever more difficult not to talk to Olivia about her lost sister, especially when we boat past the old house, or the island still named for Selena—she would have turned thirty-six that April. So many stories about Selena that I know Olivia would love. But

Riding Loonie-back
PHOTO BY CHARLES VOISIN

I also know I have to wait until she's better able to comprehend such world-shattering information. Maybe when she's eight or so. I guess I'll know—but it will be hard.) Olivia and I had a good time on the lake and in the lake nearly every day, and one hot day we went swimming four separate times.

On a cool morning when dark clouds threatened rain, we put on our rain jackets and reef shoes and walked down toward the dock. I caught a glimpse of brown velvet in the woods across the stream, and reached out a hand to Olivia's shoulder. She looked over, and I put a finger to my lips as I pointed toward a yearling deer twenty-five feet away. We all stayed frozen for a couple of minutes, checking each other out.

Little Pink Butterfly Hood

Later that morning we walked up the gravel road to our neighbor's house to pick up a food container we had left there while visiting a few days before. On the way back, I led us through the woods, assuring Olivia, "There *used* to be a trail here." However, that had been fifteen years before, and it was largely overgrown—we had to do some serious bushwhacking. Olivia never faltered—just followed me through the trees, rocks, roots, and moss, pushing her way through the branches in her pink and purple butterfly raincoat. No complaints, no moans, no sighs—because we were sharing an *adventure*, not an ordeal. Just as last winter she was the Merida (Scottish princess in Disney movie *Brave*) of snowshoes, now she was the Merida of the summer woods.

When we finally fought through to the shore, I helped her across the stepping stones over the little stream, and we emerged at our dock. I told her I was proud of her, and she said, "Me, too!"

Rowing had long been a favorite summer exercise, and I have owned the boat pictured here, with sliding seat and outrigger oars, for twenty-four years. Most every summer day I went for a long row around the lake, feeling the satisfaction of driving my whole body into the oars as the nimble hull sliced through the water. My childhood was "sport-free," due to general ineptitude (a certain "dis-coordination" that was useful in drumming, but not in anything else), but later in life my highly physical approach to playing drums gave me one lonely athletic gift: stamina.

Misty Morning

In my thirties I took up sports like cross-country skiing, long-distance bicycling, swimming, and rowing, and discovered that even if I couldn't do them *well*, I could do them for a long time. That they are all typically *solitary* activities is telling, too. No competition, no teams, no expectations from others—recalling my definition of an audience as "strangers with expectations."

In turn, getting all physical like that made me serious about fitness, a drive that has never faltered. When I wasn't drumming, bicycling, or cross-country skiing, I was at the gym working those muscles several times a week. To close the circle, those same activities naturally helped keep me fit for drumming. The reward was that right into my sixties I could feel that while I might never be good enough, or fast enough, or loose enough, whatever—at least I was *strong* enough.

One night in Quebec a heavy rain hammered down on our metal roof (wonderful sound—nature's drum solo) for hours, and in the morning Olivia and I went down to the dock to bail out the boats. While sitting on the rowboat's wooden seat, I leaned toward the stern with the bailing cup and heard a snap—the seat had broken in half. Fortunately enough of it remained for me to keep up my daily rowing routine, at least in a half-assed fashion—which was not much of a change. (*Badaboom.*)

For some reason that summer, after all those years of "recreational" rowing, I rose to a new level of *engagement*. I reveled in the feeling while I was doing it, putting all of my strength through my back, arms, and legs into that rhythmic motion, yet my mental state was serene. I also loved how I felt good after—unlike cross-country skiing or snowshoeing (or drumming), there was no pain, just an all-over sense of well-being. Which is why we exercise, right?

An internet search for a new wooden seat came up empty, but did lead me to the sites of several builders of racing shells. Ooh—I had wanted one of those for a *long* time. A spark lit up in my brain. "Yes," I thought, "Now's the time."

I chose a builder, Jürgen Kaschper, who offered a boat with classic twentieth-century mahogany veneer, but over a thin composite hull with modern carbon-fiber hardware and oars. I placed my order for delivery next spring—ready for another summer. It's going to be so great . . .

Similar to cross-country skiing, the flowing rhythm of rowing is a subtle combination of many small cogs, levers, and motors. With much practice, they are refined into clockwork synchrony until you don't even have to think—each part of the body knows its part of the machinery. (The exact relation to drumming is obvious.) I decided I wanted to write about rowing, and when I was on the water I tried to pay attention to each of those elements and mentally put them in words. (A typical writerly exercise wherever I am, whatever I'm doing—"How would I put this in words?")

Breathe in deeply while the body slides the seat sternward, wrists twisted to "feather" the oars. Arms push forward to carry the oars back, then the wrists twist and pull up, the blades catching water. Begin to exhale as the shoulders, arms, trunk, and legs uncoil, feet hard on the footrests, the leg muscles extending and sliding you back on the seat, the whole body muscling the boat forward.

The wake surges for a moment with the propulsion, and the next time the oars meet the water a satisfying distance has been covered from the previous circles of ripples. At the end of the stroke, the oar blades curve back to feather position, legs flat for a second, the handles returning close to the body, then extend to begin anew.

Take a deep breath and repeat, repeat, repeat . . .

After a long row, I return to the dock well heated up, especially on sunny days. Once the boat is tidily lashed to the whiplines, I shed my clothes, don my goggles, and ease into the water. Down the shore to

PHOTO BY CRAIG M. RENWICK

the south is an old wooden dock that is never visited, because no house was ever built on the lot. It is about a quarter mile away, so a perfect milestone. Easing into the front crawl's natural flow, I breathe on alternate sides, every third stroke (called "bilateral breathing"), a technique I learned long ago from the late Mike McLoughlin.

Mike was a longtime member of the band's touring family, starting our first merchandising operation in the late '70s (a business continued today by his son, Patrick). Back then Mike was an open-water swimming enthusiast, and on days off would go offshore in places like San Francisco Bay. When I first became interested in distance swimming, in the 1980s, Mike explained that if I started out trying that three-stroke

Talk to the Animals
PHOTO BY CRAIG M. RENWICK

rhythm on the front crawl I would be able to develop it, but it was very difficult to adopt later. The stamina and breath control I had built through drumming helped me to master the technique, just as they aided with long-distance cycling, cross-country skiing, and rowing.

Coming up alternately on opposite sides of your body to breathe seems clearly superior, but I notice that when I'm at the Y and using the cross-training machines, which overlook the pool, I rarely see anyone going three strokes between breaths—always two, on the same side. (And when I'm on those machines, or in that pool, don't I wish I was *really* cross-country skiing, or rowing, or swimming in that beautiful lake?)

Distance swimming rewards the same economy of motion and smooth full-body technique as does rowing or cross-country skiing. (Or drumming.) I was pleased that friend Craiggie captured that particular motion—not just the picturesque splash as I kicked, but my arm emerging from the water in a relaxed curve, the wrist bent and doing no "work" until it has to. Just that trailing hand demonstrates a general principle that applies to every sport that requires rhythmic stamina. It is certainly part of the wisdom preached by my late drumming teacher, Freddie Gruber: "If the stick wants to fall, let it fall. If the stick wants to bounce, let it bounce. *Get out of your own way*."

The Roman poet Juvenal suggested we should pray for "*mens sana in corpore sano*," a healthy mind in a healthy body, and that is a worthy ideal. We can but try.

One morning Olivia noticed an old birdhouse in the garage and asked what it was. The concept puzzled her, and when we got to our "art table," I drew a quick sketch in magenta marker of a bird carrying a bug as it flew to a birdhouse. She wondered what it was like inside, so I sketched the view through the hole, with the nest made of grass and leaves.

Well, Olivia had some ideas on building a better birdhouse. She drew a larger circle, then asked me to draw the inside. The walls should be made of leaves, the floor of bark, and there should be a bird on its nest. I decided to draw a robin sitting on its eggs. One of our crayons was called robin's egg blue, so Olivia knew what color to make them. I had told her before that robins ate worms, and she took the marker and drew an amorphous shape, colored it brown, and told me it was "Mrs. Robin's favorite toy—it tastes like *worms*!"

Thinking of every need for Mrs. Robin, she added a container of worms on one side, a container of water on the other, and an "upstairs room" that she said was "full of more toys." Lucky Mrs. Robin!

Olivia wanted to title the finished work "Mrs. Robin's Home," so I outlined the letters and she filled in the colors (we just say "ROY G BIV" for short now), plus robin's egg blue for the rest. "For the sky," she explained.

Now Mrs. Robin joins the rest of our friends from the summer of 2014—Olivia the Pig and Princess Stephanie, Toot and Puddle, Boo and Buddy, Baby Loon and ROY G BIV, "Love Shack" and "Gangnam Style," Holley Shiftwell and Finn McMissile (a.k.a. Olivia and Dad), Olivia's favorite painters David Hockney and Jackson Pollock (she's David; I'm Jackson—when I requested permission to use one of Mr. Hockney's works in *Far and Near*, I shared with his representative, while agreeing to the modest fee, that after Olivia viewed some of his works in San Francisco, she stood in front of her easel and declared, "David Hockney . . . inspires me"—the lady said she couldn't think of a nicer tribute), Merida and Angus (Merida's horse), all to be remembered and treasured for the rest of our days, in the timeless and unforgettable universe of Science Island.

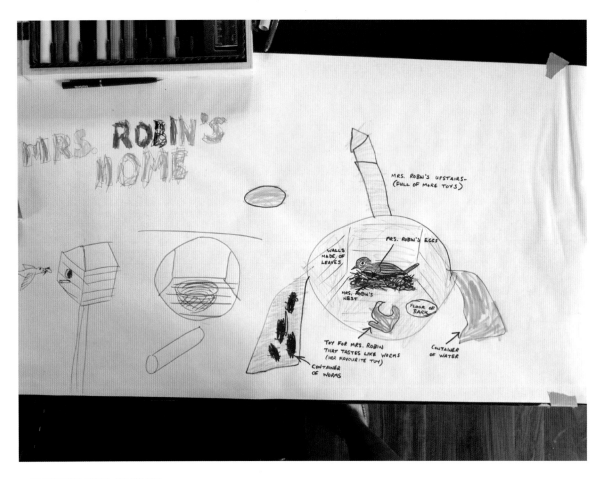

ART DIRECTION, VISION, AND COLORS
BY OLIVIA, PRELIMINARY SKETCHES
AND LETTERING BY DAD

In Front of Le Studio, 2014
PHOTO BY MARTIN HAWKES

ROCK OF AGES

While I was at the lake by myself for the first week, I was happy to be invited to the home of my neighbors (a few lakes away) Paul Northfield and Judy Smith. Their little house on Lac Cochon is elegant and comfortable, good taste evident in art, lighting, and music, and they are both fine cooks.

Thinking of cooking for other people as perhaps the most basic expression of love, I might define Paul and Judy as true "amateurs" in the French sense—giving love and taking pride in their cooking. Thinking further, other cooks I know, like our Alex and Brutus, will spend whole days preparing complex, ambitious, and superb repasts, and they are true "artists" in the kitchen. In contrast to artists and amateurs, I would have to label myself, Chef Bubba, as a "mechanic." I can wield the necessary tools and adhere to careful data of heat and time, and thus produce an edible, even nutritious, meal. But it ain't art. We live up to the motto of my cooking website, Bubba's Bar 'n' Grill: "Good Simple Food."

When I place one of my multicolored meals on the table, say salmon teriyaki with green beans, rainbow carrots, and jasmine rice, Carrie might say, "That looks good!"

In Eeyore's glum monotone, I will comment dismissively, "It probably won't kill you."

Paul and Judy also have long associations with the place that first brought me to the Laurentians—nearby Le Studio, where the Guys at Work and I recorded at various times from 1979 until 1995.

Paul was the engineer on many of those sessions, from *Permanent Waves* right up to *Vapor Trails* in 2001 (though recorded in Toronto), on the Buddy Rich tributes he and I recorded in the early '90s, and on my second instructional DVD, *Anatomy of a Drum Solo*. Judy had been with Paul all through those years and had managed Le Studio for five years in the mid-'90s. And of course they had known my "first family" all through that era. So we go back.

That night the subject of Le Studio's abandonment and ruination came up, and the very next day I had an email from Meghan at our office asking me to do an interview for the guys at Banger Films (makers of the *Beyond the Lighted Stage* documentary). They were making a show about one of the Guys at Work, Geddy, and wanted to talk to me.

It was *immediately* obvious where that interview had to take place.

A few days later, on a pleasantly cool and overcast afternoon, I put the top down on the Z8 (Zed 8, when it's in Canada) and took the short drive to meet the Banger crew. The route was what I think of as back-backroads, mainly gravel, and in one way it might seem a shame to subject a beautiful car to all that dust and flying stones—but in reality it was absolutely the right thing to do. Another one of those times when I heard Matt Monro singing "On Days Like These" on my inner radio as I cruised through the rolling woodlands.

I pulled up in that familiar driveway for the first time in about fifteen years. From time to time I had heard it was abandoned and crumbling, but had never gone back to look.

At the moment of arriving, and even on the way there, I felt some emotions bubbling up. I kind of pushed them down for the moment—unsure exactly what I was feeling, or would feel. Later I realized that the experience was really just too much to process all at once—because no other place on Earth had been more important in my life.

Sounds like hyperbole, maybe, but it wasn't "larger than life"—it was exactly life-size.

My memory replayed a flashbook of numberless days and nights, weeks and months, summers and winters, the songs, the albums, the laughs—it was a long emotional parade of memories. Yet at least the ghosts there were *happy* ones, so it was enjoyable to wander among them.

Our first visit to Le Studio was in the fall of 1979, to record the basic tracks for *Permanent Waves*. After making the previous two albums, *A*

Video Shoot, Le Studio,
circa 1979-80
PHOTO BY FIN COSTELLO

Farewell to Kings and *Hemispheres*, in rural Wales and London, it was a comfortable change to find a place we loved that was only a six-hour drive from our homes.

(My first drive up there, on a glorious autumn day, was in the black Mercedes 6.9 sedan I bought in 1978, just after Selena was born, as my idea of a "family ride." What a crazy big muscle car that was—one of the few in my multiwheeled life I wish I had kept.)

In subsequent years we returned to record and mix *Moving Pictures*, our most successful album ever, then to mix a live album, *Exit: Stage*

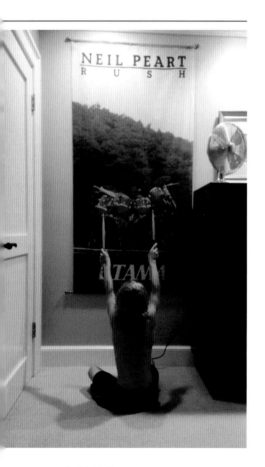

Rockin' It Forward
PHOTO BY TAYLOR HAWKINS

Left. There wasn't much for us to do on that project except occasionally approve performances and balances, so we started messing around with other things. Alex built and crashed radio-control floatplanes; Geddy learned everything in the world about baseball (his new passion then), and I did a painstaking nut-and-lug restoration of an old set of Hayman drums that were lying around the studio basement. Apparently they had belonged to Corky Laing, drummer with Mountain, and when I had cleaned and oiled the tension casings and installed and tuned new heads, I liked the way they sounded.

Each of us eventually started fooling around with our instruments, and wrote "Subdivisions"—I remember the Guys at Work coming up to me in the driveway of the guest house while I was polishing my Ferrari 308 GTS (black over red—gorgeous) and playing the demo for me on a cassette player. We soon recorded a demo of it, on which I played those Hayman drums.

In the summer of 1982 we returned to Le Studio to record that song properly, and to put together the rest of the *Signals* album. During those sessions, the Tama drum company asked for a portrait of my new drumset, the prototype of the "Artstar" series, in candy apple red. (The shell design was inspired by the Haymans—I asked Tama to replicate their relatively thin shells, because I liked their bright attack and warm resonance.) I dreamed up the idea of doing a photo shoot in the middle of the lake—setting up the drums on a swimming raft that was moored offshore from the studio. With our band crew and the studio guys helping, each piece of the four drum boards on which the stands were mounted was ferried out by rowboat, followed by each of the drums and cymbals. I canoed out there, then sat and played while microphones were recording from shore (interesting experiment, but never used for anything). Art director Hugh Syme and photographer Deborah Samuel floated around me in a pedal boat while Deborah snapped away, and the resulting image was used by Tama on a large fabric advertising banner.

That banner was popular with a younger generation of drummers coming of age in the '80s (because in that era of rampant drum machines, there weren't that many "real" drummers and drumsets to get excited about). My friend Taylor Hawkins is the drummer of the Foo Fighters, and is twenty years younger than me. Taylor told me he searched out one of those banners for himself not long ago, to honor a teenage fantasy—but that it now hangs on his son's wall. Nice—corrupting yet another generation!

Then, in the long winter of 1983–84, we were back at Le Studio to struggle with the making of *Grace Under Pressure* (one of our "trouble child" records). Our visits to Le Studio became more sporadic as we experimented with "settings" again, recording and mixing in the English countryside, in London, on the tropic isle of Montserrat in the Caribbean, and in Paris. (Because we could.) In the '90s we returned to Le Studio with Rupert Hine and Stephen W. Tayler to record the basic tracks for *Presto* and *Roll the Bones*, and with Peter Collins and Kevin "Caveman" Shirley for the same on *Counterparts*.

Around that same period, Paul Northfield and I recorded the Buddy Rich tribute albums in New York City, then brought them back to Le Studio to mix. Later that decade, starting in the summer of 1997, my world came crashing down piece by piece, like a bad country song ("My baby died, my wife died, my dog died—and my best friend went to jail"). During those "wilderness years" (see *Ghost Rider*), I did not pick up a pair of drumsticks for two years. In the summer of '99, I had an urge to quietly, privately see how I felt about drumming. Under another name (a covert operation—ha, "black ops"), I booked the little back room at Le Studio (called "The Far Side") for a couple of days. My local friend Trevor helped me sneak in my old yellow Gretsches, and I spent some time setting them up and tuning them. I sat behind them and picked up the sticks, curious to see if I could still play, really, and maybe how I felt about it.

Le Studio 2014:
A Farewell to Things

What I found myself doing that day was *playing my story*. I thought I was just hitting things aimlessly, but suddenly I felt the narrative that was coming out of me—or maybe through me. "This is the *angry* part—this is the *lost* part—this is the *journey*."

It was kind of spooky. (To jump forward in time briefly, that "narrative" idea became the inspiration for the solo I performed on the R40 tour in 2015. I decided to approach it as though I were just sitting down at the drums to play a story, and would later title it, "The Story So Far.")

So, to consider Le Studio at all was to consider a lot of my life that had been centered on that place, and so much of my best *work*. It felt good to reflect on it all now, with pride and relief that it was over. Because I wouldn't want to do any of that again.

The Door of Doom

Sketch by Alex, Early '80s

Why?

If this door could talk, it could share some reasons why . . .

The thick soundproof door simply leads between the control room and the recording room—but sometimes those few steps represented a hard, painful journey. You would pass through it after listening to a playback, on your way out to try it "one more time." Or ten. Or a hundred. I will never forget the sound of that latch (made for a walk-in freezer, like in a slaughterhouse, I guess). As you pushed in on the round knob, the spring compressed with a dull rasp, the latch opened with a metal-against-metal swipe, and it ended with a hard, cold "snick."

In the days of *Permanent Waves* and *Moving Pictures*, for example, we would first have spent a few weeks at a country place in Ontario working on the songs. We arrived at Le Studio with some songs ready, some mapped out, and at least one yet to be written. So we ended up playing each of those songs many, many times, all of us in the room together—making a *heck* of a racket as we flailed through and worked out the arrangement, our parts, the interaction with the other guys' parts, sonic issues, and the overall performance. It was utter chaos, which made the constant repetition all the more necessary.

In recent years we have learned to do all that detail work separately, adding nuances to our own and each other's parts in a "leapfrog" fashion. Tweak the arrangement on a demo, add a sketch for the drum part, update the bass and guitar parts to suit, then redo the drums to raise the level of "action and interaction." After all these years we automatically play "to" each other organically (and pretty much helplessly), so that's not an issue, and this method allows for the more improvisational approach I prefer in recent years. Thirty years ago my drumming was more compositional, and thus the endless repetition actually served me well in creating those intricately detailed drum parts.

But it *hurt*. No one wants to relive pain, and thus I do not "wish I could live it all again." But still, there are many, many good memories from those days.

As I stood in front of the low, weathered building with the Banger crew, I described the recording of the intro for "Witch Hunt" on those very steps. On a night in early winter, with a few snowflakes in the air, we set up a microphone outdoors and acted out the vigilante scene. The rabble-rouser was played by yours truly, shouting out nonsense like, "We've got to stand up for law and order!" and "We have to protect our *children!*" The mob I was inciting to mayhem was made up of the Guys at Work—band, crew, and studio guys.

"Right over there . . ."
PHOTO BY MARTIN HAWKES

Another thirty-four-year-old memory emerged as I led the Banger camera and crew around to the back of the studio building, where the lake appeared through the trees. I described the recording of the intro for "Natural Science" down by the lakeshore. On a cold night late in 1979, Alex and I stood at the water's edge in winter coats and gloves, holding rowboat oars and canoe paddles. As we stirred the water, a pair of microphones (for stereo) on stands nearby captured the sound effects for the "Tide Pools" section. (Considering all our experiments with sonic environments and music-making gadgetry—digital recording, electronic instruments and sequencers, midi interfaces, drum triggers, digital sampling—that studio represented a kind of "Science Island," too.)

All these years later, after standing and looking out at that lake again, fairly overwhelmed by so many flashes of memory, I turned back toward the building. Shading the reflections with my arms, I looked through the plate-glass window into the recording room. I saw the parquet floor where my drums had been set up so many times—where I had "faced the music," and faced that cursèd control room door.

The studio building sits at one end of a small kidney-shaped lake; at the other end is the guest house—a large, multibedroomed dwelling, beautifully decorated by owner Andre Perry and his partner,

"My drums were set up just there."
PHOTO BY MARTIN HAWKES

Yaël. Also apparently abandoned now, the guest house was augmented by a smaller building, "The Little House on the Driveway," usually shared by a couple of crew members. Commuting between there and the studio in summer, you could take a rowboat, canoe, or pedal boat, or in winter, cross-country ski. On summer nights you could drift in a boat in the middle of the lake, in perfect silence and utter darkness, the bright Milky Way sweeping across the sky.

In the winter of 1980, when we were working on *Moving Pictures*, and a few years later for *Grace Under Pressure*, I made two "commuter" ski trails: one over the ice and snow around the lakeshore, and one through the woods, on land. I took the lake crossing in the daytime, or if there was someone with me. (Alex had a brief flirtation with cross-country skiing the first winter, when we were taught by the late Robbie Whelan, then assistant engineer and invaluable member of the recording team—remembered in "Not All Days Are Sundays," in *Far and Near*.) Even in the deep freeze of a Quebec winter night, beaver holes or flowing springs could make open ice treacherous, so when I was alone I took the "overland" route. Through the dark woods, my previous parallel tracks in the snow were faintly visible by moon or stars, and skis tended to follow those grooves easily enough. But I have never forgotten one snow-covered boulder in the woods that *always*, time after time, made me start and think, "Bear!" A momentary thrill of fear tricked me every time, just for that split second of atavistic terror. Certainly we are all hard-wired to respond to stimuli like that—anything that looks or sounds like it might *eat* you.

In the early '80s we stayed in the guest house for long stretches, working at the studio for months at a time, refining songs and arrangements, recording tracks and overdubs, and mixing. Being fairly close to home made it easy to have family members visit, or to take breaks in Toronto—unlike the years when we worked in Wales and England. In the space of just a few years the three of us flew Concorde about thirty times.

At Le Studio, we also played a lot of volleyball. We had a court marked out with vinyl tape and a few floodlights on two-by-four stands above the net. We would stop work an hour before dinner and play, usually with enough guys for four or five on a side, and after work—starting at midnight or 1 a.m. and sometimes continuing until the light of dawn appeared. (In high summer at that latitude, the sky would start to pale about 4:30 a.m.) The floodlights illuminated the playing area, more or less. An errant ball rolling off into the darkness could be a problem. As autumn brought down the leaves and then the snow, we would rake or shovel the court every night and keep playing as long as we could.

The following passage was written for a bio and tourbook essay for *Presto*, in 1990. (Funny that I first referred to the Guys at Work as "Rash" in that story—a joke that would recur over twenty years later in comedic films to accompany the *Time Machine* tour.)

Commuter Lanes

A long day's work behind us, we gathered outside, charged by the cool air of early summer in the Laurentians. We doused ourselves with bug repellent, then gathered on the floodlit grass, took our sides, and performed a kind of St. Vitus Dance to shake off the mosquitoes. Occasionally one of us hit the ball in the right direction—but not often. Mostly it was punched madly toward the lake, or missed completely, to trickle away into the dark and scary woods. ("*That's okay; I'll get it.*") We were as amused by Rupert's efforts at volleyball as he'd been by our songs but, indeed, all of us had our moments—laughter contributed more to the game than skill. And if the double-distilled French refreshments subtracted from our skill, they added to our laughter.

Between games the shout went up—"*Drink!*"—and obediently we ran to the line of brandy glasses on the porch. Richard the Raccoon poked his masked face out from beneath the stairs, wanting to know what all the noise was about. *"Richard!"* we shouted, and the poor frightened beastie ran back under the steps, and we ran laughing back onto the court. The floodlights silvered the grass, an island of light set apart from the world, like a stage.

On this stage, however, we leave out the drive for excellence; no pressure from within, no expectations from others. Mistakes are not a curse, but a cause for laughter, and on this stage, the play's the thing—we can forget that we also have to *work* together.

Work together, play together, frighten small mammals together: Are we having fun yet? Yes, we are. And *that*, now that I think about it, is why we do what we do, and why we keep doing it. We have fun together. How boring it would be if we didn't. Not only that, but we work well together, too, balancing each other like a three-sided mirror, each reflecting a different view, but all moving down the road together. As the Zen farmer says, "Life is like the scissors-paper-stone game: None of the answers is *always* right, but each one sometimes is."

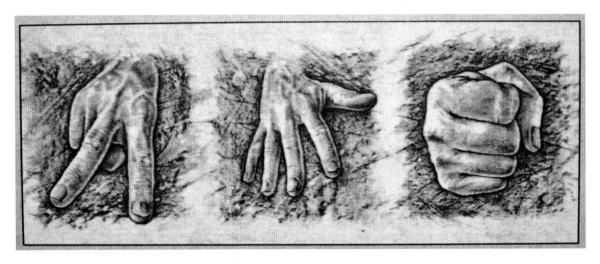

ARTWORK BY HUGH SYME

Those reflections from over two decades ago make a good segue to the part of the story the Banger guys wanted me to address: Geddy. Having said that Le Studio was the most important place in my life, it follows that the most important collaboration in my life has been with Geddy. That's all I really wanted to say on camera—though I don't think those actual words occurred to me until later.

In any case, the interviewer, Sam, had his eye on "the show" they were making. Naturally enough, he was looking for some incisive remarks from me, maybe some kind of "dirt"—if not *blood*. Preferably bad blood. He was careful about it, trying to bring me around to that sort of nitty-gritty by apologizing for "being like a three-year-old, asking the same question again and again." But a complex relationship that has endured for over forty years is not going to be defined in a sound bite. It's like asking a spouse of that duration to define the other—tread carefully!

I am often reminded of when Carrie and I were first getting to know each other, late in 1999. She had worked in human resources (loathsome name) for some big corporation and asked me, "What do you think your friends would say is your worst flaw?"

My immediate answer was, "My friends wouldn't say anything bad about me!"

She said, "You're being *evasive*."

But honestly, I didn't *think* I was. I was simply puzzled, and even now can't imagine such a scenario.

Perhaps it represents yet another echo of the line from the song "Presto" that I often cite as being always-and-forever true, "What a fool I used to be."

Then, in talking about Geddy, Sam also wanted me to presume to *analyze* why the guy is the way he is. Oh no, no, no.

Not entirely unconnected, since a 2014 story called "Magnetic Mirages" I have been pondering the theme of how each of us has been both wired and warped into seeing the world a certain way, and reacting to others from that stance. Mostly we are unconscious of those constraints and, I'm beginning to think, fairly helpless to be different. That has grown into a paradigm shift in the way I look at other people and their behavior. "They can't help doing what they can't help doing."

How we are wired and how we are warped shape our characters, and only strength of will, and occasionally extensive therapy, can change that. Some people are wired badly, and some are warped even worse. We usually don't choose our friends with maddening wiring and warpage, but all of us deal with people like that among our own guys at work, and perhaps in extended families. A lot of quirks and toxic behavior you might find exasperating, even enraging, really can be stepped away from in that phrase. "He can't help it." (Or "she," of course.)

When I say that my closest collaboration has been with Geddy, it is not to diminish Alex's role in our music. After all, Alex is our

Writing "Natural Science," 1979
PHOTO BY FIN COSTELLO

Musical Scientist, the Funniest Man Alive, and a shamefully under-rated and thoroughly wonderful guitar player. He can improvise so fast and freely he is hardly aware of it—we often laugh about how Geddy will ask him, "Wait—what was that?" and he only shrugs and says, "I don't know." That's why when the two of them are working on musical ideas, they have to record every second. And if we talk about bluesy, soulful guitar solos, I feel the passion and inventiveness of Alex's solos may only be rivaled by Pink Floyd's David Gilmour.

But the musical relationship between bass player and drummer, the rhythm section, is famously tight (or ought to be!). And of course the bond of trust necessary between lyricist and singer is even more intimate.

Posing in front of Le Studio that day in August 2014, I told the camera that as bass player and drummer, the communication between Geddy and me operated on three levels: 1) auditory, when we listen to what each other is playing and respond to the ideas, accents,

Still Making Me Smile
PHOTO BY CRAIG M. RENWICK

and patterns; 2) verbal, when we discuss different approaches we could take together and try them; and 3) something that verges on the *telepathic*, when suddenly we're both playing an interlocking pattern, onstage or in the studio, and laugh out loud.

I explained how the lyrics were completely subservient to their purpose—to be sung—and that if Geddy found something awkward to sing, I changed it. If he found something pleasurable to sing, I tried to write *more* like that!

Because surely the essence of collaboration is making each other happy, yes?

1970s Postcard

Conjuring the Happy Ghosts
PHOTO BY MARTIN HAWKES

This photograph is from almost forty years ago, and as of August 2014, that very piano sits among the ruins. Inexplicably, it has been left to molder away in the summer's damp heat and the winter's brittle cold.

My feelings were running high during that visit, but I could not quite define them—words failed for a time. Some people described the place's abandonment as "sad," but wandering through those rooms did not make me feel that way. What I felt was more like *lucky*, with an overriding sense of *gratitude*—that we had been fortunate enough to live and work in a place like that, all those times, in every season. And others like it: Air Studios in the tropical paradise of Montserrat; the "quaint" British residential studios like Rockfield, the Manor, and Ridge Farm; and Bearsville and Allaire in New York's Catskill Mountains. In today's lean and hungry music industry—for better and worse—such facilities are all part of a vanished world. Certainly it will be a long time before a rock band will ever again enjoy and be nourished by such artistic and playful retreats.

That, to me, is the *really* sad part.

Among the many prominent artists who visited Le Studio over the years, from David Bowie to Keith Richards to Tina Turner, in the early '80s the Police worked on their *Ghost in the Machine* and *Synchronicity* albums there. The idea of ghosts and spirits, as in their great song "Spirits in the Material World," suggests that the scarred shell of the building must still be haunted by something ethereal, something ineffable. But I felt like the ghosts must be "happy" ones, and I was proud to see my younger self among them.

Clockwork Angels Tour
(Bubba the Bearded Lady, Too)
PHOTO BY CRAIG M. RENWICK

GIFTS OF TIME

At the end of the *Clockwork Angels* tour in the summer of 2013, the Guys at Work and I had played seventy-two shows, and with my riding partners, Michael and Brutus, I had covered 28,000 miles of motorcycling.

Us three band members agreed then that after touring and recording fairly incessantly for the previous ten years (not to mention almost thirty years before that), we would not even *talk* about work for at least a year.

Thus I had a true sabbatical in 2014, as in the excellent Wiki definition: "In recent times, 'sabbatical' has come to mean any extended absence in the career of an individual in order to achieve something. In the modern sense, one takes sabbatical typically to fulfill some goal, e.g., writing a book or traveling extensively for research."

Moonrise, Sunset, Homeward Bound

In my case, I only modified that to "staying home extensively for research." And looking back, I guess it only *seems* coincidental that around that same time I leased the Hallowed Bubba Cave. At first I only wanted a garage where I could keep a few old cars, but then, in one corner, I put a desk and a chair. Suddenly—let the heavens open and the angels sing!—a *sanctuary*—a place to hide out and write with silence, solitude, and an inspiring view of gritty urban functionalism outside, and pretty silver cars inside.

A sabbatical combined with a sanctuary promises a magical, or at least alchemical, mix. Soon I was settled into a weekday nine-to-five routine at the Hallowed Bubba Cave. (The adjective was suggested by Stewart Copeland. I had thought of naming it the Sacred Bubba Cave, after his home studio, the Sacred Grove, but after visiting, he thought I should up it to Hallowed.) The combination of time and place was pleasant and productive, and, well, I loved it.

Among plenty of letter-writing and shorter pieces for magazines and friends' books, I was able to spearhead a new Bubba's Bar 'n'

Grill calendar for 2014. I had first made that happen for 2012, and they require a surprising amount of work and time, so don't get made every year. (And alas, people don't seem to care much about fine-art calendars in these digital times.)

The whimsical title I came up with for the calendar led me to put together a book, *Far and Near: On Days Like These*. The stories had all appeared previously on my website, but moving to print required editorial supervision and new writing for the beginning and end. At the same time I was contributing to the development of the graphic novel of *Clockwork Angels* with Kevin Anderson, artist Nick Robles, and the fine editorial team of Ian Brill and Jasmine Amiri. Then Kevin dived into writing *Clockwork Lives*, a spin-off from the *Clockwork Angels* universe (as I describe it, "We invented a world we like so much we can't stand to leave it!"). I was happy to be *available* to keep up with Kevin's prolific pace—even hoping to write a couple of the stories myself.

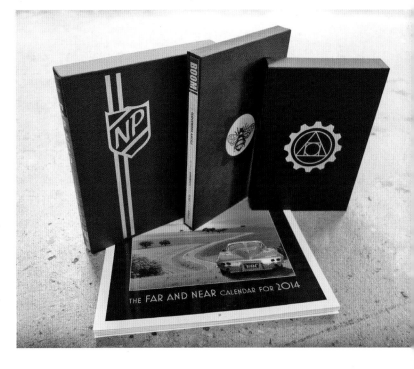

(Alas, the ostensible subject of this book—the R40 tour—belayed that desire. But I did get to help Kevin with a couple of worthy passages about "imaginary music," and I am grateful for that little dabble into speculative fiction.)

Outside my weekday office hours, I could begin and end my days at home, being around at breakfast and off-to-school time, and picking up groceries on the way home and cooking healthy dinners for Carrie and Olivia. Weekends were sacred Family Time, staying home or sharing activities like weekend getaways to San Francisco, the exquisite Ojai Valley (model for an early film version of Shangri-La—as Olivia once remarked at age four, "Ojai has *real* magic"), or Palm Springs. To give Mama some time on her own, Olivia and Daddy would go ice skating, roller skating, to playgrounds and museums, and make lots and lots of art.

Life felt absolutely complete to me, and I realized that I felt *done* with all the rest. Not in any bitter or jaded way—quite the contrary. I simply felt that fifty years of playing drums, forty of them with Rush, might be enough for these old bones.

Hearing loss alone would be a valid reason—but even in that regard I look at the bright side. (Just made that way. It bothers some people.) It is ironic that the damage was not from the actual *drumming*, but occurred in the late '70s and early '80s when I had crappy distorted monitors cranked up painfully loud to be able to play along with primitive sequencers. Thus my hearing loss is much worse than the other Guys at Work have suffered. However, fifty years of playing drums have been rewarding enough that I will not haggle about the price. Like the line I adapted from the great novelist John Barth for "Bravado" (with his approval, which I was proud to receive by letter in 1990), "We will pay the price, but we will not count the cost."

And anyway, hearing aids are very *advanced* these days!

Artistically, at that point in my life prose writing was outlet and fulfillment aplenty, and—without criticizing anyone (there will be no score-settling or grudge-bearing here)—let's just say prose writing is . . . uncomplicated by other personalities. Plus it was so much less stressful and punishing than touring, mentally and physically. Maybe I didn't have to do that to myself anymore—maybe I had *earned*, in every sense, the right to step out of the ring, "to withdraw, as from battle."

(A quote from Bob Dylan leaps to mind. When asked how he reconciled his wealth with his values, he said, "For every dollar I've earned there's a pool of sweat on the floor."

Good old Mr. Zimmerman also nailed the purpose of art—to inspire. "What else can you do? What else can you do for anyone but inspire them?")

Even after a couple of years, the *Clockwork Angels* album still seemed as good as I could do, in lyrics and drumming. That feeling had never happened before. As a band, I felt it stood as the masterpiece we had spent our career working toward. We were not going to beat it. The subsequent tour, featuring the Clockwork Angels String Ensemble, likewise felt like a high-water mark that did not need to be challenged.

These were new states of existence for me, who had always been sure I could do better, better, better.

("A man's reach should exceed his grasp, or what's a metaphor?" Marshall McLuhan, after Robert Browning.)

So, as I stood poised on that metaphorical stepping stone, with peaceful waters all around, I had a decision to make. Not just about my own life, for it would affect a great number of others, too. The Guys at Work, our families, our crew and their families, manager Ray and his employees at the Toronto office, and just regular people who might want to see us play together again—quite a "crowd," so to speak. Around my solitary island ripples and waves stirred the once-placid surface in ever-widening circles of turbulence.

In the fall of 2014 I agreed to travel to Toronto and meet with the Guys at Work—Alex, Geddy, and manager Ray. My plan then was to tell them I was "done," or at least that I was not interested in touring the following year. In my secret heart of hearts, the one tiny door I left open was that if one of the guys said he *really* wanted to do it one more time, and wasn't sure he'd be *able* to in another year, I would have to . . . surrender.

Well. Of course Alex didn't know about that little door, or that my decision hinged on it, but he said *exactly* that—explaining that his creeping arthritis was affecting his hands, that he really wanted to play live again, and didn't know if he would be able to do it in another year. (In such situations, the three of us often imitate the emotionless, underplayed delivery of a British army officer expressing outrage in a cold monotone: "My god. You bawsted.")

Realizing I was trapped, I got back to my hotel that night and stomped around the room in a mighty rage and an attack of extreme Tourette's. But soon I surrendered to the wisdom of my late drum teacher, Freddie Gruber—a motto carved in wood on the desk at the Hallowed Bubba Cave.

"It is what it is. *Deal* with it."

British statesman Benjamin Disraeli (1804–1881) said, "Never complain; never explain." I respect that, and am pretty sure I am not a complainer—however, I can never resist trying to *explain* myself. Unfortunately, to some people that can sound the same as complaining. I remember an interview with Jennifer Lopez, at a time when she was being mercilessly dogged by the gutter media and paparazzi. She was asked what it was like to live like that, and she paused before answering, "Well, I mustn't seem to be *complaining*."

(Just ran across this journal note from later in the tour, before I found the Disraeli quote: "'I Don't Want to Complain, But Let Me Explain,' said nobody ever. Until me, now.")

But what I wish to explain is that my reluctance was not selfish—or not *entirely* so. During the previous tour it had become apparent that my absence was very hard on Olivia. At three and four years old, she could not understand why Daddy was away, but it felt wrong to her. She was disturbed emotionally and even physically, developing nervous tics and "acting out" behavior. Forty years of touring have taught me how to "compartmentalize" the things I am missing—family and home—and as I have said before about Olivia, "I can stand missing her, but I can't stand her missing me."

At least now that she was a little older I could explain things better, and we had developed good ways to communicate when we were apart. Art is the language Olivia and I share, together or apart, and from my motel room or backstage we connect visually on my iPad or even cell phone. I will be ready with pen and paper, knowing Olivia will say, "Draw something for me." Then off she will go into flights of fantastic scale, yet with infinitely specific details.

Art with Olivia *Bubble Guppies* in Egyptian Garden

Following her directions, I sketch and occasionally raise the result to the screen to show her as I go. A thoughtful friend gave me a set of double-ended pencil crayons (Americans call them "colored pencils"—so *literal*) that were compact enough to carry on my motorcycle. Thus this tour, over a couple of sessions together, I was able to produce some finished works for her. The main value is that we end up spending an hour or so face-to-face like that, where a typical conversation with a five-year-old would long have "expired."

So much of life on Planet Olivia is represented in this collaborative work. Olivia's little hand shows four fingers—a secret sign of ours—because that's what the Bubble Guppies have. I explained to her that it's kind of an inside joke going back to the earliest cartoons by Walt Disney, who felt five fingers made the hands too big.

Olivia is my art director, in meticulous detail, and she is the final colorist. Dad just tries to follow her highly detailed instructions for the outlines. She specifies each costume, each painting—like the central character Oona's in the style of Jackson Pollock's "Autumn Rhythm," and Nonny's (the "Aspy" of the diverse Guppies) of lipsticks in various shades, in the style of Andy Warhol. Olivia had just learned about those artists at preschool. Another of her fascinations shows in the Ancient Egyptian art in blue-haired Gil's painting (he's the schlemiel of the Guppies) and the wall behind the garden. On that wall is the goddess Ma'at, and Olivia will tell you she represents harmony, justice, and truth.

Here's one we did by long distance on a piece of printer paper when I was in Montreal and Boston. It featured her new "friends" from an animated show called *Team Umizoomi*. (Yes, each time she finds a new favorite show I have to learn to draw the characters—I just print them out and copy.) Milli and Geo enjoy their pancakes, while our dog, Winston, looks on, and Olivia is about to steal some pancakes from Bot's tray. Milli's enormous pigtails on the flowered helmet have superpowers, as do the "nipples" on Geo's, while the dog ears on Olivia's helmet show that she is able to change into a dog that can talk like a human.

I just draw what she says—and of course both of us prefer to be *together* when we do it. That is the invisible loss faced by touring musicians—the moments, the people, the places, and especially the children. How to measure that? The moments we miss we *lose*, not for a day or a month but forever.

Eastern religions instruct us to be mindful of each moment, and I do practice that awareness of my own time and place—often. I have been with Olivia, drawing or ice skating, and thought consciously, "Instead of doing this I could be in Indianapolis, or Denver, or Virginia Beach today." And of course, been instantly grateful that I *wasn't*.

No offense to any of those places, or the highways between, but my favorite name these days is Dad.

So I Had This Idea . . .
PHOTO BY CRAIG M. RENWICK

BACKSTAGE BYWAYS

After that meeting in Toronto in November, when I agreed to three months of touring and thirty-five shows, the work of planning those shows had built with ever-increasing intensity for five months.

And "building" the show is how it started to feel, as we worked on the concept for a reverse-chronology presentation, employing the skills of many artists in theatrical staging and video arts. (One of the pleasures of our profession is giving other artists the opportunity to do *their* best work.) Eventually our traveling circus would fill eleven trucks and carry sixty-two people with five buses, two motorcycles, and one chartered jet.

Right from that first November meeting, song suggestions rocketed among the three of us. We needed to narrow down a list for production reasons, and for us to be prepared to play them. We agreed fairly easily on ones we could retire for a while, often those we had performed recently, and the "indispensables" (fans know what they are!). We dredged up a few discoveries from the past, like "How It Is" from *Vapor Trails* (2002), which we had never played live, and "Jacob's Ladder" from *Permanent Waves* (1979), unplayed since that tour—a mere thirty-five years ago!

As I saw the way the setlist and production were growing and listened to some of the songs from the late '70s we were considering, I had a whimsical thought that first triggered a smile, then an affirmative nod of my head. "Yeah. Gotta do it."

What if in addition to using the current iteration of my "modern" setup, during intermission I switched to a replica of the black-chrome Slingerlands I had played in the late '70s? Double bass drums, open concert toms—bad ergonomics and all.

The idea seemed irresistible to me, and I was soon meeting with the artists and artisans at Drum Workshop to begin work on designing and building both sets. Here is an essay I wrote for the *R40* tourbook—a section we always called our "equipment pages"—which gives a little background on the hardware side of my workplace.

Black Chrome Slingerlands, Circa 1977
PHOTOGRAPHER UNKNOWN

These *R40* drums are a time machine that spans an incredible 1500 years. Around 500 CE was the beginning of the Dark Ages in Central Europe, when the Roman Empire was crumbling and overrun by . . . what sounds like a bunch of heavy-metal bands—the Visigoths, the Ostrogoths, the Vandals, the Byzantines, the Saxons, the Bulgars, the Huns.

Meanwhile, along the banks of the Olt River in present-day Romania, a mighty oak tree toppled into the water and was gradually buried in silt. Centuries, generations, and historical epochs passed, while that oak's wood gathered supernatural density from the pressure of its airless tomb.

In 2014 that log was raised, and its wood was acquired by Drum Workshop. I tried a few prototype shells and knew I wanted my new drums made from that log—the wood offered exceptional tonality and projection.

Through the development of DW's "Icon" snare series, I learned about laser-cut inlay work, and we applied that technology to an update of the *R30* drumset design. Each of the logos and even the red oblong frames around them (deliberately evoking Keith Moon's "Pictures of Lily" kit, my teenage dream) are made of inlaid hardwoods. The hardware is gold-plated, as seemed appropriate for an "anniversary" tour.

It will soon be no secret that I am playing two separate sets on this tour: one "modern" arrangement like I have been using for the past twenty-five years, and one like the setup I played for almost twenty years before—double bass drums, open concert toms, ride cymbal hard right. Its look is modeled after the black-chrome Slingerlands I played in the late '70s, but DW's version far surpasses those in tone, resonance, playability, and "shininess"! The hardware is plated in black nickel, for a murdered-out look that will be perfect when I am asked to play for the Ostrogoth Vandals or the Byzantine Huns . . .

Monsters from the Deep

Each drumshell in both sets was made from that single Romanian River Oak (DW uses the slogan "1500 Years in the Making"; I prefer "Monsters from the Deep.")

The cymbals are all Sabian Paragons, with a couple of new sizes in the mix—19-inch and 17-inch crashes. Sticks are by Pro-Mark, the heads an ever-changing variety of DW and Remos (always experimenting in that area). The Roland V-Drums (with custom DW shells), MalletKat, KAT trigger pedal, and Dauz pad go through Ableton Live running on a MacBook Pro.

Lorne "Gump" Wheaton continues to keep all that good stuff working and looking wonderful, as he has for almost fifteen years now. Recently a friend asked the two of us who was the bigger "pain" to work with, and after a pause, I replied, "We don't really have trouble with each other—just *other* people!"

Gump laughed and agreed . . .

Not surprisingly, I much prefer playing my modern drumset, which has evolved into a more cohesive instrument. For example, all of the toms blend into one chord, instead of the two separate chromatic arrays of the high concert toms and lower closed toms. The only unfortunate result in the show was that I ended up soloing on the "retro" kit, in the second set, which I would rather have done on the modern setup—more comfortable, and more "musical." But "deal with it," et cetera, and I was well enough pleased with the results. Wailing on the timbales was fun, and the big "gong drum" on my right was a dynamic powerhouse.

Chimes and Rushmore Profile Onscreen
PHOTO BY JOHN ARROWSMITH

The idea of adding the dramatic orchestra chimes (a.k.a. tubular bells) for songs like "Jacob's Ladder" and "Xanadu" had been the same kind of "gotta do it" decision. They made a melodic and theatrical addition to the show—the crowd loved it, and so did I.

Starting at the beginning of March, I rehearsed on my own for a full month at my home away from home, Drum Channel. One major highlight is the *commute*—fifty miles up and back on the Pacific Coast Highway every day in one of my old silver classics—alternating the DB5, the E-Type, and the Ghibli, each for a few days at a time.

Gump and I got the new gear sorted, and I began playing along with the recorded versions of the songs—a little more, and a little harder, every day. By the second week when I was sweating through two sets of clothes, I knew I was "getting somewhere." At the end of the day Gump handed me an Advil gelcap to take before driving home, and even then I would stiffen up during that hour and climb out with a groan. But as I always say, I hurt all over, not in any specific place, so that's okay.

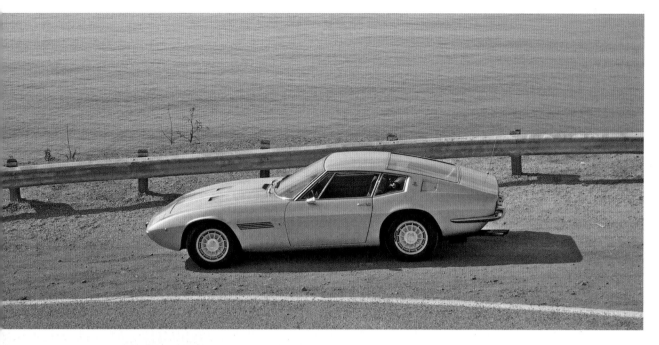

1973 Maserati Ghibli SS

"What was I thinking?"
PHOTO BY CRAIG M. RENWICK

During the same time the other guys were doing their "homework," and in April we got together for band rehearsals. Alex and Geddy had generously agreed to do them in Los Angeles this time, rather than the usual Toronto, allowing me to have more time at home. They are both grandfathers, while I am a "late-life dad," and "Uncle Alex and Uncle Geddy" understand that five-year-old Olivia likes to have her daddy around.

People laugh when I say I like rehearsing better than performing, but it's true. While I understand the reality that I can't have one without the other, rehearsing offers all the same challenges without the stress and demands of working in front of an audience (those "strangers with expectations"). Some would rhapsodize about the energy amplified by the crowd, and there's something to that. But it has to be measured against being able to be at home mornings and evenings—having breakfast in my own kitchen and sleeping in my own bed. These small blessings cannot be appreciated without knowing their lack.

The Guys at Work
PHOTO BY CRAIG M. RENWICK

Here's how I described the mindset of rehearsing ten years before, in *Roadshow: Landscape With Drums—A Concert Tour by Motorcycle.*

I was giving it everything I had, straining and sweating, and in fact, I was already playing for an audience, though they were imaginary. It is a defining trait in my character and attitude toward performing that no audience is more unforgivingly critical than an imaginary one. They knew exactly how well I was supposed to play, and whether I had or not.

Every time you push yourself to your absolute limits, mentally and physically, and as the standards rise, you're like a high-jumper continually raising the bar. On a good day, you might clear it, but the rest of the time you just fall on your ass.

A journal note I made during band rehearsals this time was titled "My Metric Century"—because in March of that year I had turned sixty-two-point-five years old. In long-distance bicycling a major goal is a Century, a hundred miles in one day, but sometimes less ambitious—or less masochistic—cyclists choose what is called a Metric Century, a hundred kilometers [*please* say "*kill-o-meters*"], or sixty-two-point-five miles.

Under that title I wrote, "Lucky days, these. PCH opening, traffic patterns, physical health, family equilibrium."

"PCH opening" referred to a long stretch of the Pacific Coast Highway on the way to Drum Channel that had been closed for *months* due to mudslides—it reopened two days before we started. "Traffic patterns" noted that my commute to the band rehearsal place was on one of the busiest freeways in the country, but good fortune had the heavy volume in the opposite direction each way. The first time I drove there on that notorious 405 I had the conscious thought, "That was *way* nicer than it had any right to be. What city am I in?"

The rehearsal place was part of a vast warehouse where many bands stored their equipment, and one entertaining pastime was watching all the different road cases cross the loading dock every day. Like a classic rock playlist, there was Def Leppard, Van Halen, Kiss, Fleetwood Mac, REO Speedwagon, Boston, and on and on. Some of the less prominent names these days, like Billy Idol and the Black Crowes, I was just glad to see they had work. Because it would be awful to want it and not have it—certainly worse than having it and not wanting it . . .

The ceremonial "Ghost Rider" photograph was taken on the morning of my departure from home to the production rehearsals and first show in Tulsa, Oklahoma. It is the latest in a series begun in 1998, in a setting I will always love. With my motorcycle or car, when I travel that way I like to pause and repeat the framing—facing west on old Route 66 toward Amboy, California, with Roy's Motel and the Amboy Crater in the distance.

In the middle of that day's necessarily long freeway slog, I had allowed myself the luxury of crossing the Mojave by two-lanes, from Palm Springs to just north of Amboy, where I joined Interstate 40 for the rest of the day. (I-40 to R40—perfect.) That may have cost me an hour, but repaid me well in enjoyment.

Even that seemingly straightforward journey took some logistical planning. The first consideration was that I didn't want to fly from Los Angeles to Tulsa. My quality ratio of flying to road travel is simply between "bad" and "good," and if a journey can be done by road in less than a day, I'll do it that way.

In any case, a long motorcycle ride seemed the proper way to kick off a big tour, and this route was an especially sweet echo. Our thirtieth anniversary tour, R30, had also begun with a long ride on I-40, to rehearsals in Nashville (described in *Roadshow*). But that 2,000-mile crossing had taken three days, and though this one was "only" 1,500 miles, to maximize time at home I needed to do it overnight.

So . . . strategy.

On the appointed day in late April, Dave set out with the bus and trailer from his home base in Nashville. I had pulled the meeting point of Grants, New Mexico, out of my head as being roughly 750 miles from

my house. From previous crossings I knew that distance was about "right"—to cover some miles without suffering too much. Back in the fall of 1996, Brutus and I had taken refuge in Grants one night, coming the other way on a long cross-country ride. That night I had bought a book about the area in the motel lobby and learned that Grants was named after three Canadian brothers who built the railway running through, and that the town had experienced a uranium boom in the mid-twentieth century. Location, accommodations, and history—all seemed good reasons to aim for Grants.

As a professional driver for twenty years, Dave has crossed the country more than a few times. He and I agree that of all the cross-country freeways, Interstate 40 is the most "interesting." Going east, the scenery changes from California desert (100 degrees at Needles) to the high-elevation pine forests around Flagstaff, then down to the red rock desert of New Mexico. The nostalgic remnants of old Route 66, which I-40 largely replaced, remain colorful and entertaining along the roadside in billboards and attractions.

Michael and I had ended up riding separately—he was late showing up at my house, so I just left. (No fun standing

Rendezvous in Grants

in the driveway with all your riding gear on, straddling a silent bike—not wanting to disturb the neighborhood, even with the BMW's inoffensive purr.) I texted him my intended route and figured we would almost certainly connect somewhere along that highway. But we never did—Michael followed me into the truck stop at Grants to meet the bus a half hour behind me. And that was fine, I never mind riding alone. It's having someone to talk to at the end of the day that's nice. Even if that someone is Michael. (Longtime readers know the two of us are "the best of frenemies," and maintain our day-to-day equilibrium by constantly "venting" at each other. I still like to tell the story of how one time Michael delivered a load of bitter and obscene rhetoric on me, and I said, "I love that you feel you can talk to me like that—but I really wish you wouldn't." One admirable quality Michael does have is that he's not "moody"—not the kind of person who is a different person every day, like many people we know. Nope, not our Michael—he's the same person. Every. Day.)

The bikes were tied down in the trailer, and Dave drove us through the night to a Château Walmart in Elk City, Oklahoma.

For this traveler, many an adventure has begun in a seemingly mundane Walmart parking lot. After each show, driver Dave ferries Michael and me to my chosen dropoff point for the next day's ride, then parks for the rest of the night. These days truckstops are increasingly crowded and noisy, while Walmart parking lots welcome overnight campers as potential morning shoppers. And the reader will likely be aware that in the twenty-first century Walmarts are *everywhere* in North America—over five thousand "outlets" as of 2015.

No one could say how many small towns have been gutted—indeed, have lost their hearts and souls—and how many thousands of little businesses, once someone's dream, have been beaten down. In small towns around the rural United States I see the sad rows of shuttered ruins where a former "downtown" is reduced to not much more than a post office. But people vote with their dollars (as do their elected representatives!), and it is the suburbs where Walmart truly rules. One time I arranged with Dave to meet Michael and me at a Walmart north of Toronto, on Major Mackenzie Drive. Michael and I turned off the highway there and followed our GPS units to the wrong Walmart, not once but twice—because on that same suburban street within five miles of each other were *three* Walmarts. So a Château Walmart is almost always available where I plan to begin a ride—and I just realized that when scanning the map I might subconsciously choose where to start by the likelihood of a Walmart. Keep things easy and predictable, which of course is exactly why Walmart exists—and why they are located near the same offramps as Holiday Inn Express, Denny's, and Flying J truckstops.

In the morning Michael and I unloaded the bikes among early Elk City Walmart shoppers and carried on another 300 miles, by my chosen backroads, to Tulsa. We would arrive in time for the first production rehearsal that night, and so even before the first show Michael and I had ridden over 1,000 miles.

Earlier that winter of 2014–15, Olivia and I had been doing a lot of ice skating at rinks in Los Angeles and San Francisco. As with teaching her snowshoeing, or how to kill deer flies, I called it "nurturing her inner Icechucker." It was Michael who started calling us Canadians Icechuckers, with multiple levels of cultural insensitivity.

He says we come from the socialist dystopia of Icechuckerland—which, according to him, is pronounced like "Northumberland."

That spring Olivia had started roller skating, so I bought skates of my own. I brought them with me for that week in Tulsa, with a big empty arena to ramble around in. The first time I showed up backstage on those eight wheels, the crew guys were visibly . . . *alarmed*. Apparently worried I was going to fall and hurt myself—and threaten their livelihoods. I could only laugh.

I hadn't thought about that for a second, having roller-skated throughout my youth. (Though perhaps I might have reflected that this was no longer my youth!) In my teenage years in the mid- to late '60s, the social center for young people in St. Catharines was the roller rink. The hits of the day played as we skated—slow songs like "Cherish" and "When a Man Loves a Woman" for Couples Only and Ladies' Choice, fast ones like "Wipe Out," "Good Lovin'," and "Psychotic Reaction" for Boys Only. Later in the evening live bands—often Toronto blue-eyed-soul outfits—played on a stage in the corner. In the summer of 1969, a version of the ever-changing band I was in, the Majority, was the "house band" there.

On one or two tours in the late '70s, roller skating had been a backstage pastime for a number of us Guys at Work. Arena floors and outside hallways were spectacular for it. On more recent tours I often saw our pyro guy, John "Boom-Boom," zooming around backstage parking lots on inline skates with our merch guy, Patrick. When Boom-Boom saw me rolling around the loading dock, he immediately sent the runner out for a pair of wristguards he insisted I should wear—because he had been hurt that way one time. All this concern made me laugh inside, thinking, "If they only knew . . . ," meaning the dangers to life and limb I faced on the motorcycle *every day*.

The expression "to shoot yourself in the foot" is often misused, like in cases where people deliberately sabotage themselves in some way. The real meaning is quite the opposite. Coined in World War I, it referred to soldiers who gave themselves a self-inflicted wound rather than be sent into the slaughter of the trenches. So shooting yourself in the foot was not a self-defeating act (so to speak—ouch), but one of *self-preservation*.

One episode in the Artie Shaw biography tells of him working around his home with an axe, splitting firewood, when a mishap almost took off a finger. Chillingly, Shaw described how at that moment he experienced a fleeting thought that actually *cheered* him: "The very first thought I had was, 'I'll never have to play the clarinet

Roller Derby Bubba
PHOTO BY RICHARD SIBBALD

PHOTO BY RICHARD SIBBALD

again.'" You never know what's going on under the surface—even your *own* surface. But I don't *think* I had anything like that in mind.

Though . . . there was that other time. Back in March I had been ice skating with Olivia and friends the day before I would start drum rehearsals. I hadn't thought of it as being risky or foolish, but at one point I was on the ice holding hands with a five-year-old on each side. Suddenly one was falling forward while the other toppled behind, and I felt myself going over backward. There was just enough time on the way down to think, "Uh-oh."

I landed on my side and my elbow, the impact traveling up to my shoulder, which seemed to be hurt the worst. Shaking it off, I kept skating, rotating that shoulder to keep it mobile. I was relieved when I went to work the next day and it didn't affect my playing. However, a couple of weeks later I woke up one morning with a swollen, tender red bulge on that elbow. It turned out to be bursitis—a whole new disease I had never heard of before, waiting to be experienced . . . in my Metric Century.

Anti-inflammatories kept it under control, though every time I tried to stop taking that unpleasant medication (disturbing my digestion, sleep, and even concentration), it would flare up again. I ended up having to take them for about two months, and the disturbance to

PHOTO BY RICHARD SIBBALD

my onstage concentration was a real nuisance. It seemed I had to be doubly on guard against "lapses," and it was thus twice as exhausting, mentally.

In any case, inviting the reader to follow me on a backstage tour around the arena on roller skates seems like a good way to introduce some of the setting and characters. With so many Guys at Work on the entire production (over sixty), there is no way to introduce them all without overwhelming the reader. But, as Willy Loman's wife said in *Death of a Salesman*, "Attention must be paid."

Rolling down the outer hallways, I passed the main production office. The heartbeat of everything in so many ways, from early morning load-in to late night load-out, it was presided over by C.B. He has been our production manager since 1996, though we have known

each other since 1974, when C.B. worked for Kiss's sound company. Our new production assistant was a French-Canadian named Lydia, and she would prove to be a sweetheart of efficiency and good cheer.

Farther down was "Drysdale and Co." (after the tight-fisted banker on *The Beverly Hillbillies*), the office of tour manager Liam, which also carried the drudgery of tour accountant—payroll, expenses, settlements. Liam has been with the band since before I joined, working his way up as the operation grew from a crew of two to sixty-two—of which he was Supreme Commander.

Venue security chief Tony shared an office with artist liaison (press, photographers, meet-and-greets, guest lists, and more) Kevin, while Frenchie ruled over a makeshift kitchen in a hockey dressing room. Traveling with ten road cases and assorted coolers, Frenchie had been our self-described "nutritionist" since 2002. And it is true that few working conditions are more important to the three of us than nutrition. To keep up our output of energy, we need to eat well. Frenchie's soup is justly famous, and he prepared our meals to individual preferences (steaks for Alex; fish or chicken for Geddy and me). Even Frenchie's after-show sandwiches, prepared for my bus every night, were masterpieces of care and creativity—never the same combination of breads and fillings twice.

Our meals in the dressing room were carried in by Donovan, who has served for eleven years as our road manager. That is a catchall title for a job that ranged from traveling with the other two and looking after their needs to producing any object requested from his cavernous roadcases.

Nearer the stage I greeted the band crew, like Tony "Jack Secret," with us since 1977, usually in the "keyboard pit"; Alex's tech of a few tours, Scottie, at stage right; and Geddy's man Skully at stage left— among the vast collection of vintage bass guitars the two of them had assembled in recent years. I also might run into stage manager George (since about 1987, and we had known each other since childhood in Port Dalhousie), and monitor guy Brent (since 2004).

Behind the stage I had to get up on my toe-stops and step carefully over heaps of cables running from the control consoles for the moving lights and rear-screen projections. Many of those technicians were a good-humored bunch of French-Canadians from a newly hired video company from Montreal. The director of the film portions of the show and the live-camera action, Dave, has been with us since 2002.

The R40 production required a great number of props, especially for the ever-changing amp line as it "devolved" through time. Carpenter Cliff had a full-on woodshop set up near the loading area to work on all that, and he and many other crew members were busy throughout the show moving them in and out. Above the stage (and above all our heads) hung 40,000 pounds of speakers, light trusses, and video screens, all positioned by riggers Jerry and James.

As I skated out front, between the rows of seats on the floor, I arrived at the fenced-off audio consoles, ruled since 2004 by our front-of-house mixer, Brad—chief of the audio crew for a few tours before that. Behind Brad's setup, on a riser, was the lighting board and the Mighty Herns in command, as he had been since 1974, joining at the same time I did, as our first road manager and later as lighting director.

As for the danger to life and limb in that roller-skating expedition, and two or three other occasions that week, I had a couple of stumbles, but never did fall. What's more, for the rest of the tour I never again had the time and energy on a show day to put on those skates.

PHOTO BY JOHN ARROWSMITH

This, Too, Is Oklahoma
PHOTO BY MICHAEL MOSBACH

A SENSE OF PLACE

From time to time in my stories I have inserted a series of what I call "cliché buster" photographs: me on my motorcycle in the pastoral countryside of New Jersey, banking around a corner in Iowa, or railing through a ninety-degree bend in an Indiana cornfield. As one who has traveled a myriad of byways and landscapes in the United States, surely as widely as any living mortal, I have seen every stereotype, and every exception.

The above photograph was taken on Winding Stair Mountain, in the southeast corner of Oklahoma. The peaks behind are the Ouachita Mountains (surely where "Wichita" comes from as well), which bridge Oklahoma and Arkansas, and were once part of the Appalachians much farther east. Winding Stair is an important setting in the novel

True Grit, though replaced in the two film versions by Colorado and New Mexico.

Michael and I were returning from a day-off jaunt to Hot Springs, Arkansas, before the first show in Tulsa. Even this little side-trip had called for some strategy to make it possible, with Dave driving us south from Tulsa after the final rehearsal to McAlester, Oklahoma. (You know where we parked.)

But there was another mighty cliché buster during our stay in Tulsa. We were working there for a little over a week, rehearsing as we would be performing—every second night—so Carrie and Olivia joined me for a few days. At first Carrie hadn't been impressed by the notion of spending a week in Tulsa, but we all ended up enjoying our time there very much. The hotel was good, the staff were friendly and helpful, and Olivia and I shared some good times at the pool.

On a day off Dave drove the family in our bus (Olivia delighted by that: the first time in her life riding in a vehicle without being strapped into a car seat) up to Bartlesville, Oklahoma. We stopped at the Woolaroc Ranch, named for the woods, lakes, and rocks of its setting in the Osage Hills. The 3,700-acre working ranch was founded in 1925 by Frank Phillips, of petroleum fame—and wealth. He made

This, Too, Is Iowa
PHOTO BY MICHAEL MOSBACH

it an unparalleled monument to the American West, the pastures stocked with longhorn cattle, bison, elk, and even exotics like ostrich and water buffalo, while the main buildings house what must be the world's finest collection of Western art and artifacts.

Around the town, Carrie and Olivia encountered more friendly people, and an attractive park with a classical ensemble giving a concert. While they were out I was looking from the tenth-floor window down at the pool, and noticed it was filled with a crowd of burly white guys, many bald, but with luxuriant beards. Then I noticed a few pairs of them were obviously cuddling (there's no other word), one standing behind the other with his arms around him.

They were "Bears"—a subset of gay men who identify by their size and hairiness. It turned out to be a formal gathering, called the "Green Country Growl" (the area around Tulsa calls itself "Green Country"), and they had booked many of the hotel's facilities, including the pool. They even wore nametag laminates on lanyards everywhere and gathered in hirsute and husky pairs in the restaurant in the mornings while Olivia and I colored. Like some of the other stories I have touched upon or glanced at, there's much more to this tale—but the major deal is clear: *It was happening in Tulsa, Oklahoma!*

I was surprised and delighted; others might be shocked and appalled—nevertheless, it demonstrated a sea change at work in America.

Considering these themes in words and pictures—the cliché busters of all kinds, like mountains and Bears in Oklahoma—an early title I thought of for this chapter was "THIS, TOO, IS AMERICA." Yet we experienced moments in places that *were* absolute stereotypes, in the best sense.

Back in the early summer of 1997, on the *Test for Echo* tour, Brutus and I had slept on the bus to Ogallala, Nebraska—coming from a show in Denver that time, I think, on the way to one in Dallas. That day we rode south through Kansas, with a pause at Dodge City (because it was there—and we grew up on *Gunsmoke*) and onward into Oklahoma. Late in the day the weather started to kick up, dark clouds looming in with gusty winds. We pulled over to put on our rain gear, and I took a photograph of Brutus holding his plastic rain pants as they were whipped to horizontal. (The image exists *somewhere*, but in the prehistoric world of slide transparencies—relics of a past age.)

In late afternoon we took shelter in the town of Fairview, Oklahoma, at a small motel called the Heritage Inn. Parked in front of our doors, the owners' son, about ten, admired our motorcycles. He asked me where we had started that day, and when I told him Ogallala, he went wide-eyed and breathed, "Oh my!"

The way he said it, you knew that's how his mother talked.

Across the street was a diner called the Queen's Kitchen, and it was late evening when we sat down. A uniformed state trooper was dropping off a boy and girl with their mother (presumably the "Queen") before starting his shift. The boy was around ten, the girl maybe eight, and they were set to work refilling salt, pepper, and sugar containers at the other tables. As they worked, the girl sighed with fatigue and martyrdom, and the boy snapped indignantly, "*You think you're tired, ha-ha-ha!*"

Since that day, Brutus and I have repeated that line many times at the end of many long rides.

Not Madison County
PHOTO BY MICHAEL MOSBACH

Here's the reference to Fairview in *Roadshow*, transcribed from a journal note when I was considerably more "lyrical" than my terse notes tend to be now.

And about those who bewail the loss of "regionalism" in America. Whether or not it's worth regretting, it's definitely still *there*—if those armchair anthropologists would get off the interstate! Away from the cities and beltways, away from the suits and logos and trailer-trash TV talk shows, there are still a million pockets of "Americana" out there, small-town gas stations and diners where you will meet hillbillies, aristocratic southerners, weathered ranchers, overalled farmers, solitary fishermen, burly loggers, apple-cheeked grandmothers, and friendly, decent folks. And a million landscapes, from snowy mountains and starkly majestic deserts to white picket fences and maple trees on Main Street.

Consider Roy's Motel on Route 66 in Amboy, California; the Queen's Kitchen in Fairview, Oklahoma; the Wheatleigh Inn in Lenox, Massachusetts; the Hammond Family Restaurant in Madison, Indiana; the Cowboy Café in Tilden, Texas; and La Maison de Saucisse de Lac Artur, in Louisiana's Cajun country. All part of the Great American Theme Park.

Naturally, in the early days of this tour Olivia, Minnesota, stood out for me because of my dear faraway daughter (who *loved* this photo), but it is just the sort of small town celebrated on that list. After ten years, some of those name-checks no longer survive, but the truth of it remains. Always seeking that proof, when Michael and I were crossing Oklahoma this time I routed us through Fairview—the first time I had seen it since 1997—and was delighted to see that it remained an exquisite little western town (around 2,500 people), apparently thriving. The wide main street (yes, called that) was authentically wide enough to turn around a stagecoach (an important historical link), with full-size pickups angled into the curb on both sides.

The Heritage Inn was just down the street, looking exactly the same (pleasant to think that maybe it was run by the "Oh my!" boy, now about thirty years old), though the Queen's Kitchen was gone. Well, it had been eighteen years. When I did an online search for that diner, I found a couple of obituaries for ladies who had worked there, and my own above mention of it in *Roadshow*.

A few days later, in another state, I was riding through a small town like Fairview and spoke the words out loud in my helmet, "Hello, America—I've missed you."

This seems a good point at which to share that the previous year I had become an American citizen. After living in the U.S. for fifteen years, it seemed like the right thing to do. I would always retain my Canadian passport (and the maple syrup in my veins), so that was not a problem. In a strange and unlikely way, it would also make me feel a little more in control of my own destiny.

At the time of getting my green card, after marrying Carrie in 2000, an immigration lawyer asked me if I was planning to pursue citizenship. I said, "No, I don't think so."

"Well," she said, "the only advantage is that a citizen can't be deported."

That stayed with me. Because, as I like to explain it, "You just never know when you're going to *have* to commit a felony, right?"

(I do get some funny looks after that explanation—but having made a home and family in the United States, being deported would be a problem.)

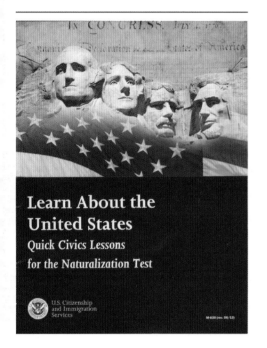

My green card was expiring in 2014, so I decided I might as well become "naturalized," as they call it officially. After several months of paperwork, fingerprinting, photographs, applications, interviews, and written and oral tests (most Americans could not have passed—"The House of Representatives has how many voting members?" "How many amendments does the Constitution have?"), the ceremony was scheduled for November. It was held on the far eastern reaches of metropolitan Los Angeles, at a convention center in the suburb of Ontario—named by visionary brothers George and William Chaffey after the Canadian province. Born in Canada, they moved to Southern California in the late 1800s. They pioneered irrigation techniques and created a "model colony," and named another nearby community Etiwanda, after a Six Nations chief in Ontario, Canada. So it was a fun coincidence to take my Oath of Allegiance in an American town named after the place of my Canadian birth.

The letter confirming my ceremony advised me to "dress appropriately for this solemn occasion," specifically no jeans, shorts, or flip-flops. The vast Ontario Convention Center was only one of five huge complexes around Los Angeles County where citizenship ceremonies were held, sometimes for thousands of people at a time. When I arrived that morning a ceremony was already underway in a huge exhibition hall, and later I crowded into those same rows of seats among 1,015 "huddled masses" from ninety-three countries. At least that many "supporters," friends and family, waited outside, where they could buy red, white, and blue flowers and balloons. While we waited, the big video screens showed a list of the top five

countries of origin for that day's new citizens: China, El Salvador, the Philippines, Guatemala, and Mexico.

Obviously the event meant a lot more to most of those people than it did to me. My change of status was just a *convenience*—and an *inconvenience*, to have spent so many hours dealing with bureaucracy, and that day having to drive fifty miles across the width of Los Angeles in morning traffic.

And I did have a minor problem with the part of the oath that obliged me to forswear loyalty to any previous "prince or potentate, state or nation." It seemed perfectly possible for me to remain loyal to the American Eagle, to the Maple Leaf—and to My Queen.

It is hard to explain, especially to Americans, what a "monument" Queen Elizabeth II, crowned the year I was born, has represented in my life. All through my childhood her portrait was the centerpiece

Personal Salute from a New Citizen–May 2015

of every schoolroom, post office, bank, postage stamp, and coin. Later in my youth and maturity I spent a number of years living in England, off and on, which deepened her "symbolism" for me. During her Christmas television address in 1997, when she talked about her horrible year—the death of Princess Diana, the devastating fire at Windsor Castle—she seemed to be talking about *my* horrible year, and the death of *my* princess. Carrie likes to jokingly refer to her as "Your Queen," but somehow she is that, My Queen.

So I had to perjure myself a little there. And mumble through the godly bits. (Canadians of my generation grew up on American television, chiefly, and knew the Pledge of Allegiance early on, from *Romper Room*. It amazed me to learn much later that the "under God" part was only added to the "One nation" line in the 1950s—the Eisenhower years seem an unlikely time for that constitutional breach.)

The swearing-in ceremony was well produced, in the theatrical sense—lighting, staging, and seating. The lengthy speechifying and reciting the oath ended with a video speech from President Obama that expressed and exemplified everything that is *good* about America—he welcomed us all with warmth, dignity, sincerity, and hope. Unfortunately, that high point was followed by its polar opposite—a music video from some country singer that was corny, breast-beatingly patriotic, unconstitutionally religious, and embarrassing. By then I was just thinking, "Please let it be *over!*"

I was wearing my Order of Canada lapel pin, and as I finally lined up at desk 11 to pick up my certificate of naturalization, the lady behind the desk pointed to it and said, "What a pretty flower!" With a smile and a thank-you, I corrected her, "It's not a flower—it's a *snowflake*. It's a Canadian thing." She smiled back.

My first act as an American citizen was hitting the drive-thru at In-N-Out Burger on the way to the freeway. Perfect. (A Californian institution since the late 1940s, now slowly expanding into other Western states, In-N-Out is still privately owned—shown in one way by the quirk of Bible verse numbers hidden on their packaging. In Eric Schlosser's *Fast Food Nation*, In-N-Out Burger was the *only* chain given good marks for both the quality of their ingredients and their treatment of employees.)

When I got home and described the citizenship event to Carrie, she said, "Didn't you feel at least a *little* emotion?"

I said, "Yes—when I had to *betray* My Queen."

Still, my "lenses" had to be different with this new status, and during my travels on the R40 tour I found I *was* observing the United

States, the country and its people, just a little differently. I was not just passing through anymore; in some strange way, I *belonged*, I was part of it. That thought could be frightening, I admit.

But this Icechucker still has a maple-leaf-shaped heart that swells in the snowy woods, and maple syrup and even hockey flow in his veins forever. I plan to keep my home in Quebec and always aim to be there in February, the heart of winter, and August, the heart of summer. While in California, I will maintain regular injections of maple syrup, continue to be polite and considerate to others, and often go ice skating with Olivia and her friends Bunny and Puppy and their New Englander dad, Jeff.

You can take the Chucker out of the Ice, but . . . like Stephen Colbert put it, I Am America (And So Can You!).

Frosted Nebraska
PHOTO BY
MICHAEL MOSBACH

SHOW ON THE ROAD/
SNOW ON THE ROAD

Sometimes a motorcycling destination is worth a longer nighttime bus ride, and a bouncier sleep. Other times circumstances force it. On the day of the Tulsa show, while checking over my motorcycle, I discovered a bind in the back wheel, like the brake caliper dragging on the disc. My mechanical abilities are pretty much limited to oil changes (though I'm *very* good at those!), so it would need to be taken to a BMW dealer. Fortunately there was one in Omaha, near the next show in Lincoln, and Michael called ahead to let them know we'd be bringing it in. I transferred my tools and such to the spare bike (the older GS that usually lives at my home in Quebec) and drew up a plan that would get Dave close enough to Omaha, while Michael and I could head west across Nebraska.

My journal note after the first show in Tulsa sets a pattern of observations that would resonate through the next thirty-four shows.

Show report—after all that preparing. Pretty good overall, except for two hardest bits, in "Headlong" and "Monkey Biz."
 Made it through, anyway, in every sense.
 Feeling pretty good about *everything* right now.
 It cannot last . . .

Thus spake a man well versed, and sometimes cursed, in performing, travel, and life. Ten years ago, for *Roadshow*, I made a collection of church signs around the Bible Belt. The best one might be "WANT TO MAKE GOD LAUGH? TELL HIM YOUR PLANS." I wouldn't give him the satisfaction. This pilgrim has endured enough of God's laughter in sixty-two-point-five years. If there's anything I have learned in my Metric Century, it's not to tell *anybody* my plans! (Or my failures.)

The new solo theme I had conceived for this tour—just sit down and start telling a story—was working pretty well, I thought. Through band and production rehearsals, as I built up the improvised framework, I had felt a strange "vacuum" about that solo, because nobody

A Peaceful Moment at Work
PHOTO BY CRAIG M. RENWICK

else in the band or crew had mentioned anything about it. I was going on faith and determination—and sometimes those have to be "sufficient unto the day." (Good derivation on that phrase, too; from the New Testament: "Take therefore no thought for the morrow, for the morrow shall take thought for the things of itself. Sufficient unto the day is the evil thereof.")

After my dear friend Matt Scannell had seen the show a couple of times, he said, "I really like what you're doing in the solo—it's like you're telling a story." That lit me up inside, and I gave him a big hug and said, "Thank you!" Later on another friend, Chris Stankee, a Berklee-schooled drummer who works for the Sabian cymbal company, said, "That solo is like the ultimate combination of you as drummer and you as lyricist." He also received a hug for his trouble.

The afternoon of the Lincoln show I was crouched on the floor of the bus amid a tapestry of paper maps. After our show there, we had a day off before the next one in St. Paul, Minnesota, and I had a large area of possible exploration between. I began by glancing over the map of the central states, for the bird's-eye view. Sometimes I even start by scanning the opening pages in the road atlas (the Book of Dreams) that displays the entire country—helpful for the "meta" planning, including looking at other cities we would be performing in, to divide up my areas of exploration. For example, I might be thinking, "We'll head west tomorrow—save the Mormon Garden of Eden for Kansas City." (No joke—you'll see!) Then I would go to the more detailed state maps to find the smallest roads through the most "interesting" areas and possible overnight stops.

("Interesting" is subjective, of course. An early writing teacher, Mark Riebling, said I should *never* use the words "beautiful" or "interesting" because they were meaningless to anyone who didn't know what might be beautiful or interesting to me. Your basic principle of "show, don't tell"—it was up to the writer to *make* something beautiful or interesting. I have always tried to follow Mark's advice, hence the quotation marks.)

After I did my waves and bows in Tulsa and ran to the bus, Dave drove us north most of the night, to York, Nebraska. Once Michael and I were up and away, Dave continued to the BMW dealer in Omaha. (Thanks to them for excellent service and delivery.)

Rainy Nebraska
PHOTO BY MICHAEL MOSBACH

Rain and cold shrouded us across Nebraska and back—the rare day that actually got colder through the afternoon, from the chilly mid-fifties to the positively frosty mid-forties. (Wind chill at fifty mph well below freezing.) The "Rainy Nebraska" photo's scenery, captured between showers and thunderstorms, is not as picturesque as most I would choose, but it feels evocative. The narrow two-lane over a gently rolling landscape ("hummocky," I called it in my journal), the

sprays of early summer green along the roadside and the cottonwoods in the draw (always wanted to use that archetypal Western phrase), the brown contours of the freshly tilled and planted fields, the railroad crossing, the science-fiction farm buildings in the distance, the bleak gray sky. There are even a few center-pivot irrigation rigs (long silvery trusses on wheels)—a device that puzzled Brutus and me in our early travels in that area: "How do it work?"

After hours of cold rain and falling temperatures Michael and I were happy to take shelter at an offramp oasis in Ogallala. Usually I took the time to look around a town for possible independent motels, but that day we checked into the first chain motel we came to.

Ogallala Offramp Oasis

Not yet having planned our route for the day off after the Lincoln show, I couldn't know we would be starting right back in Ogallala in about thirty hours.

Perhaps it is only long habit that makes me prefer to find my routes on paper maps, with the tactile details they seem to reveal—and that's the perfect word. I do not so much design a route as study the page for a while and let the "right" roads be *revealed* to me. With highlighter pen, I stitch together a complicated thread of Rand McNally's thin red lines, gray lines, and, best of all, the broken gray lines—the unpaved roads. The term "adventure riders" has become tarnished with overuse, but if it's adventure a motorcyclist is looking for, it will likely be found on those roads.

(In recent years those paper maps are increasingly hard to find. We used to start every tour by buying the Rand McNally boxed set of all fifty states, but now Michael has to collect them piecemeal online, and they are dated more than a decade ago.)

Unless we have to get into a city for work, I avoid all major arteries, *especially* divided four-lanes (heavy traffic, low speed limits, and frequent intersections), and any settlements with more than a single stoplight or two. Once I have joined the puzzle (as it often feels) with my blue highlighter, we move into the modern digital world. I pass the map to Michael and, kneeling at his computer, he transfers the route (often with much mumbling of profanities) to his mapping program, "Mother." She sometimes dislikes those broken gray lines and won't let Michael place the route there—keeps ignoring my desires, and the paper map's information, and offering her own "interpretation." Michael will warn me that we have some "mystery roads" coming up, as the routes are downloaded to our onboard units—called Doofus and Dingus since we first started using GPS, in 2004. Even in their fifth generation they still often earn their names by . . . misleading us. If I look at Dingus's directions in a city I know well, like Toronto or Los Angeles, I see how wrong-headed it sometimes is. So I know that would be the case when it leads me through Chicago or Salt Lake City.

This photo happened to be taken on an afternoon when I was drawing the Texas portion of a route to carry us from a dropoff point at a Château Walmart near Oklahoma City toward the next show in Austin, Texas. Though a little out of time, it illustrates some basic principles in my way of navigating through America.

At that very moment I was working out possible ways to sneak around Wichita Falls—too big to get caught up in, but like many "hub" towns, most nearby roads were magnetically drawn to it. For that night I was considering Abilene, Texas, as a possible destination (emphasis always on *possible*—reflecting that church sign again). Abilene appealed for the usual mix of reasons—big enough to have motels and restaurants, small enough to get into and out of easily, and . . . a pretty name.

So, circling back in time a week or so, I was in the same position on the floor with a few maps and my highlighter, contemplating the day off between Lincoln and St. Paul. Scanning the map around and between those points, my eyes immediately went to western South Dakota and its many attractions. Not that it was anything like "around and between those points," but it might be doable, with a little strategy.

Brutus and I had ridden through that area on the *Test for Echo* tour, in 1996–97—almost twenty years before. I laughed and told Michael how back then Brutus and I had been planning a ride from Durango, Colorado, where our wives had joined us on a break to explore the Four Corners region together, to the next show in Cincinnati. Looking over the map (the big one of the whole country that time!), I pointed

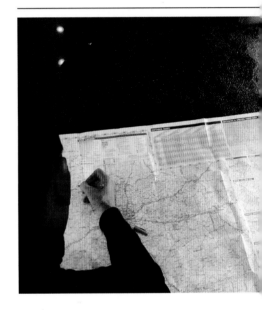

Pathfinder
PHOTO BY MICHAEL MOSBACH

to Mount Rushmore and asked Brutus if he thought we could make it there "on the way."

Of course it was nothing like "on the way"—it would add 500 miles to a journey that was already 1,500 miles, and we only had four days to get to that show in Cincinnati.

But, Brutus being Brutus, he nodded and said we could do it. Me being me, I said, "Let's." The highlight of that cross-country ride remained the area around the Black Hills—the spectacular sight of Mount Rushmore, a stop at the memorial of Wounded Knee, and crossing the Badlands, all remained powerful in memory. I wanted to see them again—but this time the ambition could again be defined as a long shot.

It would also require some help from bus driver Dave, with me for all those nineteen years since *Test for Echo*.

The Lincoln show was a little better than the one in Tulsa, but still marred by a few rough spots—it would not be until the third show, in St. Paul, that I thought we hit our groove. (That was just the internal critic, of course—in every case the audiences were cheering and happy, and that was exhilarating. Friend Matt Scannell attended

"The Rig," Château Walmart
PHOTO BY MICHAEL MOSBACH

the fourth show, in St. Louis, with some friends, and reported that on the way out "strangers were high-fiving each other." Nice.)

From Lincoln, Dave drove us west through most of the night, right back to the Château Walmart in Ogallala, Nebraska. Despite never getting to sleep after a show until about 1 a.m., I set my alarm for a painful 7:00 (again, uncomfortable but worth it). Dragging myself out of bed, I turned on the coffeepot (preloaded by Dave) and sliced and squeezed the oranges into the electric juicer, then into the glasses frosting in the freezer overnight. After a few minutes of quiet time with juice and coffee, looking out the bus window at the day's weather and early Walmart shoppers (justly famous on the interweb), I went back to wake Michael—with the usual rattle of the curtains over his bunk, and a grunt quiet enough not to wake Dave, earplugged in the bunk below. Michael responded with an echoed grunt, and we had "communicated."

(That phrase echoes a private joke Michael says I can share. One morning I woke him as usual with a drum tattoo on his door—I often favored a two-bar snare roll that ends "Don't Be That Way" on *Sinatra Swings* [just noticed it's a slowed-down version of "Wipe Out"!]—not

Ogallala Walmart, Morning Shadows
PHOTO BY MICHAEL MOSBACH

knowing he had a "guest" in his room. Michael responded with a grunt that might be spelled "*Mer*"—an imitation of Jon Stewart imitating Dick Cheney. Michael's guest, mystified by waking to a drum pattern on the door answered by a grunt, said, "Um—was that some kind of *communication?*"

He laughed and said yes, it was.)

After some cereal and bananas, and another cup of coffee, we started suiting up—wearing every layer we owned. We also had electrically heated vests, though a moral dilemma arose when Michael said he hadn't brought his. ("*I didn't expect cold weather,*" he whined. Blahblah.) I offered him my spare vest, only to discover that his worked, but mine *didn't.* What do you do in a situation like that? If you're like me, you shut up and accept it. If you're like Michael, you keep moaning dramatically at every stop about how cold you are—all except for the part the vest warms. (So your inner core from which the *blood* flows, then.)

On previous days I had been watching the weather carefully, so I knew it would be cold, and that significant snow had fallen in the Rapid City area. Thus I was prepared for my plans to be stymied that way, and would adapt as necessary. Apart from that church sign again, I prefer to follow the eternal gospel from Freddie: "It is what it is. *Deal* with it."

In past years I had ridden through part of the Sand Hills of Western Nebraska, and remembered the area as desolately pretty and surprisingly *dynamic.* Like the backroads of Western Idaho or central Missouri, say—not that many *turns,* but lots of ups and downs—the pavement laid like a ribbon over the undulations. On that unseasonably wintry morning in mid-May, the snow was at least . . . picturesque.

Over the years Michael and I have developed an efficient approach to catching photographs on the fly. If I see a background, a piece of road, or a roadside view that seems worth capturing, I will wave Michael over and tell him where I want him to stand and where I'd like him to focus. (Always funny when I say, "Make sure the rhododendrons are in the shot," or "Get both the Joshua tree and the saguaro," whatever. He has no interest in such matters and considers it bizarre that *anyone* does.) I will do a couple of ride-bys for him, while he fires off multiple exposures. "Spray and Pray," he calls it, and it works—though I have a lot of editing to do after a ride. When trying to capture the rider amid a *big* landscape, I encourage my riding partners, Michael or Brutus, to climb up high beside the road for the best angle. That sometimes causes some grumbling, but I try to set the example myself.

This, Too, Is Nebraska
PHOTO BY MICHAEL MOSBACH

The few photographs I take are more of the "Pick and Click" variety, as I typically choose a "safe" angle looking up the road and wave Michael to ride through. If we are in a particularly scenic area, he will know to stop somewhere ahead and "spray" me in both directions as I ride by. Using that leapfrog method we manage to take a lot of photographs without costing too much time. Because we *always* have a lot of distance to cover.

On the subject of riding shots, I have been intrigued by a difference of taste among people. I usually prefer the shot of the rider from behind, because then the viewer may imagine actually riding behind him, on the same journey. Michael and many others I ask prefer the head-on shot, with the rider coming out of the scenery toward the viewer.

So I just encourage Michael to shoot both angles and use a variety of both—for each kind of viewer.

My first target that morning was Wounded Knee, South Dakota, at the humble monument where Brutus and I had stopped all those years ago. The sad histories of Native Americans and Canadians had

attracted my sympathy and interest for many years, and Dee Brown's *Bury My Heart at Wounded Knee: An Indian History of the American West* (1970) remains one of the important works. I was pleased to learn from my friends at Wikipedia that "the title is taken from the final phrase of a twentieth-century poem titled 'American Names' by Steven Vincent Benét. The full quotation, 'I shall not be there, I shall rise and pass/ Bury my heart at Wounded Knee,' appears at the beginning of Brown's book. Although Benet's poem is not about the plight of Native Americans, Wounded Knee was the location of the last major confrontation between the U.S. Army and Native Americans."

That final phrase bleeds tragedy and shame, and the interested reader is encouraged to seek out Dee Brown's book. (Driver Dave is also keen on early American history, especially of the West, and both having read that book many years ago, we agreed that we wanted to read it again now, knowing so much more of its context.)

One telling detail glares on the roadside sign—something I noticed when Brutus and I were there nineteen years ago. The painted text has been touched up over the years, but the same title remained, "MASSACRE OF WOUNDED KNEE," with the word "massacre" being a very obvious patch over something else, on both sides of the sign. Presumably the original caption was "BATTLE OF WOUNDED KNEE."

It was no battle . . .

Standing in that place and reading of the events of December 29, 1890, and subsequent

The Snows of Nebraska

days, brings on the same haunting chill as visiting the many Civil War battlefields in the mid-Atlantic states, the World War I killing grounds in Belgium, or the Vietnam Memorial in Washington: not just so many individual ghosts, but the dark pall that is humanity's worst curse—faceless, impersonal murder.

Just as Michael and I were putting our gloves back on and preparing to ride away, a massive old GMC Suburban full of Native youths pulled up beside us. A young woman got out and stepped through the slush to me, clutching a hoody around her tattooed neck to guard against the chill. She asked if we could "make a donation."

I said, "A donation to what?"

She said, "Gas."

I smiled at all that might have meant, and all it *did* mean, in this modern world and the ancient one of those youngsters' ancestors. I turned to my tankbag and dug out a twenty for her.

As they drove away, Michael asked, "What was all that about?" When I told him, he said, "Nice trick—just after you read all that horrible stuff and the white guilt is fresh, they hit you up!"

I said, "At least she didn't say, 'God bless you,'" and he laughed at that.

Around my home in Westside Los Angeles panhandlers often stand at the long red lights leading onto the Pacific Coast Highway. When I call over an unfortunate one and hand over the bill, if they give me the "God bless you" line, I shake my head while saying, "This has nothing to do with God—it's between you and me," as I point my finger at them and smile.

Sometimes they are taken aback, but one guy I encountered a second time, and as he started to say it, I raised a finger. He smiled wide and said, "I remember—'just between you and me,' right? I like that."

I smiled back and said, "I like it, too."

After a brief stop at Wind Cave National Park (no time to visit the cave, but enough to collect the passport stamp), we rode on through the snowy hills, now stippled with pine trees, to the Crazy Horse Memorial. It was begun in 1948 with the grandiose ambition of becoming the world's largest sculpture and has been funded only by private donations. It is fittingly located in the Black Hills, which had been promised to the Sioux by the American

Crazy Horse in Progress
PHOTO BY MICHAEL MOSBACH

PHOTO BY MICHAEL MOSBACH

Two Riders Were Approaching . . .
Badlands National Park

government "forever"—until gold was discovered there.

Since Brutus and I had paused for a quick look at the Crazy Horse Memorial in our "head-long flight" back in 1997, the face has been completed (top right profile). Sometime in the distant future, the work will reveal his horse and pointing arm—which some elders claim is an obscene cultural insensitivity, equivalent to George Washington raising a middle finger on Mount Rushmore.

Which, fittingly, was our next "roadside attraction" that day.

Our journey had been roughly northward so far, but after pausing to marvel at that truly monumental array of presidential faces (once again decoratively laced with snow), we turned east and looped under Rapid City and headed for Badlands National Park.

The term "badlands" sometimes refers to areas where nothing grows, or where there is no water, but in this case came from the

difficulty of getting the pioneer wagon trains through the area. I thought of their struggle often as I looked around at the landscape we rode through. Without roads, they would be very bad lands indeed.

Shortly after the "Two Riders" photograph was taken, showing the wide-angle view, we saw some huge dark masses among the snow-patched grasslands. Four bison were grazing along the road, two of them right on the narrow strip of gravel and dirt. I stopped and put my feet down, thinking. They were ornery beasts, and *huge* (up to 4,000 pounds), and I wasn't sure how to proceed. What if they were a bull and his harem, and my approaching motorcycle became a "red flag"? I would have nowhere to ride or run from a charging bull.

Straddling the bike, I waved Michael alongside and said, "I'll ride through and make them mad—then you follow and I'll film the results!"

He made one of his droll "oh, ha ha" faces, and I said with icy scorn, "Don't worry—it's not *mating* season. They won't want to . . . *molest* you."

I went ahead, slowly, keeping my distance as much as I could. Fortunately there was no *charging*, but one of them started galumphing up the road ahead of me. I tried to stay back and far to the road's edge, but it kept going for the longest time—with me thinking, "All

"I'll go first!"
PHOTO BY MICHAEL MOSBACH

it has to do is *stop* and I'm crashing into a 4,000-pound *wall.*" To my relief it finally humped off into the grass and snow.

Meanwhile, as Michael and I rode among the snow-covered "via points" and exciting wildlife that day, stopping often for photographs—especially through the unique landscape of the Badlands—Dave was driving the bus up through the middle of Nebraska to the lower middle of South Dakota. Assuming Michael and I accomplished all our missions, we would meet Dave at a dot on the interstate called Murdo. Michael and I would sleep aboard while Dave carried us a few hundred miles east to Sioux Falls. From there we could unload the bikes again and ride to the show in St. Paul.

The short version is that the day's journey went as planned (though we arrived at the Badlands visitor center twenty minutes too late and I couldn't get the passport stamp—but that was a minor disappointment). After over 500 miles and almost twelve hours of riding, Michael and I were safe and warm on the bus, toasting the day's hardships and rewards with Macallan 18. I've said it before and I'll say it again, "Magic happens—but it often requires some planning."

And luck . . .

This, Too, Is Texas
PHOTO BY MICHAEL MOSBACH

AGAINST THE WEATHER

"So we beat on, boats against the current, borne back ceaselessly into the past."

That wonderful final line from *The Great Gatsby* applies so perfectly to this tour—I certainly did a lot of "beating" (and took a lot, too), and the show we were presenting went back in reverse chronology musically, and in its production, with stage sets devolving around us. The places Michael and I visited on days off were usually rural areas and small towns that seemed pleasantly out of step with the modern world of big cities and arenas.

"Boats against the current" can be likened to "bikes against the weather," because in just the first couple of weeks we experienced every kind there is, from desert heat to snow to torrential rains. The opening photograph was taken on a rainy day in East Texas, the Piney

Woods region, near our overnight stop in Nacogdoches. (Another destination chosen for its convenient location in an area I liked to explore—*and* for its name. The next evening at dinner before the show, when I was talking about it, Geddy said, "You just like saying that name." I nodded enthusiastically, "*Yeah I do!*").

The sheer volume of rainfall that day was greater than I have ever experienced on a motorcycle—all of our so-called waterproof gear was overwhelmed, and the roads were constantly awash. Though at least still navigable—it was just the beginning of a continuing deluge that a week later badly flooded that whole area of Texas. Talking to a lady at the motel in Nacogdoches that evening, I said I was thinking of parking the motorcycle and building a boat.

In Oklahoma and Arkansas we had been menaced by thunderstorms, always carrying the threat of tornadoes. It occurred to me that we didn't have a "strategy" for that, and as Michael and I discussed it, I decided that if a twister was coming my way I would lay my motorcycle on its side, keep on all my protective gear, and crouch down beside its 600-pound bulk. Michael agreed that would be about the best we could do—and it felt good to have a "tornado strategy."

Journal note:

> First priority night and day—look up weather.
>
> Strange to be back glued to Weather Channel—satellite maps, live storm reports.
>
> Tornadoes all around us for days.
>
> Global weirding.

Those nights on the bus, or evenings in the motel, I was reading *Head Check: What It Feels Like to Ride Motorcycles* by Jack Lewis. A veteran of America's Iraq "adventure" as an army staff sergeant (in a Psy-Ops, or Psychological Operations company, of all things), Jack Lewis first came to prominence in *Motorcyclist* magazine, where I encountered his work. He is a fine writer—sometimes powerful and dark (a soldier returning to his Pacific Northwest home recalls Hemingway's "Big Two-Hearted River," only with motorcycling rather than fly-fishing as the vehicle), but more often he is light, witty, lively, and funny. From *Head Check* I picked up a term from his military career, "situational awareness," that certainly applies deeply to motorcycling—and not least to *weather*. (Like having a tornado strategy.)

A few scattered journal notes jotted down at moments and places like this, or in the motel room at the end of the day:

Noah Comes to Nacogdoches
PHOTO BY MICHAEL MOSBACH

Back to "What day is it?"

"Edge of seat" life of traveling, performing, keeping everything together—exhausting. Not boring, certainly—rewarding, even—so vital—but takes so much constant effort, and will.

Traveling is like performing, always on the ragged edge of "doability."

My arms weigh 200 pounds each.

Just faced a critical test. After long, hot (though *peaceful*) day, ending in a mighty flail of wrong GPS destination, then motel ridiculously complicated to get to. Looking in the mirror as I washed my face, thinking about all that, and asking existential question:

"Was it worth it?"

No hesitation—yes.

I am glad to report that rural Texans *do* continue to drive "friendly," as the "Welcome to Texas" sign encourages. It's different in the cities, like everywhere, but Texas has a lot more country than city.

Farther south in Texas the enemy was heat and humidity— mid-nineties and slimy. In *Far and Near* I wrote about the devastation wrought by hydraulic fracturing, "fracking," in North Dakota and in the mesquite ranchland surrounding the little South Texan cowboy town of Tilden, a place I had admired since 1996. (Also name-checked in the earlier *Roadshow* excerpt.) Now a few years on from when I wrote about those "unnatural disasters," still nothing was really known about the effects of pumping a slurry of up to forty different chemicals under high pressure a mile or two underground to force out the oil and gas. Naturally, water for drinking and agriculture is down there, too, and the industry has been allowed to grow completely unchecked—offering the irresistible political currency of "creating jobs" and "reducing our dependency on foreign oil." Both commendable goals, if secondary to pure economics—but an operation like that ought to be done *carefully*.

Even above the ground, it leaves an awful mess—including burning off the "excess" (meaning "currently unprofitable") natural gas in flares that

Roadhouse and Rain, Poynor, Texas
PHOTO BY MICHAEL MOSBACH

PHOTO BY MICHAEL MOSBACH

brighten the night even in satellite images. No one has been able to *prove* that fracking is bad, but it sure doesn't sound like a good idea. Or *look* like a good idea, up close. So I didn't have the heart to go through Tilden (or do any more ranting on the subject) but skirted the area to the south, just to have a look-see. On one long stretch of two-lane leading from nothing to nowhere, just horizon-to-horizon

Mesquite Plains
PHOTO BY MICHAEL MOSBACH

mesquite, I noticed ominous signs in federal red, white, and blue: "FUTURE INTERSTATE CORRIDOR 69." We began to overtake and pass trains of lumbering semis belching black smoke as they hauled crude metal tankers. Speeding up to get by them, our wheels shuddered over humps and ripples in the road's surface from their constant weight. Hordes of identical rigs crouched together in shambolic road-side lots, like giant robot caterpillars. Occasionally we passed massive

FAR AND WIDE

installations of raw metal pipes and cylinders towering over the mesquite, and always miles and miles of security fencing—higher, tighter-meshed, and more forbidding than the window-pane mesh and barbed wire local ranchers used to favor. (Why does an oil operation need security fences? There's nothing to steal, and little to see, so what's to hide or protect? It's just *suspicious*.)

Mesquite Francklands
PHOTO BY MICHAEL MOSBACH

Usually I like to show "pretty" pictures, and would avoid unsightly traffic or industry, or crop it out, but on this one I left in the towering wellheads, utility poles, and tanker truck to the upper left, and the forbidding fence lining the far roadside. None of that was there even five years before.

New Orleans was a welcome "intermission" in the run, in every way. Michael and I took three days off the bikes while I had a visit from

NOLA

Carrie and Olivia. We all enjoyed our time in that great city, eating well and wandering around the enduringly unique French Quarter (though apparently historically it's more Spanish than French). Olivia learned to imitate a deep Southern drawl from a cab driver from the airport: "He a cornbread, collard green, hamhock eatin' foo'."

It was also Olivia's first Rush concert, and she *loved* it. I had thought she might last a song or two, but she danced and air-drummed right to the end. Manager Ray arranged a "box" for them, high up over everything, and Olivia couldn't get over all the people.

"There must be two thousand and eighteen people," she said.

Ray laughed and told her, "Actually there are about *eleven* thousand!"

Olivia looked puzzled. "Are they all here to see my dad and Uncle Alex and Uncle Geddy?"

When Ray assured her they were, she said, "That's too silly."

Then she wondered, "Do they know he's my dad?"

Ray laughed and said, "They probably do."

During intermission she came backstage and ran up to me, arms raised for me to pick her up. Still wearing her big red "ear defenders," she was *so* excited that she bounced in my arms.

"Daddy! It was *great*! I only didn't like the shipwreck" (rearscreen video in "The Wreckers," to her an echo of the dark beginning of *Frozen*, a movie she finds rightly unbearable) "and the *explosion*!" (pyro-man Boom-Boom's fireworks in "Far Cry").

At breakfast the next morning in the hotel restaurant, with our sketchbook and markers, Olivia wanted me to draw her onstage. She should be playing drums (left-handed, of course), with her tongue sticking out, while Uncle Alex, Uncle Geddy, and Daddy should be on the screen behind her.

You might think she had "plans" . . .

I stayed in New Orleans with them for the day off after the show, then in the evening Dave drove Michael and me through the night to Tallahassee. Michael and I set off for a fairly pleasant ride on the backroads toward Tampa—until we had to get on the interstate near the city and were exposed to the nightmare that is Florida drivers. (Just the opposite of the Texas slogan—more like "Drive Unfriendly.")

"*Honey, don't let me commence!*" is a fitting echo from New Orleans—a Truman Capote story about an old "madam" in Jackson Square who frequently begins her speeches that way.

Let us move on to the joy of riding in North Georgia, the Carolinas, the Virginias, and the neighboring corner of Tennessee. That's the heart of the Appalachian Mountains, and as good as East Coast riding gets.

After the Tampa show Dave faced another all-night drive, to the north side of Atlanta. (Of course the "sleepers" also faced that all-night drive, which can never be as restful.) We actually parked right near the venue for the next show, and Michael and I rode out early to meet friend Wes (Porcupine Tree guitarist and fine solo artist) and his wife, Becca, in Suches, in the mountains in the northern part of Georgia.

Cherohala Skyway
PHOTO BY MICHAEL MOSBACH

A few tours ago Michael and I rode around that region and neighboring corners of North Carolina and Tennessee with Wes and Becca. Becca had grown up on motorcycles, riding behind her notoriously fast father, and back then Wes told us, "I usually just let her lead, and try to keep up." And that's what we did. (See "A Winter's Tale of Summers Past," February 2009, in *Far and Away*.)

Astonishingly, it was now seven years later, and in the interim

Wes and Becca had welcomed son John Wesley Dearth IV (JWD4, or Jay) into the world. He was almost four now, and Becca had been on "maternity leave" from motorcycling all that time—these few days in the southern Appalachians were her return to serious riding.

Wes told us they had been for a good ride the previous day, and he was glad to see that Becca had been "staying safe"—though once a sportbike rider had passed them, and Becca charged off after him and reeled him in (a motorcycling term I hope is self-explanatory). "Just to know I could do it," she said.

Back in 2008 we had all stayed at a fantastic little resort and campground devoted to motorcyclists, Two Wheels Only, in Suches, Georgia. It had closed a few years later, and when Michael and I rode by last tour I saw it was shut down and abandoned. However, a former customer, Bill, bought the property and reopened it with many improvements—*such as* (impossible not to pun on "Suches") the charming little cabins we stayed in this time.

After leaving some luggage there, we set off on a day-ride together toward the mountainous border country of Georgia, Tennessee, and North Carolina. I had been prepared to follow Becca around once again, but she said she didn't want to lead. I asked her to write down a list of the roads, and we set off on a nice long loop of twisty two-lanes that took us to a favorite lunch stop of theirs in Tellico Plains, Tennessee. It was one end of the Cherohala Skyway, a scenic little road spanning Tennessee and North Carolina that, like the Blue Ridge Parkway or Skyline Drive farther north, is only there to be *pretty*. We made a number of photo stops along there, Michael wielding his manly camera to capture the three of us riding, along with the majestic scenery around us. At one stop he started complaining, "Maybe *someone* with a camera might take a shot or two of me?"

So a little farther on I pulled off the road and humored him.

A journal note I made one evening in a motel:

Just realized the way I talk to Michael is the way I talk to myself. Nasty, withering, derisive, sarcastic—yet with occasional grudging approval. Like today thinking I had forgotten extra water, and cursing myself, then finding a bottle in my bag and thinking, "See? You're not so bad!" Sometimes I do have to laugh out loud at myself.

It sometimes happens that toward the end of a long ride something takes hold of me—like what Jack Lewis describes as "a horse that can smell the barn." It always happens on a challenging road, late in the day, and some of those rides have been unforgettable. Riding into Death Valley for the first time, under a full moon, was one of those—another happened in Tuscany, when Brutus and I had crossed the Alps from Austria and been held up with some bike trouble. By evening all of the Italians seemed to be off the road, and it was just me racing ahead of Brutus. (He always sensed when I was "possessed," and just let me go.) Winding through the exquisite countryside, framed in a supernatural golden light, my world shrank to the bike and the road.

That day on the Cherohala, we still had a couple of hours to ride back to Suches, and dark clouds were bringing in the rain that was forecast for the evening. Once I was sure we had enough photos, I

This, Too, Is Michael

Blue Ridge Parkway
PHOTO BY MICHAEL MOSBACH

started "smelling the barn." I rode off and surrendered to that spell, that determined pace. I threaded the curves in a rapid rhythm, eyes like a ray on the apex and the exit, keeping everything smooth and quick. Occasionally I glanced in my mirrors and saw a single headlight behind—"Probably a sportbike rider," I thought, and I wicked up the pace a little—to *keep* him back there. Like Becca said, "Just to know I could do it."

Curve after curve, mile after mile, that light was still there, and only later did I learn that of course it was Becca. Wes said after, "I haven't seen her smile like that for a *long* time."

I asked him, "Is it a sin to dance with another man's wife?"

Wes laughed and said, "No, it's not!"

Although the newly renamed Two Wheels of Suches was officially closed that night, the owner had invited us to stay in the cabins and use the main building. We had a friend from our previous visit, Mimi, a schoolteacher who lived across the road and helped out around the place. In collaboration with Michael's arrangements (and our credit card), Mimi brought us dinner in her car from a nearby town.

Through the evening, rainshowers came and went, heavy and light, and between them fireflies twinkled in the trees. The one other guest was Patti, riding a Suzuki touring bike with clutch trouble, and we invited her to join us. We had food and wine aplenty, and laughter carried in the air.

In Atlanta we were joined by a guest rider from a couple of previous tours, Toronto percussionist and GS rider Richard Moore. I told him later we had given him a two-week motorcycle tour—in three days! After the Atlanta show Dave parked us in Greenville, South Carolina, and in the morning the three of us rode west toward Tennessee on some of the East's finest little roads—including the famous "Tail of the Dragon," Deals Gap, with "318 Turns in 11 Miles." As reported on previous visits, the celebrated place has become a circus for motorcycle and car clubs, but remains an undeniably wonderful and technically demanding stretch of road.

From there we cruised the Foothills Parkway (another sweet little road built only to be pretty, though less celebrated than the others), and back east through Great Smoky Mountains National Park to Asheville, North Carolina, and the Biltmore Estate.

Another long story short—it is a massive showplace of château-style (and I don't mean Walmart) mansion and gardens on 4,000 acres built for a Vanderbilt heir in the late 1890s, the Gilded Age. In America, it can only be compared to William Randolph Hearst's San Simeon in California. I first heard of the place from motorcycle magazines, because it was a popular setting for manufacturers to introduce new models—a glamorous backdrop amid spectacular riding country.

A fairly good hotel stands on another part of the Biltmore grounds, and Michael and I have stayed there several times. (See that same story, "A Winter's Tale of Summers Past," for a charming previous encounter.) The last time, though, had left an unpleasant aftertaste, and I almost led us somewhere else that day. But I decided it had been the *person*, not the place.

And I was right. When we pulled up in the late afternoon, George the doorman welcomed us enthusiastically, saying he had been sure we would never come back, and how sorry he was about what had happened. Then the director of security, Victor, came out to share delighted greetings, and how terrible he had felt about it—for two years.

That time we had pulled our bikes under the front portico, and while we unloaded, Michael conferred the Order of the Palm (paper imprinted with dead president) upon George to let us keep the bikes there. We had done so before—there and at many other fine properties (I still treasure a photo of Brutus's and my bikes parked in front of the Hôtel de Crillon overnight on the Place de la Concorde in Paris). We had also talked to Victor at the time, and they were fine with our out-of-the-way parking spots.

However, just as we were leaving our rooms for dinner, Michael got a call from the manager, an unpleasant woman, saying we would have to move our motorcycles. We ignored her and went for a fine meal in the restaurant, only to find when we came back that she had recoded our doors. We had to wait (silent and fuming) while a red-faced bellman let us in to get our bike keys, then go out into the drizzle, in our dining clothes, to move the bikes.

George told me he said to her later, "You realize you just did that to a guy who has published five travel books?"

Deals Gap
PHOTO BY MICHAEL MOSBACH

FAR AND WIDE

Biltmore House
PHOTO BY MICHAEL MOSBACH

When I asked him what had happened to her, George smiled and said, with obvious satisfaction, "She's gone."

He mentioned that he was planning to attend one of our Toronto shows later that summer, and I quietly asked Michael to arrange some good tickets for him.

Next morning the saddle of each of our motorcycles was decorated with a red rose. That's a first!

Michael and I teased Richard about having chosen to ride with us for the only two nights when we were staying somewhere *nice*. On nights off we usually just settled into a modest motel somewhere, preferably with a nearby restaurant, and took what there was. From the Biltmore we rode to the following show in Greensboro (the band in a good groove now, with the performance consistent, though exhausting for us all). We had a night off before the final show of the run, at an amphitheater outside Washington, DC. Michael, Richard, and I spent that day on the backroads of Virginia and West Virginia, and I noted later that it provided every kind of road you could possibly want.

Switchback gravel? Single-lane paved? Third gear sweepers along the river? Logging roads? Picturesque little towns? Views of distant forested mountains? Sunny sky, wet roads?

That last was a result of our good luck in dodging the day's few showers, riding through a place that had just been rained on. The wet pavement steamed under the returning sun.

Altogether it was a pretty serious test of all kinds of riding techniques, from the loosest to the tightest, I might say. And we were always ready to adapt to surprises like the debris washed down into this one-lane hairpin in West Virginia.

Dangerous Curves
PHOTO BY MICHAEL MOSBACH

Best of all, the day ended at another unforgettable destination, the Homestead Resort in Hot Springs, Virginia. Established in 1766, even before the *country* was, it is a place of elegance and splendor—the only destination in America where we pack a suit and tie for dinner. When Michael pulled up at the Homestead's imposing entrance to check us in, he was a little surprised when the doorman said, "We were expecting you today." For years we have always stayed there before or after the DC show, but never thought they "noticed" us.

The following day, when we were parked at the amphitheater in Bristow, Virginia, Richard said, in a tone that might have been admiring or just tired, "You guys are *hardcore*."

I presented him with one of the stickers we had been given by the BMW dealer in St. Louis, our "main guy" these days, for bikes and advice.

The sticker reads: "YOU CAN FOLLOW ME, BUT YOU'RE NOT GOING TO MAKE IT."

I said to Richard, "You made it."

And really, we all did. Michael and I made it through almost 7,000 miles of motorcycling, and the Guys at Work and me through the first twelve shows. Though for that last one at the Bristow amphitheater I was under attack from a bug that gave me stomach cramps, general malaise, and light-headedness—but everyone else seemed to have a good time.

Then up painfully early next morning for a long flight and a brief few days at home, before a long flight back east toward the next show in Columbus.

Richard and Bubba,
Homestead, May 2013
PHOTO BY MICHAEL MOSBACH

Back to the bikes, back to the drums, and back to the celebration of forty years of music—and my Metric Century.

So I beat on, bike against the weather, borne back ceaselessly into the past . . .

MISFIT MIDDLE EIGHT

"Nowhere is the dreamer or the misfit more alone"
"Subdivisions," 1982

I know, I know—"Never complain, never explain."

That's why this little tale about being a misfit is *itself* a misfit. I didn't want to sully the flow of other stories, for the reader's sake, and have accentuated the Gypsy Motorcycle Drumhead and not the Misfit. Yet his story needs to be told as well, because in so many ways it illuminates all the others. And (I console myself) it might help other misfits.

In pop songs, the "middle eight" is a separate section, nominally of eight bars, different from the rest of the structure. In the great pop song of life, some of us are the verses that move things forward, many join the choruses that chime in together to multiply the power, and some, alas, are the oddball middle eights.

At family dinner one night, six-year-old Olivia asked her mom and me, out of nowhere, "What kind of person is an *oddball?*"

I chuckled ruefully and said quietly, "Me." Carrie laughed and said, "Mm-hmm." Then I said to Olivia, "I'm afraid *you* might be an oddball, too—sorry!"

But at least in these times, and in her progressive schools, Olivia will never be messed with psychologically and emotionally in quite the same ways Dad was. Like at age eight, halfway through grade three, being moved into grade four, then the next year from five into six. "Accelerating," they called it, with the best intentions, but it meant I started high school before I had even turned thirteen—at least two years younger than my classmates, at that most delicate age. Whatever other damage that asymmetry inflicted, I became intensely self-conscious, reserved, private, and forever the misfit.

I guess I can only blame genetics for the hyperthymia. Insert another rueful chuckle, for alas, that joke has often been on me. The energy and productivity that "annoys other people" sometimes sours them all the way to *envy*, apparently for the seeming reproach to their energies and accomplishments. Envy is not pleasant to give or receive, but you can only do what "fits" your "mis."

When Carrie first met my mother in 2000, they had tea together at a Toronto hotel. Carrie asked Mom what I was like as a child, and she sighed and said, "He was *always* weird." (I think she meant, "He was always a *misfit*.") Later, when Carrie asked to view some home movies from my childhood, she was disappointed when every time the camera pointed at me, I ran out of the shot. Child is father to the man.

The situation in the opening photograph (and it *was*, alas, a *situation*) began, as trouble usually does these days, with an email in early 2015. "*Rolling Stone* wants to do a cover story on you!"

My immediate feeling was ambivalence. "Oh, all right. Maybe. But . . ."

That reaction, I promise you, is not jaded and cynical, but wise and experienced—over the years *Rolling Stone* had never been kind to us, and "it could all go horribly wrong." Plus there would likely be demands and conditions, and we were in the middle of band rehearsals.

Still, I remained optimistic, thinking, "Maybe it will be a good story—and maybe they'll use an exciting live shot for the cover." (As a young fan I always preferred concert photographs of my favorite bands to posed ones—still do.)

I generally enjoy doing interviews, person to person. It is not easy, as anyone who has even interviewed for a *job* will know—and similarly, it requires a sustained effort to appear at your "best," in clarity, tact, and imagination. When it goes well, the exchange can be stimulating. In the course of trying to be clear and articulate about drumming or writing professionally, sometimes I air thoughts that are new and useful, in understanding what I do and why.

(I still think of a young journalist from the early days, the mid- to late '70s. He was a tall, shambling Midwesterner, in his early twenties—like us—who conducted a bright, amusing interview with us, then wrote an incisive piece that actually *illuminated* what we were about. His ending line remains with me forty years later. After airing some misgivings about our music, he closed with, "I just want to give them a big kick in the direction they're going.")

Anyway, that same day the Guys at Work chimed in that they felt strongly we should "co-operate" with the *Rolling Stone* people. "At this stage of our career," et cetera. I could already sense that, once again, I was *trapped*.

And once more I defaulted to the Freddie Gruber position. "It is what it is. *Deal* with it."

So, here's the Roadcraft Principle: "When people you love want something very much, you have to try to help them get it."

Can anyone argue with that principle? That has been my advice to, for example, late-life second-time-around reluctant dads. (Yes, including myself.) You can't tell yourself how to feel, and no one else can tell you how to feel. (Though how they will try!) But you *can* tell yourself what to *do*.

You can say, "I will help."

In the context of another complex relationship, a band of brothers over four decades, there will be differing opinions on matters that are not deep. Band activities and appearances that you personally might not care to do, but in the grand scheme of principles and integrity, they are not of any consequence. So for the sake of peace and goodwill, you go along.

A documentary about the band is pitched to management, and then to the Guys, and you think, "No, no, no." Because you have always handled your *own* autobiography—in just such settings as this book—and have no desire to be otherwise documented. And you know they'll end up consuming a lot of your time. And you'll never watch it—so it will have none of the value of music or writing, where you will actually enjoy the making, listening, and reading.

But the others want to do it. So you say, "I will help."

Needs must when the devil drives.

That is a quaint old English expression I admire—it would make a good rock lyric, were I not "withdrawn" from that battle, too. It traces back more than 600 years, and, oh, what knowledge of human nature it expresses! We can't help doing what the devil makes us do.

And one of the devil's worst torments for some of us misfit angels is . . .

Award shows.

Not awards themselves, *per se*, because sometimes they can be very meaningful—I am always proud and grateful for any nods from the drumming community, for example. And a streetside tribute like this is fun! (I always wanted to go there and "collect," but never made it.)

Show business award shows, though, are all about (guess what?) *show business*. Some actors and musicians I know confess they only attend them for their wives, who want to dress up and be glamorous. And fair enough—"needs must . . ."

Sometimes an award is offered *only* on the condition that you attend and be "part of the show." Which, again, is of zero interest to this Bubba. But naturally it feels good to be appreciated.

And—oh yes—what an irresistible opportunity here for an aside about the 2005 Grammy Awards. "*¡Jesu Cristo!*" quoth Bubba. That year, by some fantastic miracle, my drum solo from the *Rush in Rio* DVD, "O Baterista!" (The Drummer), was nominated for Best Rock Instrumental Performance.

Venice, California

A *drum solo gets a Grammy nomination?* There was no question I would show up for that event: honor, respect—all good things.

Listed among such other "secondary awards" as Best Hawaiian Album, Best Polka Album, and Best Tejano Album, the Best Rock Instrumental Performance was not part of the big prime-time show on television. The B-list awards were presented in the afternoon, off-camera, in a convention hall beside a vast sports arena in Los Angeles.

Accompanied by manager Ray and our wives, I dressed up and really tried to "man up" for it. To just *surrender* to the experience and take it as it came.

But alas, it could not be borne. The afternoon part was tolerable. (Brian Wilson was the "sentimental winner" in my category, and I could not resent that—and the fact remains forevermore that a drum solo was once *nominated* for a Grammy.) When the show moved into the Big Room, though—our seats well back on the arena floor—the showbiz factor amped *way* up. On three or four separate stages, colored lights flashed in non-stop action while dancers tumbled and cavorted, and singers came and went. It was all slick and carefully staged, but none of the performances linger in memory. (Well, except for the *cheesiest*—but we won't get into that. Might offend someone.)

During commercial breaks the audience suddenly flurried up and into motion, like a flock of starlings startled from a field. Stars and seat-warmers traded places (the viewers at home mustn't see an empty seat!) as nominees and presenters were led by handlers through the shadowy aisles.

Some gangsta rapper was mentioned in a nomination, and behind me a fat white guy in a suit and tie started jumping and screaming. The gangsta's accountant or business manager, I presumed. And you know—good for them! He obviously did his part well, and I'm for that, in every way.

It's just that it has *nothing to do with music*.

As the hours went by I thought I was "enduring" it, but my mood seeped away into a dark pool of simmering anger. It was everything I despise, and I couldn't *wait* to get out of there.

So let that state of mind carry us into the dark, simmering pools of . . . photo sessions.

Do I like having my photograph taken? Naw. It's fine when I'm *doing* something—playing drums, for example, and I'm all for it when riding my motorcycle through fantastic scenery. But *posing* for the camera is another thing. I'm like the Amish people who, contrary to popular belief, aren't actually averse to being photographed—they forbid *posing* for photographs, because that shows vanity.

Bubba agrees—and has since childhood.

Though vanity is not the worst of human failings. I once thought that was pride, then I decided it was envy—one dark pool of wasted energy on both ends. But now I believe the greatest predator is really vanity's evil cousin, narcissism. People equate the two qualities, or failings, but they are quite different. Vanity is usually a harmless indulgence, while narcissism at its worst is a vicious personality disorder. It is relevant to the professional situations under discussion that during my motorcycle musings on this tour I was trying to hammer out the difference between vanity and narcissism.

I thought of a line in my "scrapyard" of unused lyrical ideas, one I had wanted to use in a song for a decade or more: *"He wears a motorcycle jacket in a limousine."*

Rhythmically, the line just *rocks*, all on its own and, though it never found a home, it is a fine little portrait of narcissism. (One idea was to put it in a song called "The Rock Star and the Model"—but that sort of easy parody never inspired me. Nor was the irony lost on my own "profession" and Carrie having earned her way through university in Paris by modeling.)

The classic double-breasted, multi-zippered black leather jacket Marlon Brando wore in *The Wild One* was called a Perfecto—the prototype for thousands of future poseurs. Like the unnamed rock-star character in my line, people adopting the Perfecto look don't want to *be* a motorcyclist, with all its discomforts and dangers, but just *look* like one. In a limousine, a nightclub, or—on the cover of a magazine.

Vanity looks in the mirror with delight, a closed loop affecting no one else, while narcissism looks at *others* as a source of delight—seeking to make an impression, confirm an illusion, and usually (because narcissism is an essential marker of a sociopath) use that illusion to some advantage of their own. The vain person strutting down the street will check out his or her reflection in the store windows—the narcissist will be checking out his or her impression on *you*.

Such people are common enough in the "arts and entertainment" fields, where they use their vanity in a cynical effort to manipulate people, to create a marketable image. "Packaging" is an apt metaphor for how the cynically manufactured "product" offered as music or other forms of entertainment might be wrapped in . . . a motorcycle jacket.

Andrew and Bubba
PHOTO BY CARRIE NUTTALL

As a band, our ideal relationship in photography was with the late Andrew MacNaughtan, our "staff photographer" through the '90s and the Noughties. Simply by hanging around a lot—even suffering through two tours as personal assistant—Andrew captured innumerable moments of each of us just being ourselves. Only a trusted friend can achieve that kind of "access," and when we needed a formal portrait for a new album or tour, Andrew understood that I, at least, was impatient with that kind of thing. He would either organize a studio session so tightly that we could be in and out in less than an hour—or get us outdoors somewhere, where I was always ("naturally!") more comfortable. Or he would let me read!

In recent years my drumset portraits and such have been shot by another friend, Craig Renwick, and he can always get a genuine grin out of me. Being photographed in a studio by a stranger, without even my drums to hide behind, is simply "not interesting." Not rewarding, not worthwhile.

The *Rolling Stone* interviewer, Brian Hiatt, visited us at the rehearsal hall, watching us work and talking casually during breaks with each of us and our crew members. After, I drove him in my DB5

Vapor Trails Portrait, 2001
PHOTO BY ANDREW MACNAUGHTAN

to the Hallowed Bubba Cave for a wide-ranging and stimulating talk, continuing at a favorite local Argentinian restaurant. Following manager Ray's counsel, I resisted saying anything "final," and just steered around those questions.

From the conception of this tour I had wanted to call it "The Rush Fortieth Anniversary Farewell Comeback Reunion Tour." You know, to

get all that out of the way at once. (Another title I like now is "Forty-One and Done.")

But none of the other Guys wanted to be that "straightforward," and under advisement from Ray, I didn't want to be perceived as the *villain*, either. Have people in the audience holding up signs every night with unhelpful messages like, "NEIL—DON'T KILL RUSH!" (Consider the maniac who shot Darrell Abbott in 2004 for "breaking up Pantera.")

So, for the press release we approved a waffle along the lines of the "last major tour of this scale." Brian had to accept that as the "official word" on the subject, and I am told that in the end his story was positive and fairly insightful.

But I never, ever read any press about myself—in accordance with the long-ago advice of a novelist mentioned earlier, Tom Robbins. I wrote to him after reading a particularly savage and humorless review of one of his novels in the *New York Times*, saying that I wanted him to know his *readers* didn't share that opinion. He wrote back and said he never read his reviews, "because if I believed the good ones I would have to believe the bad ones, too."

That was great advice—and what a gentleman he is to have written back to me. I glean from his recent non-fiction book, *Tibetan Peach Pie*, that he often wrote back to his admirers. That is another rare habit we share—I don't know of anyone else who does it. For twenty years, from 1974 to 1994, I answered every letter that came my way, spending whole days typing up individual responses and personally signing postcards to each one. For all those years I was able to keep up with them, even through the era of our greatest popularity in the early 1980s. I suppose it worked because I kept *quiet* about it—that helped keep the numbers down. Because what changed was *the internet*. Suddenly everybody was telling everybody everything all the time (pretty good definition of social media!), and the flood of requests coming in multiplied beyond my time and energy. Still, in the years since then, I have continued to send countless thank-you notes and signed gifts to as many

Postcard Images, circa 1982, 1986, 1992 1982, 1986 BY DEBORAH SAMUEL, 1992 BY ANDREW MACNAUGHTAN

strangers-with-expectations as I could. But now . . . well, sorry, I am retired from that, too!

Tom Robbins also mentioned that sometimes others passed on comments from his reviews and such, and I have shared that experience, too. Apparently Brian Hiatt wrote in his story that I seemed friendly, not like the guy who had written "I can't pretend a stranger is a long-awaited friend" ("Limelight," 1980). I expect that was just an irresistible riff, because he was experienced enough in the ways of the "business" to understand the line's real meaning and the distinction that a meeting between him and me was *professional*. No expectations beyond having a good, honest conversation. (Amazing how many times in the years since "Limelight," younger musicians, and even actors and athletes, achieved a little fame and told me, "I get that song now.")

As a traveler—and even as a grocery shopper, hiker, old-car driver (as opposed to old car-driver), motorcyclist, and dad—I have constant encounters with strangers that are simply nice and "neighborly." The difference is easily defined, I suddenly realize, in a way that most everyone should understand. The key is the way I defined an audience early on: "strangers with expectations." The only awkward kind of encounter for me is meeting a person like that—a stranger with expectations. Thought about in that way, it happens to everyone, whether you're confronted at your door by a missionary or a pushy salesman or a feverish fan—you are not equals if the other person *wants* something from you, right?

(I will wager most women have felt that discomfort around a "stranger with expectations" often enough.)

John Cleese writes about a particular kind of stranger-with-expectations, the "selfie-seeker," in his memoir, *So, Anyway . . .*

> In the old days people would ask for a photograph of you, but now it's always, *always* . . . *with* you. Presumably so they can show their friends, "Look there's *me* with . . . what's-his-name."

I am glad I am not alone in my discomfort with that situation. And I know of many celebrities, the introverts among us, who feel the same. Posing for a camera with strangers is uncomfortable enough to make us avoid it, however difficult it is to refuse *gracefully*—graciously. But I try, maybe offering to sign something for the person if they wish. But they never do. That generation lives by the demand "pics or it didn't happen."

My Kind of Selfie–
with Some Trees and Snow

Mr. Cleese explained how he handles the selfie requests.

I'm really not sure why this "Sorry to interrupt you but can I have a picture with you?" irritates me so much. Perhaps it's the idea of providing photographic proof for the rest of eternity of the moment I stood next to someone I'd never set eyes on before. In the past, I have to confess, I sometimes responded to the request by saying, "What, to commemorate the fact that we met four seconds ago?" But now I have taken to replying, "I'm sorry but I'm afraid I don't do that," delivering the line with a fatalistic smile that hints that the interloper is asking me to betray some deeply held religious principle, and that the matter is consequently out of my hands. This has failed only once, at a South African airport in 2013, when it infuriated a fellow passenger so much that he wrote to the *Cape Argus* about it.

When the *Rolling Stone* cover shoot was scheduled, a request came
in for all my physical dimensions—for the "stylists." Oh dear, no.
I wrote in response,

Many people have tried to "style" me over the years. I recall in 1974,
early on our first tour, our managers said they thought I might "do"
as a drummer, but I "ought to dress different." On a day off in Atlanta
my bandmates made me try on some of their stage clothes. That—
ladies and gentlemen of the jury—is how I ended up in a kimono.

A possible cover portrait idea was proposed, a close-up of our three
faces, with all of us wearing black shirts. And see, I could *understand*
that. In answering, I explained the difference between "art direction"
and "styling," as I had learned it. In the early '80s the three of us were

2015 a.k.a. 1976
TOURBOOK PHOTO BY
CRAIG M. RENWICK

photographed by one of the greatest portrait photographers of the twentieth century, Yousuf Karsh.

At his studio in the grand Château Laurier hotel in Ottawa, he asked if we had brought white shirts, as he had asked. We hadn't heard about that request, but would have just snorted at the notion anyway— "We don't wear *uniforms*." Mr. Karsh was visibly disgusted that his command had been ignored. (He was a wonderfully tyrannical character—once when his assistant told him the overhead lights in the ballroom couldn't be adjusted separately, Mr. Karsh erupted, "That is not an answer that I can accept! That is *not* an answer that I can accept!")

Mr. Karsh told us he had photographed three American astronauts like that—and later I saw that portrait framing three semi-profiles of the characterful faces of Michael Collins, Buzz Aldrin, and Neil Armstrong, each wearing a simple white shirt. I saw what he meant, and from then on I understood the difference between art direction and style.

On the day of the *Rolling Stone* shoot I walked into the big photo studio and saw three or four long rails of hanging clothes, mostly black. Alex and Geddy were trying on some stuff, and the very nice wardrobe lady was urging me to try this and that. I just held up my hanger, like a shield, and said, "I brought a black shirt!"

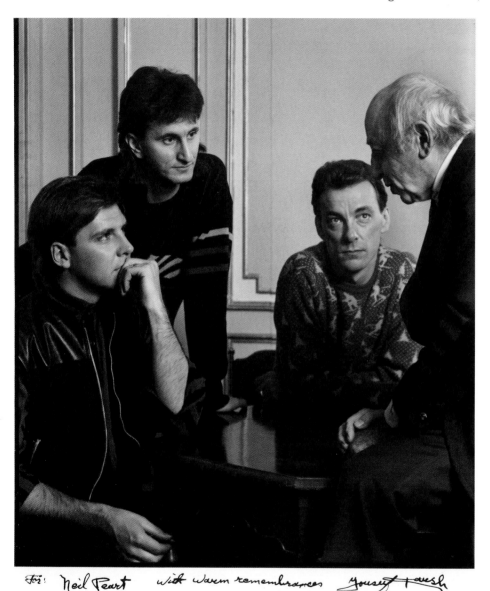

For: Neil Peart   with warm remembrances   Yousuf Karsh 1984

Us with Karsh

Carrie had worked for many years as a professional photographer, and an assistant before that, so when she asked to attend I said okay. But then the "stylists" (a committee by now) even tried to get *her* to "reason" with me. I just held up a finger to her: "Don't interfere."

I was getting tense by then.

The photographer, Peggy Sirota, was a high-spirited, energetic, determined lady. (As Geddy said during the shoot, when she stepped out of earshot for a moment, "She's a pistol!") Peggy came up to me privately in the makeup room and said, "I know everybody else has tried, so I guess it's up to the photographer now."

I said, "What do you mean?"

I am tempted to put her timeless reply in twenty-point type, to show how it was received in my brain. Perhaps the reader may imagine it that way. Or at least please read it very slowly, to savor every word.

"It is my job to try to make you look a LITTLE bit cool."

(Even raising her thumb and forefinger, a quarter-inch apart, for that "*little.*")

I was dumbstruck.

She went on, not unkindly, "I know those are probably your favorite pants—"

Whoa! I saw in a flash of stunned disbelief that the whole concern was that my *trousers* were too baggy! That was what prevented me from being "a *little* bit cool"?

Now, I understood it truly was her job—not least in the sense that if she made me look "a little bit cool," it would make *her* look cool. Same with all the stylists—that old commercial, "If you don't look good, we don't look good."

Michael Collins, Buzz Aldrin,
Neil Armstrong
PHOTOGRAPH BY YOUSUF KARSH

I get it, and it's not wrong—just wrong for this Bubba.

Still trying not to be "difficult," I even agreed to try on some of the silly "skinny jeans" they offered. Ha—the tiny things wouldn't go up past my *calves*, and I came out holding the hangers, shaking my head.

So they asked if they could just *safety-pin* the back of my pants, tighten them up a little?

I . . . surrendered.

Needs must when the devil drives.

The crew set up a few different backdrops and lighting arrangements and, as we worked through them, at one point Peggy said to me, "You've been giving me the same face all day. Could you change it up—maybe drop the smile?"

Now, see . . . if I have to pose for a photographer, I have *one* goal: to look nice for my mother. From the earliest days, when Mom attended our concerts she always complained that I never smiled onstage when I was drumming. ("Ma! It's *hard!*") So I made a silent deal with myself that I would always smile for a posed photograph.

I told Peggy, "I just want to look nice for my mother," and she left me alone about it.

Somewhere I picked up the trick that you should look into the lens as if you're looking at your dog—or your child (or your mother!)—and that helps. A friend behind the lens helps, too.

Then came the Gratuitous Raincoats. (A fine band name.) On a hot, sunny day in Southern California, they wanted us to wear matching raincoats. The other two agreed, and I breathed a sad little "fine." For this setup Peggy wanted Alex and Geddy to hold their guitars and me a pair of sticks. I never mind that for a photo—my tools, after all—though bear in mind I had to sit there with safety pins up the back of my formerly baggy trousers.

Smile for Craiggie!
PHOTO BY CRAIG M. RENWICK

FAR AND WIDE

Peggy said she wanted *action* and urged the Guys to rock out on their guitars—even got the assistants to play "Tom Sawyer" on the sound system for them to "jam" to. She wanted me to drum on the back of that wooden chair, and when I said I couldn't do that (wood against wood, right?), she said, "Just pretend then."

Now see, if I'd had a high-hat, I could have played for an hour, happily. But not on the back of a chair. And no, I could not "pretend."

The line I draw seems so clear to me—*for* me. When we make our comedic films, for example, I will act in any silly way—wear the dumbest costume of gnome or bearded lady. Do anything if it's for *comedy*.

But for the sake of looking "a little bit cool," I don't do costumes or "acting." I am not fourteen-and-a-half. (Probably wouldn't have done it then, either.) For this Bubba, it is wrong—*inauthentic*.

For Comedy, Anything
PHOTOS BY MICHAEL MOSBACH

PHOTO BY PEGGY SIROTA

"You gotta make your sixteen-year-old self proud."

Even back in the days of music videos, I could not "lip-sync" a drum part—I learned it note for note and *played* it, for real, full-out, every time. Some directors would want me to remove part of the drumset to get the camera closer, or tilt a cymbal out of their lighting, and I would say, "Sorry, can't do it." My principles were simple: "I'm the drummer; you're the director. I will play the drums; you make a video of it." Likewise, the drumset doesn't change for the lighting; the lighting changes for the drumset—isn't that *obvious*?

Anyway, Peggy saw my expression, and the sticks immobile in my hands, and realized I wasn't going to "play along." To give the lady credit, she suggested I throw the sticks on the floor and continue making "that face." I was happy to oblige her. No acting necessary . . .

Later that afternoon, driving onward to the rehearsal place, I tried to figure out my scattered feelings. Why did I feel so agitated and uncomfortable inside?

I realized I felt like I had been *bullied* all day.

My simple plea, "I just want to look nice for my mother," had left me feeling like I had been a horrible uncooperative diva who everyone would hate ever after.

It was not a good feeling.

But I played well at rehearsal that day . . .

"Time to RAWWK!"
PHOTO BY CRAIG M. RENWICK

Monument, Colorado, June 29, 2004
PHOTO BY KEVIN J. ANDERSON

MIRACLE IN COLORADO

9

One morning in February 2015, I was working at the Hallowed Bubba Cave and received a call from an old friend, Rob Wallis. For close to twenty years, with his longtime partner Paul Siegel at Hudson Music, we had collaborated on a series of drumming DVDs. Just a few weeks before, Rob had been in Southern California, and we had gotten together at the Cave with a couple of other East Coasters who were also in town for the annual musical instrument makers' show, NAMM.

Like many good friends who have many good friends, Rob and I are not in frequent contact, maybe once or twice a year. But to add to the truly *paranormal* aspect of these events, Rob had just been out shoveling snow around his house. He thought of my affection for winter and snow sports, and snapped a selfie to send to me.

When Rob went indoors, he picked up a mysterious voicemail. An elderly lady said she was calling from Colorado Springs, then launched into a story about her husband having found a duffel bag years ago then forgetting about it in their garage. Recently she was clearing out the garage and found the bag again. She said there were papers in it with my name on them "dating back to 2004," "a very nice watch," and, somehow, Rob's telephone number.

As Rob recounted these facts to me, he sounded hesitant and mystified—it made no sense to him. I knew right away what it *had* to be—though my brain was reeling at even the possibility.

It had been *eleven years ago*.

Veteran motojournalist Brian Catterson has joined Michael and me for two or three days on every tour since *Vapor Trails* in 2002. His rides with us always seemed to be accompanied by thunderstorms, torrential rain, blinding fog, and even sudden blizzards. The summer of 2004 was no exception, as Brian rode with Michael and me for two days off between a show in Houston and one at Red Rocks in Denver. It was Rush's thirtieth anniversary tour, *R30*, and as we travel back to that time, I have a handy "vehicle" for the journey. The events in question were carefully documented for the book I wrote about that tour, *Roadshow: Landscape With Drums, A Concert Tour by Motorcycle*.

We pick up the action in Colorado, on June 28, 2004. The previous day Michael, Brian, and I had ridden up through New Mexico's fine backroads to Taos for the night (with thunderstorms), and that day across Colorado (with roadside snow, rainshowers, and even thick flurries at the summits).

Nearing Denver in early afternoon, I waved to Michael and Brian and split off where highways 24 and 285 divided. I was heading east to spend the night with Kevin Anderson and his wife, Rebecca, near Colorado Springs, while Michael and Brian rolled on to Denver to visit Brian's brother.

[Blurry focus time shift to June 2004. From *Roadshow* . . .]

. . . the dark clouds finally began to release their showers, so I settled into a more relaxed pace. As the road descended, I just stayed with the flow of traffic, taking it easy on the wet road. I began to encounter lines of vehicles backed up at traffic lights, and at one of them, just after Manitou Springs, a small pickup pulled up beside me. A bearded

Snowy Selfie, February 4, 2015
PHOTO BY ROB WALLIS

man in a park ranger's uniform leaned over and called through his passenger window, "You dropped one of your boxes back there."

I automatically looked to the rear of the bike, saw that my right-side luggage case was gone and felt an immediate chill of alarm and fear. The hardshell cases were locked onto the frame of the bike, so one of them coming off was like, say, losing the trunk of your car.

"About a half mile or a mile back," the ranger said.

Thanking him, I made a U-turn at the lights and raced back up the divided highway a mile or so, then turned around and rode back in the drizzling rain, slowly scanning the roadside. At first I hadn't been too upset, thinking I would surely find the case lying beside the road and everything would be okay, but I didn't see it.

Still hopeful, I thought, "Maybe I didn't go back far enough."

I turned around again, sped uphill a couple of miles this time, then circled back and rode slowly over that same stretch of road, desperately scanning for that luggage case. It wasn't there.

I tried again, riding back a little farther this time, but there was no sign of it.

I started to get upset, going over in my head all that was in that case. Some of it was replaceable, of course: a few clothes, the "little black book" of our itinerary, a spare faceshield for my helmet, tire repair kit, some maps,

Western Colorado Summer!
PHOTO BY BRIAN CATTERSON

Monarch Pass
PHOTO BY BRIAN CATTERSON

"Never one around
when you need one"
PHOTO BY BRIAN CATTERSON

Swiss Army alarm clock, *Cycle World* baseball hat, and the venerable plastic flask half full of The Macallan. (Precious, but replaceable.)

Then I began to add up the irreplaceable items, like my shaving kit and medicines, my phone and address book, a copy of *Traveling Music* with all of my proofreading notes in it, the little Zeiss bird-watching binoculars Jackie had bought for our East African safari in 1987, and—worst of all—the Patek Philippe watch Carrie had bought me for my fiftieth birthday and the Cartier engagement ring she'd given me in 2000. I didn't wear them when I was riding or drumming, but I liked to have them with me, in what ought to have been a safely locked case.

Where was it?

One corner of my mind knew this wasn't the *worst* that could happen—my imagination always allowed for the possibility of extreme, fatal disasters. But at the same time, having barely survived some tragedies that weren't imaginary had left me permanently fragile. I lived and functioned inside a thin armor of "adaptation" that was easily pierced, and I was feeling bad about this lost case, near tears. I stopped at the side of the road, lit a cigarette with shaking hands, and tried to think what to do.

Nothing I *could* do, really, except hope. Perhaps some Good Samaritan had picked it up, a fellow motorcyclist tossing it into his van or pickup. As a Canadian, I naturally hoped it hadn't inconvenienced anyone, but maybe the fallen case had landed in the road, blocking traffic, and a cop had picked it up.

From the time the case fell off (caused by the failure of a five-dollar bolt, it turned out) until the ranger told me about it and I raced back there, not more than ten or fifteen minutes could have passed. [Later I learned I wasn't the only new BMW GS owner that dropped a luggage case, either—I shoulda sued 'em.] But I would still hope for the best. It was the way I was made.

At least I still had the directions to Kevin and Rebecca's house in the map-case on my tankbag. It was getting late in the afternoon, and still raining. I decided to carry on, get to their house, then try to deal with the situation. Following the directions onto I-25 and north in the chilly drizzle, I climbed again from 6,000 feet at Colorado Springs to 7,000 feet at Monument, before getting lost in a maze of tree-lined roads in the rainy twilight.

Some of the street names made sense, but something seemed to be missing—I couldn't find *their* street. Worse, I didn't have my phone book, so I couldn't even call them. I headed back toward the interstate and stopped at a little strip mall. A dentist's office was just closing, and the nurse gave me the missing piece of information. When I had copied down Kevin's directions from his email, I had missed one line, one street name where I was supposed to turn.

After all that, and 734 kilometers (458 miles) of mountain riding, I was tired, cold, wet, and feeling low. When I pulled up in front of their house, I tried to pull myself together and prepare to be sociable. Kevin walked out into the driveway to meet me and I began blabbering about what had happened.

[I think first I asked if he had any whisky.]

> [Blurry time shift again—to four or five days later,
> up in Washington State. Still from Roadshow . . .]

When the bikes were parked outside our adjoining rooms at the M&M Motel in Connell, Michael and I performed the Macallan ritual, then split up to have our showers and quiet time. Turning on my cellphone to check for messages, I paused to listen to one from my brother, Danny. He wanted to make arrangements for him and his family to meet us the next afternoon. I made a mental note to call him, erased the message, and listened to the next one.

KJA and NEP, June 29, 2004
PHOTO BY REBECCA MOESTA

It was a man's voice I didn't recognize, and after he gave his name, he went on to say he had picked up my luggage case. It was "all intact," and he had drilled it open and found my phone book, with my cellphone number inside. When I realized what I was hearing, my mind went *electric*, and I thought, "Omigod—I've got to play this for *Michael!*"

He had been skeptical about my earlier optimism and, indeed, by that point I had resigned myself to the loss. Now I couldn't wait to show Michael there *were* good people in the world. My finger went down to save that precious message, but out of habit, shock, and fatigue ("fatigue makes you stupid"), I realized—even as my mind screamed, "No-o-o!"—I was pressing the "Delete" button.

My head dropped, and I stared at the phone and my traitorous finger in disbelief.

Even then, I didn't think it would be a big problem. Surely we could trace the number of that incoming call. Or the Good Samaritan might call back; he had sounded like a good guy.

I went next door to Michael's room and told him what had happened. He looked at me, shaking his head, and I snapped, "*Shut up, man*—he'll call back!"

You would think so, but so far, Michael had been getting nowhere with the phone company and we had decided to be proactive. After a local investigator had failed to turn up any clues, or any witnesses, Michael arranged to place a good-sized ad in the Colorado Springs newspaper. We offered a "substantial reward" for the return of the luggage case and gave Michael's 800 number. We ran it for a few weeks, but no response.

In Michael's case-hardened (ha ha) view of humanity, he figured the guy would eventually find the valuable watch (in a zippered side compartment of my shaving kit) and change his mind, deciding, "Oh well, he didn't call back—it's mine." But I still had faith—or at least hope.

[Blurry focus time shift back to the present day]

But the years went by—a *decade* went by—and the lost case slipped from memory. But as I talked on the phone from my office in sunny Los Angeles to Rob in snowy New York on Tuesday, February 4, 2015, all of that flooded back. But from so long ago, I could hardly absorb it.

How many times in the past ten years had readers of *Roadshow* asked me if I ever got that case back? I'd always had to give a rueful shake of my head and say, "Unfortunately, no."

And now—*presto change-o!*—that luggage case and its contents were back in my life. Imagine losing a suitcase or a cardboard box full of close personal possessions for over ten years. At first the vanished items would be achingly real and personal, and their loss would hurt. With the passing of years, the objects cease to be "attached"—or you cease to be attached to *them*—and they are all replaced in your life by new versions. Like one of those time travel stories where a person or object can't appear twice in the same place—these are a phantom shaving kit, gold watch, binoculars, ring, and so on.

Right after that loss, I replaced the BMW luggage cases with aluminum Jesse cases that *couldn't* fall off—their ads showed the bike being lifted by the luggage mounts. I was never able to trust the BMW cases again.

Right after I got off the phone with Rob, I had to call Michael. He would not believe it either. I also decided to enlist his help in getting it back—I simply felt so overwhelmed by this news that I wasn't ready to face it directly yet. As the saying goes, I "couldn't deal."

Fortunately Michael and I were friends with a police officer in a neighboring Colorado town. Because his duties are sometimes of a sensitive nature, we'll call him Leo, for "law enforcement officer." (In fine dramatic irony, Michael got to know Leo at around that same time, 2004, during a local investigation into a psycho-stalker who was threatening violence against me. From the

Later That Summer–
Snazzy New Cases
Tupper Lake, NY

three of us dealing with the worst side of humanity, homicidal mania, now we were dealing with the best side, simple goodness.)

I asked Michael to call the lady, and when he suggested to her that we would send someone around to pick up the bag, she became audibly nervous.

"Oh—I don't know . . . who . . . who are you going to send?"

When Michael explained it would be a uniformed police officer, she seemed comforted. I also requested that we arrange for Leo to give her the "substantial reward" our newspaper ads had promised eleven years before. And I insisted, "Don't take no for an answer."

Leo met the lady, Carole, and her husband, Rusty, in a park on a blizzardy February day. He had learned they lived in a nearby trailer park. Carole did most of the talking, and Leo got the feeling she was "genuine and good"—"there was a sweetness to her."

They were both in their seventies, weathered with hard living, and had only been married a few years. Rusty was a lifelong tradesman, with toughened hands and layers of paint-spattered clothes. Beside his mobile home he kept a couple of sheds full of tools and equipment, and he had stored my bag there until it was covered up and forgotten.

It turned out Carole had taken the lead in contacting me because as the "new broom" in his life, she had urged Rusty to tidy things up. In turn, when the long-lost bag appeared, he asked her to find its owner.

When Leo handed him the envelope, Rusty did not open it. Leo said, "The only time he really spoke was to tell me how impressed he was with the way the bag was packed and that he knew the guy that owned it rode motorcycles and was a serious traveler. Carole never asked who the watch belonged to but thought it had to be important to the owner to cause so many people to call her. I thanked them and they walked back to the trailer park together."

I was glad Leo gave them a thousand dollars—it would mean something to people in those circumstances. A day or two later Michael played me a voice message from Carole saying how they hadn't expected anything as a reward, and were very delighted by "the dollar amount."

Once Leo had sent the bag back to me, I had to decide what to do about it—all the stuff *in* it.

For example, of the two identical Patek Philippe watches, which one would I *keep*? I would sell one to pay back the insurance company (yes, I know—it's like a twist on a humorous turn of phrase I see lately:

Lost June 2004 –
Found February 2015
PHOTO BY LEO

It Still Worked!

"'*Let's give the insurance company back their money*'—SAID NO ONE EVER."

But Bubba and the Professor agree it's the right thing to do.)

So I have to choose between the sentimental value of the first watch and the much longer-term possession of the second—less than two years versus ten years. I think longer shared experience and well-earned patina trump the old one's history; I would keep the newer one I had. Besides, the older one had been sitting in a garage all that time in the extreme weather of high-elevation Colorado, alternately baked and frozen solid. It's going to need some work. I did wind and set it, and it worked overnight, but the oil must need replacing, at least. And the leather strap, too, likely—it carries a terrible stench that affected everything in the bag. Under those same temperature extremes, it seems the Macallan degraded into a corrosive liquid that ate through the cap and leaked away. The result was a foul, pervasive reek, pungent and faintly nauseating.

As I started to put the story's details into words, I went back to Leo and asked for his impressions and more details of *how all this happened*! One thing Leo reported stayed with me: he said he asked Rusty why he hadn't searched the bag, taken the watch, or sold the items, and Rusty said, "There was something about this bag that I just didn't feel right about doing that." Leo went on, "He can't explain if it was divine intervention, goodwill, or a combination of the two, just that something told him to get it back to the owner."

Learning this background made me even more impressed by the simple benevolence of this man, and the "sweet, genuine, and good" lady making that one move—picking up the phone to make a costly call to the other side of the country, only guided by a *clue*. Leo reported Carole had first tried a few numbers from my phone book that were no longer in service. How did she end up reaching Rob Wallis, at the alphabetical end?

The very next page, inside the back cover, is where Rusty must have found my cell number in 2004, still the same—printed under "Personal Information," with this unmistakable notice in blue ink: "NEP—For reward call —."

Anyway, somehow, it all worked out. Eventually . . .

It just took a little longer—a little longer than *ten years*.

After talking to Michael, I wrote next to Kevin Anderson to tell him this amazing and completely unexpected resolution to the story. Addressing Kevin as the prolific author of wildly fantastic tales,

I wrote under the title, "YOU THINK YOU CAN INVENT A TALE OF UNBELIEVABLE MIRACLES?"

Naturally, Kevin remembered the incident well and was equally astonished.

I'm not sure if the pope would declare this a proper "miracle," with no lives saved by the magical intervention of invisible friends (new definition of religious squabbles: "*My invisible friend can beat up your invisible friend*"), but come on—what else would you call it?

In this crazy mixed-up world, all I know is, it's some kind of a story—with a bittersweet ending and renewed faith in humanity. A small dark blot in my past, with its fading nebula of pain and regret, has suddenly flared into a bright star of relief and gratitude.

You can't make that stuff up.

Time Capsule:
June 2004–February 2015
PHOTO BY LEO

10

SERENITY IN MOTION

Many photographs from our travels on the second leg of the R40 tour in June 2015 were contenders for my "opening statement" here. I settled on this humble example—because it is an action self-portrait that conveys the personal, remembered moment in the universal setting of the American Midwest. I like its geometry and palette of red, black, green, and blue, and its very *motion* suits the title theme. (The serenity part is witnessed by me feeling safe enough while riding along that quiet country lane to pull my camera out of the tankbag and snap the shot.)

It was a Thursday off between shows in Buffalo and Chicago, and after rising at the palatial Château Walmart in Sandusky, Ohio, Michael and I wended our way (never more suitable use of the phrase) south. Our onboard GPS screens showed the route I had designed the previous afternoon as a purple line, and typically, the turn-by-turn directions we followed were a complicated network of tiny country roads leading one to another—scenic and peaceful, almost always free of other traffic. The kind of roads no one travels unless they live on them.

The maps arrayed in my tankbag represent "backup navigation" for the states of Ohio, Indiana, and Illinois. In the background, the unfenced cornfield, distant farm buildings, and even the farmhouse in my mirror exemplify that sense of place. The weather was hot, around 95 degrees, hinted at by summer gloves and faceshield cracked open.

A feeling had been growing in me during these rides—a kind of "valedictory" sense, from the Latin for "saying farewell." I didn't imagine that my future life after touring would allow that "the most excellent thing I can do today" would be plotting a leisurely route from Sandusky, Ohio, to Bloomington, Indiana. That constant revelation was a little bittersweet—but mostly sweet. I had made journeys like this many, many times before, and if this was to be the last time, I would appreciate it all the more. (Tidy little verse of poetry there—or a valedictory song.)

That hot June day we would ride for eight hours and cover 358 miles of rural Ohio and Indiana. Yet in all that time and distance we were hardly ever troubled by traffic, stoplights, or stress of any kind. We just made our stately progress through pretty countryside and crossroads towns. Serenity in motion . . .

Great numbers of mystics and spiritual guides have insisted that mortals can only achieve states of serenity, tranquility, nirvana and so on if they are at rest, *without* motion. Meditating in the lotus position, say, or reclining with eyes closed in the yoga *savasana* pose. Others, like Thoreau, John Muir, or Nietzsche, would insist that such elevated states can only be attained by *walking*—hiking in the mountains, or cross-country skiing or snowshoeing in the winter woods. Yogis and yoginis would champion the tranquility of "gentle" motion, safely confined to a yoga mat, while some individuals find spiritual peace in running, swimming, bicycling, or rowing. And really, they are *all* right, in their ways. Because *ipso facto ergo bueno.*

Few people associate words like serenity and tranquility with motorcycling, but some of us discover those mind-states by motoring along on our own two wheels, out in the weather and part of the scenery, on quiet roads of our choosing.

That same day in Southern Indiana, I saw a homemade signboard in front of a small business that offered an alternative wisdom:

MONEY CAN'T BUY HAPPINESS
BUT IT CAN BUY A MANI-PEDI,
AND THAT'S ALMOST THE SAME
THING.

Yes, another quest for tranquility, on a more sensual level.

A similar plastic signboard stood in front of a small insurance office in Broken Bow, Nebraska, opposite a gas station where we stopped one rainy day. It also offered a little wisdom and wit:

ALWAYS WEAR YOUR THINKING
CAP WITH YOUR PARTY SHOES.

Indiana Byway
PHOTO BY MICHAEL MOSBACH

Everybody should follow that advice.

The photo on the next page shows a perfect little road, running north out of Indiana toward Chicago (locally they call the area "Illiana"). Sure, bad weather is coming down on us—torrential rain once again—not for the first or last time this tour. But before the storm hit I was able to experience and capture this peaceful moment. (I want to emphasize that line, on more levels than just the weather. Because in just a few days a raging storm of health problems was going to overwhelm me.)

And speaking of weather, literal and metaphorical, pollsters and pundits seeking "to take America's temperature" would find it better represented on the rural backroads than in the streets of coastal cities. In the front yards of farmhouses and small-town bungalows,

Into the Storm—Northern Indiana

crossroads churches and family businesses, little signs-of-the-times speak about faith, politics, patriotism, and—well, faith. That's most often what you see being trumpeted. Because apparently faith needs to crow.

Clearly, the "temperature of faith" rises with poverty—region to region, country to country, century to century. In our time, Radical Islam has been defined as not so much a religious war as a *class* war. Throughout history, extreme religion will always drift that way—from the Crusades to the French Revolution to Islamic jihad. People who are poor and ignorant often want easy answers, and they want *revenge*.

Having traveled the United States for over four decades, ever more intimately in the past twenty years on my motorcycle, I have measured that national temperature year after year, right down to the grassroots. After 9/11 I saw and felt the militarization of police departments, from state troopers to small-town sheriffs. Once upon a time American law enforcement officers resembled Boy Scouts, in more ways than one; now they present themselves more like storm-troopers and polarize the people that way. Hard to know where to lay the blame for a thousand little decisions—personal, local, and national—that turned a tide, but the results of that shift in perception and behavior have been tragic.

As a newly minted American citizen, perhaps in 2015 I looked with even keener eyes, but it seems that every year I watch Americans grow *angrier*, in both their faith and their politics. Just for one example, the people of Michigan have suffered enormous misfortunes and setbacks in recent decades—the decline of their central industry, automobile manufacturing, and the depopulation and crumbling of the Motor City itself. The people of Michigan seem to grow ever more evangelical, and lean more to the politics of rage.

Sample church sign in a Michigan town: "STAND FOR MARRIAGE/ KNEEL FOR PRAYER." Or a bumper sticker on a big pickup, "I'LL KEEP MY GUNS, MY FREEDOM, AND MY MONEY. YOU CAN KEEP THE 'CHANGE.'" That word choice was a slam at President Obama and liberals in general, like the sticker on the back window of a pickup with an acrostic message, "One Big Ass Mistake America." Around that time another style of pickup politics was spreading around the Northeast, a defiant protest called "rolling coal." Diesel engines were modified to collect soot so when the driver passed, say, a hybrid car, a bicyclist, or any other kind of "eco-weeny," he could floor the accelerator and blow a cloud of black smoke over them. I saw it done a few times around the Midwest, though never *on* anybody—just showing off.

Another sticker on a compact pickup (built in Asia, ironically, despite its blue oval badge—so itself symbolizing some of Michigan's problems) showed a picture of a smiling President Obama, and the phrase, "DOES THIS ASS MAKE MY TRUCK LOOK BIG?"

No, but it makes your brain look small.

But we were, after all, in Ted Nugent country.

Not to knock the authentic old wildman Ted, at least back in the time we knew him. In the mid-'70s we opened for Ted Nugent many times, and he was always professional and fair, as was his crew. Occasionally we traveled on the same commercial flights, and saw Ted approached by Hare Krishna panhandlers—a common sight in those days, though they wore wigs so they wouldn't look so "weird," and might get more donations. Ted would grab hold of that wig and raise it up high, saying, "Why do you have to hide under this? Why not just be *yourself*?" That was Ted.

We always got a soundcheck with Ted—in complete contrast to another band that was mentioned in our *Rolling Stone* profile, Aerosmith. I laughed when I heard Joe Perry had said, "I don't recall ever working with Rush."

Roosting in Michigan
PHOTO BY MICHAEL MOSBACH

Oh, for his sake I hope he was talking about his own band, the Joe Perry Project, because wow—we opened for Aerosmith *forty times*! In all those shows we never *once* got a soundcheck—not because they were mean or insecure, but because they were so *flailing*. Every day Steven Tyler held the stage and everyone else "captive," as it were, until the doors were opened. He grumbled about Joey Kramer's tempo and made him start a song again and again, or had the soundman fiddle endlessly with the digital delay on his voice. Tyler even apologized to

Geddy for it—*once*—but back then, it was just "the way they were." We felt no grudge or anything like that—we only laughed.

(And learned. I can safely say that in later years every band who opened for us got a soundcheck, if it was humanly possible.)

The point of Geddy's quote in the *Rolling Stone* story was that a decade later Joe Perry's solo band opened for us (in Lake Geneva, Wisconsin—playing for promoter Randy Levy, as I remember and Joe doesn't!), and we had to decide what to do. Geddy's and my memories agree that published reports of the dialogue at that time are more fanciful than factual but, yes, we did take the high road.

One positive note of delicious irony from those forty shows in the '70s was that while Aerosmith "carried on" there would be no opportunity to try out my drums or even warm up. I used to sit behind my drums at the side of the stage, on their little four-by-eight-foot riser on the arena floor, and whenever there was enough noise from them to "cover me," I would tap away lightly on my snare drum. Over time it improved my delicate rudimental playing quite a lot, and I would use those techniques in our music later that decade, as it became more dynamic and textural.

The flyers shown here somehow came my way and would be from late 1974, in Quincy, Illinois. They feature bands we either opened for (Ted Nugent, Savoy Brown) or opened "with" (Cheap Trick, Head East, Baby) on the popular multi-act shows of the day. Going on first of four or five bands meant a soundcheck was out of the question, and even in the show you would be lucky to get thirty minutes. (We headlined for one Pittsburgh promoter for decades after that, but never forgave him for once cutting our set to *two songs*. We opened as usual with "Finding My Way," and closed as usual with "Working Man," and in between—nothing!)

But back to Michigan in June 2015. As pictured in a previous photo, and below, it was another day of serenity in motion—with, at that wheel-spinning moment, a little added adrenaline. We had some fine riding that cool and overcast day, up through the central, more rural part of the state toward Sleeping Bear Dunes National Lakeshore and Traverse City for the night. I have theorized before that Michigan's best riding is in the eastern Upper Peninsula—Pictured Rocks and Grand Marais area—but this region had a fine selection of roads and scenery, too. In a day's ride of over 350 miles, we never touched a freeway or even a divided four-lane, just the occasional red light in a town, or a country stop sign among miles of farms and forests.

As we rode into the area of lakes, beaches, and resorts near Sleeping Bear Dunes (Brutus and I passed that way in October 1996, on the *Test for Echo* tour), we encountered more traffic, much of it families on holiday. Often their minivans and SUVs had roof racks for their sports equipment.

At one red light in a resort town, Michael leaned over and said, "What is it with white people and *kayaks*?"

Michigan Byway
PHOTO BY MICHAEL MOSBACH

Signs, signs, signs. There are so many kinds—enough to fill a science called semiotics. The example on the opposite page requires no science to decipher my riding partner's display of affection and admiration.

Framing that hatefulness is another exemplary stretch of road: a country lane in Indiana—narrow, shoulderless, patched with tar "snakes" (treacherous on hot days) and lined with spindly, off-kilter utility poles. The ragged strip of pavement is framed by distant farm buildings and a field of corn on one side and soybeans on the other. (A pattern of crops that repeats *constantly* through the American Midwest—someday I will discover the reason for that nagging mystery.) That day I saw a "welcome" sign for an Indiana town that stated modestly, "A NICE LITTLE CORNER OF THE WORLD." And it was.

Obscenity in Motion

Signs in people's front yards can tell of local struggles, too, like dozens of small placards on sticks around parts of rural Indiana reading "STOP THE WIND 'FARM.'" (Proper farming people would naturally put that word in quotes.) Its message reflects a growing friction I have observed in many parts of the United States and Canada. Call it the Energy Wars—at least of the NIMBY variety. ("Not In MY Back Yard!" "Yeah we want light and heat—but no mess or inconvenience!")

Mustachioed in Chicago
PHOTO BY JOHN ARROWSMITH

Again and again we encounter local protests for or against coal mining, oil fracking, pipelines, hydroelectric projects, gun laws and, in this case, wind power.

You can easily get semiotically paranoid, too, wondering about "the signs behind the signs." Conspiracies. (*"Just Because I'm Paranoid Doesn't Mean They're Not Out to Get Me!"*) Someone had those signs printed up, then distributed them to people who wouldn't care either way about having them on their lawns. Oil companies absolutely *do* campaign in such underhanded ways against wind and solar power, and political parties *do* create fictions like "STOP THE WAR ON COAL" to make political hay. (A fine mixed metaphor, thank you—coal and hay representing medieval sources of power, and somehow only coal endures.)

But—yon editor protesteth—the unworthy scribe doth editorialize too much.

Thus he resorteth to the time-honored dodge of a fake Hercule Poirot mustache . . .

Reverie at Rest
PHOTO BY MICHAEL MOSBACH

11

THE ACCIDENTAL PILGRIM

A helmet full of many thoughts and emotions here, as I straddle the bike at Windermere Dock on Lake Rosseau. It is early summer in Ontario's Muskoka Region, otherwise known as "cottage country," and many people from nearby Toronto and its exurbs migrate to such areas on weekends and summer holidays. (Here Michael was able to look at the passing vans and SUVs and ask, "What is it with white people and *canoes?*")

That day the theme from *A Summer Place* had been wafting through my thoughts. (What a great opening soundtrack it also made in *The Omega Man*, as Charlton Heston drove through the dead city in a Mustang convertible.) That was another subconscious song choice that was easy to identify, as I was riding through what was by definition "a summer place," as it had been all my life. The names and places were full of echoes of the past—and not without trains of thought carrying ghosts of long-ago summers.

One such spectral locomotive transports me back to childhood memories of traveling "up north" (as we called it, though not very far on the map—and way south of Northern Ontario proper) to places like this, all woods and lakes and glaciated rock. Sometimes I was camping

Above Lake Rosseau
PHOTO BY MICHAEL MOSBACH

with the family or in shared rental cottages with other families—and later groups of guys. I think sometimes we pretended to go fishing.

Another train of thought was pausing for the actual place, Windermere House, where the Guys at Work and I spent March of 1982 working on the songs and arrangements for our *Signals* album. We worked in an outbuilding that still stands behind the imposing lodge, closed in winter then and now. I wrote about a previous visit there in October 2012 in the *Far and Near* story "Witness to the Fall," and this time Michael and I stayed overnight, between shows in Detroit and Toronto.

Windermere House was a fine and gracious inn, the place and its surroundings as good as we would ever enjoy on our travels. That night I decided the finest quality an overnight stop could offer was being able to sleep with your window open.

Another lakefront scene, exactly one week before, began a darker thread behind this story. In retrospect, the day this photo of the rainy lake was taken represented a turning point—when things started to go bad for me.

Lake Placid Rain

These days when we hear about "exhaustion" it's usually because some young performer has been admitted to hospital for it—a euphemism for "overindulgence." Or sometimes *under*indulgence—in, like, nutrition.

Likewise, when people talk about "stress" it is usually translated as "anxiety." But there is a kind of extreme mental and physical exhaustion combined with stress that is actually *distress*—and the result is depletion, emptiness.

For me the tell is always the "slackjaw moment"—when I find myself standing in front of a window, staring at nothing, with my jaw hanging open.

I always reach up and push it closed, give my head a quick shake, and tell myself, "Don't be like that." (But as I noted in our song "How It Is," "You can't tell yourself how to feel." And if that's true, it's a sure thing that no one *else* can tell you how to feel.)

For decades, whenever I found myself in that condition—sometimes in the studio, but usually on tour—it would affect my physical health, always attacking my weakest part. In my twenties it was my teeth; in my forties and fifties my ears; along the way a bout of tendinitis in each elbow, and many maladies of exhaustion, from colds to anxiety to depression.

Years ago the tennis great John McEnroe told us that at the age of twenty-five he had felt "washed up." So at almost sixty-three, I'd certainly had a long run in my sport of choice. And in sports that are more about stamina than sprinting, the only factor attributable to age is *recovery time*. The band's lawyer-friend David Steinberg also represents hockey veteran Mark Messier, whose twenty-five-year career in professional hockey made him one of the all-time greats. David and Mark attended a New York Rangers game together, and David asked Mark if at age fifty-four he could still go out there and play an NHL game. After a moment's thought, Mark said yes, he could play one game—but he would never recover in time to play the next one.

Similarly, during the R40 tour, when people commented that they couldn't understand why I would want to retire when I was playing so well, I tried to explain, "Yes, I can still do it. But. It's. Too. Hard."

(Depending on the commenter, I might insert an expletive as well, for emphasis.)

I hope it goes without saying that I put everything I have into every performance—to continue the hockey theme, "leave it all on the ice." But as that output every second night exceeded the available supply of mental and physical energy, it wormed deeper and deeper into my reserves. Thus I had no resistance to any kind of physical attack.

This time the weak link was apparently my *skin*, and the chain reaction began on the long, wet ride from our dropoff point in Bath, New York, to Lake Placid.

Journal notes report:

The Next One
PHOTO BY CRAIG M. RENWICK

343 miles. Compared to what I had to do last night, and will have to do tomorrow night, a picnic.

Heavy rain for hours, everything soaked—but drying in front of the fireplace. And I'm in front of the *lake*.

And I'm drinking and I'm smoking and I'm glad to be alive.

What a great place.

Again I ask, "Worth it?"

Oh yeah.

Hours of riding under a steady downpour had overwhelmed our nominally waterproof riding gear. Droplets leaked down the backs of our helmets and inside our clothes, or seeped up sleeves and cuffs, until we were fairly soaked through. One of my boots stayed dry inside, but the other was flooded—leaving my right foot wet and cold, and the boot would not dry by morning. So I would ride another day with a wet foot—the perfect breeding ground for . . . a fungus among us. The inevitable casual exchange of socks carried it to the other foot, and at first it was just a little "hotspot" in the arch of each sole. But day by day it was growing and mutating into a fungus-eczema-psoriasis-bacterial-infection monster that would be attacking me for the rest of the tour—and long after.

Years ago I once experienced some discomfort during a show, a little pain in my chest that I immediately magnified into an incipient heart attack—but my fear was not of dying, but of "wrecking the show." When I told that to Alex later he laughed and agreed with the feeling, "Whatever you do, don't wreck the show!" Going into this tour, whatever health issues I worried about, from tendinitis to mid-solo cardiac arrest, I certainly did not spare a thought for *the bottoms of my feet*! I replaced those boots the next day, but it was too late.

However, that night on the shore of Lake Placid I was not burdened with such dark knowledge. ("Before the storm hit I was able to experience and capture this peaceful moment.") After a fantastic dinner in one of our favorite lodgings in America (a journal note: "fireplace *and* wifi—can't beat that"), I slept happily with my windows and curtains open . . .

Choosing a route back the other way across New York State toward the show in Buffalo was a shunpiker's challenge. The Finger Lakes run roughly north-south through the middle of the state, where they were gouged out by glaciers, and obstructed my attempts to connect backroads from east to west. (Talking of glaciers, through Ohio and Indiana I had been pondering why the landscape changed from flat in the north to hilly in the southern parts of those states, and wondered if that could possibly be where the ice sheets had ended—seems to be true.)

Scanning the map of upstate New York for useful backroads (several large cities to work around, too—Syracuse, Elmira, Rochester), I noticed a dot called Palmyra, and it rang a bell. Oh yes—the family farm where seventeen-year-old Joseph Smith walked into the woods one day in 1820 and had a mind-blowing revelation, then came out to found the Church of the Latter-Day Saints—the Mormons.

That history and all that followed had fascinated me for many years—just the *human* side of it. My intention is never to make fun (Matt Stone and Trey Parker have thoroughly covered that angle in *The Book of Mormon*), but rather to *marvel*, out of a true sense of wonder and awe. Wallace Stegner took the same neutral, human approach in the fine histories he wrote about them, *Mormon Country* (1942) and *The Gathering of Zion* (1964).

Mr. Stegner, a non-Mormon or "gentile" who grew up partly in Utah, speaks for me in his introduction to *The Gathering of Zion*.

> Suffering, endurance, discipline, faith, brotherly and sisterly charity, the qualities so thoroughly celebrated by Mormon writers, were surely well distributed among them, but theirs also was a normal amount of human cussedness, vengefulness, masochism, backbiting, violence, ignorance, selfishness, and gullibility. So far as it is possible, I shall take them from their own journals and reminiscences and letters, and I shall try to follow George Bancroft's rule for historians: I shall try to present them in their terms and judge them in mine. That I do not accept the faith that possessed them does not mean I doubt their frequent devotion and heroism in its service. Especially their women. Their women were incredible.

(That was in 1964, mind you, when feminism was just gaining traction in popular culture or politics. Sad to see how fifty years later, many modern-day American liberals have all but thrown feminism under the bus out of a craven fear of seeming "racist"—afraid to despise aloud the vicious treatment of women in Islamic societies, for example.)

My own interest in the Mormon story was sparked by traveling around Utah, loving the scenery and admiring the friendly people, and riding past that splendid Tabernacle in Salt Lake City. Their hard work in the Beehive State had clearly "made the desert bloom," as in the Book of Isaiah: "The wilderness and the solitary place shall be glad for them; and the desert shall rejoice, and blossom as the rose."

In past years my travels had led me to some of the holy shrines of the Church of Latter-Day Saints, and I decided we had to go to Palmyra, where it all started.

I have offered the disclaimer before that I seldom even *think* about religion, except when it's in my face—or just off the highway on the way to work!

Making a quick stop in that long ride (over 400 miles to cover, on a show day, which always lends extra urgency—but at least it was sunny and cool), I toured around the vast properties held by the Church of Latter-Day Saints in the Palmyra area. (Again thinking that seditious notion—that churches should pay taxes. If only all Americans could see for themselves the megachurches of the mid-South, vast crystal palaces of pomp and old-time religion, and the almost half a *million* individual churches that are getting a free ride. Don't forget Scientology has its own *ship*, along with vast land holdings, and many others are the same. As "not-for-profit" enterprises, a lot of people are making a nice living from churches.)

I straddled my motorcycle in front of the Sacred Grove (as mentioned, the name of friend Stewart Copeland's home studio, but he says it's just a coincidence—"the earliest places of worship"). Quietly, I registered a naturalist's observation that none of those trees were old enough to be "the remnant of an ancient forest" in 1820. One devotional painting of young Joseph Smith's revelation is tellingly titled *The Sweet Dream of a Pure-Minded Boy*, but whatever happened there, it had power and significance.

Then and later, as I ground out the tedious miles on the New York State Thruway toward Buffalo, I thought of all the charismatic men

Adirondack Morning
PHOTO BY MICHAEL MOSBACH

like Joseph Smith. (Always men—throughout history females were allowed to be visionaries of a sort, to see the Virgin Mary and such, but they couldn't take *power* from it. They were more likely to be slaughtered—I mean *martyred*—like Joan of Arc.) Consider Moses and Abraham, Jesus and Muhammad, and Joseph Smith right up to Menno Simons (Mennonites), Jakob Ammann (Amish), Charles Russell (Jehovah's Witnesses), and L. Ron Hubbard (Scientologists). All of them were undeniably visionaries, as I would define it, and apparently *believed* their own visions. Fair enough—but the miracle is that others believed *them*.

(The rest of us, or at least the rationalists, answer with Christopher Hitchens: "What can be asserted without evidence can be dismissed without evidence."

Or stand behind astrophysicist Neil deGrasse Tyson: "The good thing about science is that it's true whether or not you believe in it.")

All those prophets preached stories that absolutely beggar belief—and yet were believed. With such persuasive power and personal magnetism, these days they would be cable news anchors or popstars.

In any case, even if you are a devout believer in one of those prophets, as most people in the world are, in the back of your mind must rest the conviction that every one of the other visionaries that people believe in equally devoutly were either certifiably insane—or *made it all up*!

Wouldn't it make you wonder, just the tiniest bit?

Maybe the honeyed words uttered by those visionaries felt to their listeners like this cabin did to me after 343 rainy miles across the country roads of New York State—a place of ease and comfort, shelter and warmth, rest and reward, after my day of sufferings. No further revelations necessary—at least until dinnertime.

The word "propaganda" comes from the Catholic Church, an age-old department called *Congregatio de Propaganda Fide*, or congregation for spreading the faith. Modern-day Mormons have a similar organization called the Foundation for Apologetic Information and Research, or FairMormon. ("Apologetic" has a different meaning in religion and philosophy—more about explaining than feeling sorry.) It seems that since the defeat of Mitt Romney, their "chosen one," in 2012—at least partly because of what "gentiles" see as outlandish beliefs—Mormons are determined to "walk back" some of those perceptions. Mormons (the "Saints"—never forget it is *they* who are the Latter-Day Saints) are nothing if not practical. Businessmen first, spiritualists second. Back in the 1850s the Saints of Utah decided that statehood would be good for business, and only the inconvenient revelations about polygamy stood in their way. It took another forty years for them to gradually put aside those revelations and ban polygamy, but they did it.

(Of course there remains an orthodox splinter, considering themselves to be "holier" by sticking to Joseph Smith's words. Around the

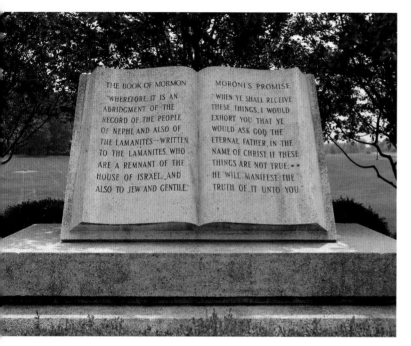

Book of Mormon Monument, Palmyra, New York

Utah-Arizona border, a couple of polygamous communities sometimes make the news. One time I rode through Colorado City, on the Arizona side, and noticed numerous multi-dwelling compounds. Wiki says half the combined population of 8,000 people are descended from two men, in a history of "cousin marriage" that has resulted in genetic problems.)

As I researched my trip to Palmyra, and a later expedition to a site in Missouri, Adam-ondi-Ahman (said by Joseph Smith to be where Adam and Eve dwelt when they were kicked out of the Garden of Eden, which was where Independence, Missouri, is now—but you knew that), I encountered the subtle revisionism of FairMormon contradicting or softening the teachings and revelations of the Elders. Once blindly accepted and venerated, now they were treated as just "some people say" sidebars. Such hot-button topics as "temple garments" (mustn't be called "magic underwear") and Joseph Smith's particularly bizarre expansions on the Book of Genesis (Noah's ark was launched in Missouri, floated down the Mississippi, and ended up on Mount Ararat in Turkey, for example) were subject to that kind of "waffling."

Adirondack Cabin

But again, not to pick on the Mormons—they're just one example of magical thinking, and far from the most extreme. Every superstition has its magic clothes—Jewish beanies, scarves, and sidelocks; priests, bishops, and popes in their fancy dresses and hats; and even the austere Buddhists in their saffron robes.

The one telling question to address to *any* religion seems obvious to me: "How do they treat *women?*" Ah, well, if you look at them that way, every single one fails miserably. But then so do our political systems, even unto the twenty-first century. Almost nowhere does a woman even own her body.

It doesn't take a cynic—maybe only a skeptic—to believe that future generations will view us as we do Ancient Egyptians or Aztecs. Fascinating, maybe, but laughably primitive. And probably a little— "horrible."

What we believed, how we lived, what we did to each other—it's not going to look good.

The Skeptic
PHOTO BY MICHAEL MOSBACH

But back to matters of the flesh—or at least, to the skin of the drummer's feet. (What I was soon describing to friends as "da agony of da feets.") By the time we reached Ontario, my feet were itching and burning, edging toward *painful*. After the day off when Michael and I rambled around Muskoka, I saw a doctor in Toronto and showed him the wreckage. I told him I'd had previous bouts with psoriasis, and he gave me some cream for that—exactly the *wrong* thing, because it suppressed the immune reaction that would have fought the fungus. Overnight it began to bloom and multiply—just in time for two shows in Toronto that would be filmed and recorded. Now even walking— even *standing up*—was becoming an ordeal.

Despite the growing "discomfort" (as medical professionals discount our mortal pain) in my feet, I didn't think it would affect my playing. That is always the bottom line, so to speak—I don't care what I have to endure as long as I can play properly. In forty years of touring, I have played through a *lot* of pain, but the only time it really bothered me was on the previous tour, in Toronto (no coincidence that stress hits harder there). My left elbow was afflicted overnight with full-blown tendinitis—awoke on the bus after a show in Philadelphia

Muskoka Backroad
PHOTO BY MICHAEL MOSBACH

with tenderness and pain. Late in that Toronto show it hurt so bad I couldn't hit as hard as I like to—and that bothered me.

Carrie and Olivia were going to meet me in Toronto for a few days, along with my mom and dad joining us at the hotel during that four-day stay. So that was a nice family occasion all around. But when it came to Olivia's idea of Dad's being able to "play properly," I would not be much use. (Except for the art.)

And you know, that first Toronto show on the R40 tour was a perfect (*horribly* perfect) illustration of exactly why stress exists. It would have been one thing if we'd been all worried about it for nothing—if nothing went wrong. But that night things went wrong we didn't even know *could* go wrong. And it started with the introduction of the very first song, "The Anarchist."

Our monitor engineer, Brent, has a separate programmed mix going to each of our in-ear monitors. That mix had been developed and refined daily since rehearsals to give us the information we needed in any given part, and not what we *didn't* need. Throughout the show Alex and Geddy are triggering things with their feet (keyboard sequences, vocal effects, bass pedals, string parts) all of which

I have to play in sync with. Some of them are accompanied by a tambourine sound as a metronome, which only I hear—meaning I have to arrive at those "events" smoothly and accurately, play through them likewise, then transition out to the next part.

Well. I started the song with the driving tom pattern, as always, but when we reached the first of those passages, the intro reprise to "The Anarchist," I was suddenly way ahead of it. I immediately blamed myself, as I do, and guessed I must be so anxious that I was pushing the tempo. Not a problem I usually had, at least in recent years, but . . . I pulled back on the tempo until it was in sync again. Then everything would be fine until the next such entry, when again I would be early, ahead of everything. I kept thinking, "What is *wrong* with me?"

It was like that all the way through the second song, "Clockwork Angels," too—and by then I was going crazy. At least I *thought* I was—and that amounts to the same thing. ("Gaslighting," it's called, popularized by the 1944 movie *Gaslight*, in which Charles Boyer's character set out to convince Ingrid Bergman's character that she is insane. Gaslighting is defined as "an attempt to destroy another's perception of reality."

Him Over There
PHOTO BY CRAIG M. RENWICK

That's just what was happening to me through those two songs.)

Before the third song, one of the backstage "geniuses" finally switched over to the backup keyboard system. Suddenly everything was fine—but of course *we* were not fine. Geddy had a problem starting "Headlong Flight" and stopped playing to switch bass guitars, leaving Alex and me unsure whether to stop or carry on. We kept playing, Geddy joined in again, and we continued on—but it was pretty much all over for us right there. We played on through the show—because what else?—but I couldn't say we "recovered." We merely *survived*.

Before the second Toronto show, Geddy described that first one as "the worst experience I've ever had onstage."

So there was that.

And now we faced a second show on which everything depended—the entire expensive and complicated filming and recording project. In contrast, back in 2008, for example, we filmed and recorded the *Snakes*

and Arrows tour over two shows in Rotterdam. The first one went great, and thus we went into the second one feeling relaxed and confident. So *both* shows were really good, and we had our pick of the performances. This time we went into the second show feeling anything but relaxed and confident. Glad to say we pulled it off, and the concert DVD turned out really well—but it didn't feel good at the time.

One bright light in Toronto returns to our hockey theme—in this case, literally, the "Hockey Theme." In a story called "Fire on Ice" (in the book *Far and Away*), I described the making of that piece of music in 2009—a theme that would introduce hockey broadcasts for a Canadian TV sports network called TSN. Drum Workshop had built a custom drumset for that project, with all of the NHL logos around

Ben and Geddy NOT "Losing It"
PHOTO BY JOHN ARROWSMITH

the shells—masked and sprayed one color at a time by DW's artist Louie Garcia. After a long display in Toronto's Hockey Hall of Fame, the entire drumset was on its way to a permanent home in Calgary's National Music Centre.

As part of that journey, TSN, Drum Workshop, Sabian cymbals, and the Hockey Hall of Fame had generously sponsored a display of those drums at each of our four Canadian shows. People could make a contribution to a cancer charity and have their photos taken with the drums. In that way we raised $20,000, and in that way it's possible I set some kind of a record—for the drummer with the most drumsets in one venue. Four, including the two I used onstage and my little warm-up set in the Bubba Gump room.

An important feature of that second Toronto show was the first performance of "Losing It." The three of us had been working on that song since our band rehearsals back in April, and played it at every soundcheck since. Our part of the song was as ready as it *could* be— without being properly "road-tested" like the rest of the night. Over thirty years after violinist Ben Mink had joined us at Le Studio in Quebec to record that song, we would perform it together live for the first time. During soundcheck before the first show, then again that afternoon, we ran through it a few times with Ben, and that night we pulled it off pretty well. (As the concert DVD shows me—I couldn't be totally sure at the time.)

With Carrie and Olivia visiting, my training in getting up early after late nights was well tested. But really it was no problem waking up with a smile to Olivia's beaming face. As we had always done in our travels, including in Tulsa and New Orleans, we let Mom sleep while we got dressed and took our sketchbook and markers down to the restaurant.

Back in the room we also created some more ambitious works.

As usual, Olivia was the art director, Dad sketched the outlines, then Olivia was the colorist. Here Olivia is shown in the style of the animated show *Team Umizoomi*. (Just when I got pretty good at drawing the Bubble Guppies! And now we've moved on to Peppa the Pig, and Shimmer and Shine—who live in a genie

Umizoomi Art with Olivia, Toronto

world, which is fun to draw.) On Olivia's bed is our golden retriever, Winston (about one-quarter scale), and her stuffed animals Boo and Buddy. Olivia's leg is poking out because, "I get too hot." Beside the bed is a smoothie cup with a straw and some books. In the other bed are the characters from the show, Geo and Milli, with Bot reading them a Bubble Guppies book. A steep, looping tunnel slide leads down from Olivia's bed, while the others have three slides, in different styles. So many great ideas—and of course for me an escape from the realities of the struggles at work, and da agony of da feets.

In our song "Vital Signs" from 1980, I wrote, "*A tired mind become a shape-shifter/ Everybody need a mood-lifter*," and Olivia is surely that for me.

12

Last Note and
Stick Toss, Montreal
PHOTO BY JOHN ARROWSMITH

GEORGE HARRISON'S EYES

The next show was in Montreal, and I think the Guys at Work and I looked at that one as a kind of "grudge match"—after the nightmare of the Toronto shows, we were determined both to play well *and* have a good time. And we did.

From there we would move on to Boston, with the usual day off before. On the afternoon of the Montreal show, I had looked around the map of the Northeast U.S. for possible destinations in that crowded part of the country. As I had done a few tours before, when I looked for "open space" on the map, my eyes were necessarily drawn to the *blue* part—the ocean. And the islands. Block Island, off Rhode Island, had made an enjoyable place to explore back then, and now I looked at Martha's Vineyard and Nantucket, and their ferry schedules.

PHOTO BY MICHAEL MOSBACH

Without giving the idea sufficient consideration, I thought it would be nice to spend the whole day wandering around Martha's Vineyard. I decided to ask Dave to drive us through the night all the way to Southern Massachusetts and the ferry dock, near Woods Hole. (I have to mention again, because it amuses me, that the U.S. Bureau of Geographic Names hates possessive apostrophes but has allowed the people of Martha's Vineyard to keep theirs—one of only five places in the entire United States—unlike Woods Hole.)

The flaw in my thinking was forgetting that we were not in the West anymore, or on the Great Plains, with long, straight, relatively smooth interstates—where you might be able to sleep through the night on the bus rolling along as gently as a sailboat in calm seas. Riding from Montreal to Southern Massachusetts would carry us over the frost-heaved roads of the Northeast, a part of the country where years ago Dave had warned Brutus and me, "Better put on your Velcro pajamas!"

Sure enough, it was a rough night, and I was awake most of it. My feet were angry and truly painful now, despite the creams I was applying. In the morning I looked out the blinds and saw we were in the neighborhood of the ferry dock, and Dave was searching for a place to park. I hobbled forward on my tender feet and said to Dave, "I bet you got more sleep last night than I did!"

Michael and I caught an early ferry over to the Vineyard (already using the familiar name, like locals) and paused for breakfast in Edgartown. The rest of the day was a leisurely tour around the island, only riding about 80 miles, but it was scenic and calm and our pace was relaxed. The island covers 100 square miles, its permanent population only about 15,000 people—though in summer that can swell to 100,000.

The place itself was absolutely delightful on a warm, sunny day in the briny air. However, on the inside I was not so sunny—my terse journal notes hint at my sorry state:

Martha's Vineyard
PHOTO BY MICHAEL MOSBACH

> Tiredest and sorest of tour.
>   Feet a fright.
>   "Slackjaw" syndrome today–
> me at my lowest.
>   Yarmulke of pain.

That last was a phenomenon I have often noticed when I am overworked physically—it seems the pain in my muscles and joints is more than they can contain or "express," and the excess gathers at the top—a dull, heavy weight under the crown of my skull.

I was noticing other symptoms of the "on the road too long" syndrome. For example, pretty much the first thing I do after arriving at a venue is loop the lanyard of our tour laminate, the crew pass, around my neck. If I take a shower, the laminate is laid out alongside the clean clothes, and goes straight back on, and doesn't come off until showtime. In *Roadshow* I described coming out of the shower and almost immediately searching for my laminate to string around my neck—then laughing to realize I was *at home*.

One of the recurring nightmares (literally, something you have bad dreams about) of touring life is being trapped outside the place you're supposed to play. Another is being trapped outside your hotel room. (One crew member was subject to sleepwalking, and twice found himself waking just as his hotel-room door clicked shut—behind his naked body. Talk about a nightmare!)

Thus it has been a similar religious custom that since the 1970s my hotel key goes in my right-side back pocket immediately, and isn't removed until I check out. Before leaving the room, I always do a "reflex pat" of that pocket—but it's always there.

When Matt Scannell and I first traveled together on a road trip, we were leaving my room to head for dinner and he said, "Do you have your room key?"

With a smile and a raised finger, I shook my head and said quietly, "You never have to ask me that again."

He got it and laughed out loud.

This time I had a moment that was a reversal of these two rituals—as I stepped off the bus one day on my way to soundcheck, I noticed I was patting my right rear pocket to check for the hotel key before I closed the bus door. "On the road too long."

That warm, sunny day on Martha's Vineyard, for the first time in many years I actually called a

PHOTO BY MICHAEL MOSBACH

halt at a shady spot and lay down for a siesta.

Just to stop, lie back on the grass under a spreading tree, and close my eyes for a while . . .

For the first time in decades, Michael had forgotten his cellphone—a talisman sacred and holy. Whenever we stopped that day, I could sense and almost see his hands twitching uncontrollably. While I lay back he asked to borrow mine and I took pity. After checking his vital social media, he looked up the story of Chappaquiddick, which we had just been discussing.

Chappaquiddick Island is a small offshoot of Martha's Vineyard, reachable by a short ferry ride, and it has long been notorious as the scene of a terrible accident. One night in July 1969 Senator Ted Kennedy gave a ride to a young woman named Mary Jo Kopechne—he said later she wanted to catch the last ferry to Edgartown, where she was staying. Yet strangely, she left without her purse and keys, and without telling her friends. Kennedy's Oldsmobile drove off an unlit bridge with no guardrails (which was *not* on the way to the ferry dock—and in fact was considered to be a *pedestrian* bridge) and overturned in the shallow water below. He managed to escape, but his companion did not.

Strangeness and scandal surrounded the tragedy, then and now. Kennedy did not report the accident until the following day, after authorities had already discovered the car and the body. He claimed

Chappaquiddick View
PHOTO BY MICHAEL MOSBACH

not to have been "under the influence of alcohol," nor to have had a "private relationship" with Mary Jo, and eventually he was let off with a two-month suspended sentence for "leaving the scene of an accident after causing injury." Whatever the truth behind that night's events (just one key question Michael posed: *"Where did he go and how did he get there?"*), it cast a pall over Ted Kennedy's chances of following his brothers John and Robert toward the presidency.

Eerily, almost exactly thirty years later, in July 1999, another Kennedy tragedy struck when John F. Kennedy Junior was killed, along with his wife and sister-in-law, when his small plane crashed into the Atlantic on the way to Martha's Vineyard to attend a family wedding.

Late in the afternoon Michael and I checked into two pleasant little cottages at a resort on the north side of the island. (Near a place name that naturally inspired Michael's puerile humor: Gay Head.) My cottage had a screened-in porch with a partial ocean view, and once I was unpacked and out of my bulky riding gear I headed out there. I brought my journal and pen to catch up on travel notes, and my camera to look through the day's photographs. But as I looked around the porch for a place to set down those and my plastic cup of the Macallan, I saw there was no table.

Somehow a line right out of the nineteenth century appeared in my head, then was spoken aloud: "A table would be useful—but lacking that, we shall not lament it."

I had to laugh at myself—as I do so often when I talk to myself when I'm alone.

However, the attitude in that speech *does* reflect one of my "adaptive mechanisms." If something I desire is not available, I do not bother regretting it. It's simply "not on the menu." Any real traveler, or self-denier, needs to develop that reflex—and next time, *bring* that thing!

Speaking of menus, as in "things not on," it seemed odd that Martha's Vineyard has strict local liquor laws of the kind usually associated with places like Tennessee or Utah—most of the island is "dry" but for two villages. Knowing in advance that our resort and its restaurant did not serve alcohol, I had cadged a bottle of red wine from the Guys at Work (they always carried many bottles of fine vintages for their after-show dinners) and brought it with us. Of course we *always* carried the Macallan—and for the first time that day instead of my much-traveled old plastic flask, we carried a bottle in a leather case with a couple of double old-fashioned glasses.

Northern Vineyard
PHOTO BY MICHAEL MOSBACH

This upgrade had been forced upon us—*forced* upon us—by a couple of bad experiences earlier in the tour. I was powerfully dismayed when two motels offered only *paper cups*. Oh no, no, no—not for single-malt whisky. For Bubba, that was beyond the pale. I assure you I am no snob about drinking vessels, and will happily sip my Macallan from a plastic cup—perhaps *especially* if it bears a Best Western logo—but not paper, or (shudder) Styrofoam. Certain basic standards *must* be upheld.

Even in the padded leather case, real glasses did not survive being jostled in a motorcycle's luggage case through a day of shunpiking. Thereafter we stocked it with Best Western plastic cups instead, and thus were always supplied with the Basic Necessities of touring life.

Once again we would sleep in a place where my windows and curtains could be open—this time to the smells of salt air mingled with the cool exhalations of woodlands on a summer night. We decided the Vineyard was a fine place.

Over dinner I told Michael about my one previous visit there, aboard the schooner *Orianda* back in 1986. That summer the boat was docked in Newport, where we were trying to sell that floating seventy-five-foot all-wood money pit. In August my family and some friends traveled down from Quebec for a cruise out to Nantucket and Martha's Vineyard.

Then as now I would always avoid flying if the drive could be done in a day, and while the others flew I drove that pleasant 450 miles across Vermont, New Hampshire, and Massachusetts. Brother-in-law Keith rode shotgun in the silver Porsche 911 Cabriolet I had then—top down all the way. I can date that long drive by my favorite song at the time, "No Promises" by Australian band Icehouse. Replayed that cassette many times that day.

After sailing from Newport to Nantucket for a night, then to the Vineyard, we anchored offshore in Edgartown. It was a weekend night, and after dinner in town we took a couple of taxis to a big disco near the airport. As dance clubs go, it was a good one, vast and dark inside with colored lightbeams flashing in the smoky air (it *was* 1986—people still smoked in bars). Another song I remember from that time was first hearing (and, oh yes, dancing to) "Smalltown Boy" by Bronski Beat (the first band to feature openly gay members, save perhaps the Village People). That song and the album, *The Age of Consent*, were favorites through the following winter. (Talking about '80s moments, I remember riding the Toronto subway to the Y and listening to them through headphones on my Walkman.)

The 1980s were a time when dance music could be great to dance to *and* to listen to—at its best, like Trevor Horn's work with ABC, Frankie Goes to Hollywood, Seal, Grace Jones, and Trevor's associate Steve Lipson with Propaganda. (All very influential to us in that period, sonically—we worked with musicians from that same circle, like string arranger Anne Dudley and flamboyant keyboard player Andy Richards.) It was the only time "dance" and "music" attained equal heights, apart from the big band era, forty years before. Timely thought, because when Michael and I were on Martha's Vineyard I was reading that biography of bandleader and celebrated clarinetist of that era Artie Shaw.

Artie Shaw was yet another American monument, a huge *life* of epic scale—both virtuoso musician *and* immensely popular, intellectual and good-looking. Married eight times, including to Lana

Bubba's Bar 'n' Grill Takeout

Vineyard Backroad
PHOTO BY MICHAEL MOSBACH

Turner and Ava Gardner, he was the first white bandleader to hire an African-American singer, Billie Holiday. Author Tom Nolan recounts a chilling story set in the 1940s, a time of frighteningly intense celebrity worship. Like the hysterical bobby soxers screaming and swooning for Frank Sinatra (starved as they were for boys in wartime), other hitmakers of the time ignited an equal madness in their fans—a.k.a. fanatics. A car in which Artie Shaw was riding was surrounded by a mob, who in their collective insanity actually *overturned* it. (This was all out of *love*—love gone mad, you could say. What is scarier than love gone mad?) Shaw crawled out, even as the "fans" tore frantically at his clothes, and ran to his hotel. *Any* normal human being would be psychologically scarred by such an experience, wouldn't they?

England circa 1977-78
PHOTO BY FIN COSTELLO

Such scares happened to the Guys at Work and me on British tours in the 1970s. We traveled in a Daimler limousine (which only *sounds* luxurious—it was cramped and drafty, especially when we were young and foolish enough to consent to tour Britain in *winter*) owned and driven by a cheerful cockney, Bill Churchman.

This photo tells many tales, not least exemplifying what William H. Calvin defined as "the Three Primal Questions": 1) "Where are we going?" 2) "When do we get there?" and 3) "Why do I have to sit in the middle?"

The quote is from a masterly book about the human mind, *The Cerebral Symphony: Seashore Reflections on the Structure of Consciousness*. The book had been an inspired choice for a 1992 bicycle trip in West Africa—the kind of journey where, for packing reasons, I tried to choose two books that would last the entire month. And traveling in a place where there is *no* other entertainment—or at least, no other *media*—books are extremely important cargo.

And, oh, *Roadcraft*! Nothing teaches you how to pack better than backpacking or bicycle touring. Everything you carry you have to *carry*, yet you need to have everything you might need. On early concert tours, for example, in a classic beginner's error, I would just throw a bunch of clothes into a suitcase, never even counting if I had the same number of socks and underwear.

With only two or four small saddlebags, or panniers, on a bicycle, I carried exactly three rolled-up T-shirts, three pairs of socks and

Djenné, Mali , 1992
PHOTO BY DAVID MOZER

underwear, three pairs of riding shorts, one pair of long pants for off the bike—especially in Islamic regions—and one collared shirt for what I used to call "pannier formal." (At the end of a month with that limited wardrobe, I would never want to see any of those shirts again.)

Another great "popularizer" of complex science, Daniel C. Dennett, said about *The Cerebral Symphony*, "Thinking along with Calvin is sheer delight. This book has the most vivid and lucid explanations of brain function I have seen, and his discussions of evolution place him in the same league with Stephen Gould and Richard Dawkins as elegant expositors in the life sciences."

On an earlier bicycle trip through Cameroon, I carried Aristotle's *Ethics* for daytime reading and van Gogh's letters for bedtime (usually in a sleeping bag with a flashlight on my shoulder), and they had been perfect counterparts. For the Mali trip I carried *The Portable Nietzsche* and *The Cerebral Symphony*—which also turned out to be nourishing and enduring treasures. William Calvin offered a poetic frame for many profound statements by himself and others on the subject of human consciousness, and touches of humor like the Three Primal Questions.

And of course on those early British tours, all of us hated sitting in that middle seat, "the hump," so took turns suffering.

After one show in the Midlands we scrambled out of the stage door through a surging crowd of denim and long hair toward the car. (Backstage security in those days wasn't what it is today, when areas are kept what the professionals call "sanitary." It has occurred to me that the Beatles might have survived longer if they had been touring in modern times of professional concert organization and . . . private jets.) After we scrambled into the back of the Daimler, Bill tried to drive away, but the fanatics blocked and surrounded the car, then started rocking it and pounding on the bodywork. (Outraged for Bill, I remember shouting out, "Hey—easy on Bill's car!")

What I felt wasn't fear, but anger, and a recoil deep inside against being *trapped*—the scar of a near-drowning experience as a boy that would later trouble me during stressful times. And of course, I learned an enduring distrust of *that* kind of "love."

In late 1974 I once looked into George Harrison's unguarded eyes. It was backstage at one of the TV shows we performed on, *In Concert* or *Don Kirshner's Rock Concert*. (On one of those tapings I broke a bass-drum head—pretty much the worst of disasters, one that can't be "played around" like another drum might be. We had to stop while it was fixed in front of the waiting live audience—though at least it wasn't being broadcast live.)

During long days of filming, many bands performed, and Billy Preston was also on that day. George Harrison was there just to visit and cheer on his friend. (Billy once said he thought the Beatles hired him to play keyboards on the *Let It Be* sessions because having him around might encourage them to be *nicer* to each other.) In the back-stage area, as George walked up a spiral staircase I happened to be behind him, and from a few steps above his head swiveled around, and his eyes bored into mine—an unforgettable look that was wary, haunted, and essentially *fearful*. And that was years before John Lennon was murdered.

Since then I have seen that look in the eyes of many other super-famous people—actors, athletes, singers. Even as a parent who lives in Westside Los Angeles, Olivia's class at school has dads who are A-list movie stars. When I encounter them at school events, I recognize their George Harrison's Eyes, wary at every turn and guarded at every approach. And of course there are a lot of school events they simply cannot take part in—other people go too weird around them. But usually they *try* to be "normal," and will even sneak into a field trip when they can. After all, their "fate" is *not* their fault, no matter what the trolls might grumble. On our second live album, *Exit, Stage Left*, we included a message in the liner notes: "We didn't change, everybody else did!" That's what happens to these people, too.

Who can believe fame is truly desirable, or remotely *healthy?* The list of casualties is long and depressing, and even those rare few who *do* seem to revel in fame, to seek celebrity at every turn, and at any cost—well, those poor souls were damaged before fame, and will be more damaged after.

Everybody ought to know the ideal is to be rich and *not* famous. (An author once commented that she was just famous enough to get a good table at a restaurant, but not famous enough to be bothered during dinner.)

Morning Ferry
PHOTO BY MICHAEL MOSBACH

Early next morning I roused Michael to pack up and ride, heading for Edgartown to catch an early ferry back to Woods Hole. On a show day, a water crossing ahead always feels like a slightly risky barrier. Once in a long while in my travels I have encountered a ferry that wasn't running, usually because of bad weather. So I'm always wary, and extra early—because show day!—but there was no trouble on that sunny morning.

Safely on the mainland, we stopped for breakfast at a great little diner in Falmouth. From there the part of Massachusetts north to the arena in Boston pretty much amounted to a congested megalopolis the whole way, so we were confined (resigned) to the interstate. I did plan one detour, to Plymouth Rock, if for no other reason than to add another "American Legend" to this story.

It is not known exactly what the *Mayflower* looked like, but it would have been much like the replica shown below. Of course many books have told the "big story," but when you actually *look* at it, the one detail you can't escape is how uncomfortable that two-month crossing must have been, with about 150 passengers and crew packed into it.

Considering all that history, you are pretty much obliged to look around the bay and try to imagine it in 1620—raw green vegetation and rippled water, nothing more—but you can't really do it.

In Bill Bryson's *Made in America*, he casts doubt on the accepted legend of the landing:

> The one thing the Pilgrims certainly didn't do was step ashore on Plymouth Rock. Quite apart from the consideration that it may have stood well above the high-water mark in 1620, no prudent mariner would try to bring a ship alongside a boulder in a heaving December sea when a sheltered inlet beckoned nearby.

(I have always wanted to share the story of another American place named after a rock, on the Arkansas River, opposite a landmark called by French explorers *la Grande Roche*, the big rock. Hence the smaller stone on the other shore—since eroded away—became Little Rock. My generation probably first heard of Little Rock in the Grand Funk song "We're an American Band," while later generations might think of the Clintons. There is actually a rumored link between "Sweet, sweet Connie" from the song and Mr. Clinton—but mustn't gossip.)

The legend of the actual Plymouth Rock itself makes a rich American story. (Malcolm X had a good quote: "We didn't land on Plymouth Rock, Plymouth Rock landed on us.") The actual boulder was identified by a ninety-four-year-old man over a century later, a claim that is still contested, but nevertheless the stone was hacked up and moved, then hacked up some more, then the remains replaced where it once was, then moved again to a place where it could be better *displayed*. An American odyssey right there.

Frenchman Alexis de Tocqueville was an early chronicler of American life, traveling widely in the early 1800s and publishing *Democracy in America*, still celebrated for its observations and insights. He wrote about Plymouth Rock:

> This Rock has become an object of veneration in the United States. I have seen bits of it carefully preserved in several towns in the Union. Does this sufficiently show that all human power and greatness is in the soul of man? Here is a stone which the feet of a few outcasts pressed for an instant; and the stone becomes famous; it is treasured by a great nation; its very dust is shared as a relic.

Mayflower Replica

When I got off the bike for the short walk to take this photo, I limped as my feet cried out at each step—they were really bad now.

Fortunately I had an ally in Boston, Matt Scannell's boyhood friend James, now a doctor—"Bro-Doc" to me. During my bout with elbow tendinitis on the previous tour, Bro-Doc had helped me a lot with suggested braces and pain relievers. That day I sent him some photos of my feet—too ugly to discuss, never mind share with anyone but a doctor.

Bro-Doc brought me some creams that we hoped would help but, really, things were so bad now that it was a classic "rearguard action." All I could do was try to stop it from getting *worse*.

At least there was one more great ride, and one more great destination, on this East Coast run. I drew up a complex little loop of tiny roads in northwestern Massachusetts and Southern Vermont, ending at the Wheatleigh, a hotel in Lenox, back in Massachusetts. My memories of that elegant refuge in the Berkshires (cited in the

"Americana" list from *Roadshow* and *R30* given earlier) go back to the *Test for Echo* tour in 1997, with Brutus and my late daughter, Selena. (By now she's eighteen years "late," and I hardly think of her—not more than . . . every day.)

I have written about that day in the Berkshires before, but it has fresh resonance now, with two of its characters gone. Starting out where Maine and New Hampshire meet, Brutus had arranged a helicopter video shoot, and for (the also "late," and also frequently missed) Andrew MacNaughtan to do some stills from aloft. Our mistake was choosing that part of the country—the backroads so overhung with trees that the two riders were only intermittently even *visible* from above. We tried again later, in Colorado, but bad weather grounded the helicopter that day.

New England Lane

Later on in the R40 tour I set out to arrange a similar motorcycling video shoot, but using crew member Sebastien's drone instead. For the backdrop I was careful to choose open country and a state where the weather would likely be clear—Arizona.

For Michael and me, our trip to the Berkshires would be another long day in traveling hours—about eight—but not in miles—only about 180. Journal note:

> Today so immaculately *peaceful*. Perfect weather, zero traffic, zero congestion, zero stress.
>
> And the place—always forget just how *great* it is. Grand, elegant, gracious, meticulous.
>
> Feet better, but still tender. Always aware of them—especially when walking—or climbing roadsides.
>
> Like that time in Mendoza—"This would be a wonderful place—if I wasn't so *tired*."
>
> Had that feeling many times.

Yes, that upscale resort in Mendoza, Argentina, blending sleek modernity with traditional shapes and textures, had been truly fantastic. It was an oasis of luxury in the heart of wine country, with the frosted Andes in the background. The trouble was it came near the end of a grueling tour in South America (the rides more than the shows, that time) in 2010. As recounted in "The Power of Magical Thinking" in *Far and Away*, when we arrived I stood in the casita among my bike bags, half out of my riding gear, feeling drained and heavy with pain.

("From my nose to my toes," as it often felt—or these days "from my Yarmulke of Pain to Da Agony of Da Feets.") That was one time I remember thinking that it was a wonderful place, but I was too tired to appreciate it. Settling into the Wheatleigh I had the conscious thought that it was an unparalleled destination, but unfortunately a little wasted on me. Because *I* was so wasted. ("The Ruins of a Man" is how I defined it for my journal.) Without that dispiriting weight, how different I would have felt in those surroundings.

Black Brook "Road"
PHOTO BY MICHAEL MOSBACH

And yet, the alternative—just *staying* somewhere and resting—had zero appeal. Another chorus of "What's the most excellent thing I can do today?" The answer would never be lounging in a hotel room or on the bus. I did not believe that resting in a hotel room for one day was going to make my condition suddenly improve. At that level of stress and exhaustion, the prescription of "rest" is measured in days and weeks, not hours. And sometimes the *definition* of rest is measured in miles.

Only three situations had ever made me decide not to ride. A lightning storm in Missouri, a snowstorm in Tennessee, and August 10, the date of Selena's death. After 1997, for many years I would not ride—and still won't perform—on that day. I would just hide in a hotel room and seek oblivion. After seventeen years, I can just about get through that day, but it is always veiled in the dark scrim all grievers know about.

Otherwise, the roads called to me, the *map* called to me—the lanes of New England as much as the Appalachians or the West. And I did find a kind of peace there.

Though undeniably peaceful, the day had not been without "mystery roads," or bits of adventure. Winding along a pleasant little two-lane in Northern Massachusetts, Doofus and Dingus told us to turn at Black Brook Road. However, the turning was clearly blocked with concrete barricades. The map showed that a detour would be lengthy, and it seemed to me I could get through or around that barricade. Michael had already given up and ridden away, but I turned down and found I could slip through the barricade. I just couldn't be sure what I was getting through *to*.

"Worth a try, anyway," I thought—we had time enough and gas. (A nice Neilogism of "world enough and time.") So I raced down the highway and waved Michael to the roadside. Shutting off my engine, I straddled the bike, raised my helmet, and just stood there, hands on hips, staring at him. As *grimly* as I could manage.

Then, shaking my head in disbelief, I said, "Since when do we run away and hide from a . . . *closed road?*"

He started blustering, "Well, I saw the sign, and the barricade, so I checked out a route around it"—pointing to Doofus's screen—"and . . ."

I cut him off with a raised backhand, "A *long* way around it, dummy. We can get through that barricade. Let's just give it a try!"

Michael–Afraid Again (Naturally)

He hissed something that managed to be racist, sexist, and homophobic in just a few coarse words.

Beyond that barricade, the pavement was broken and cut away, as if a vast sinkhole had opened up below it. Guardrails twisted down in mangled arcs into the deep, raw ravine, but there was just enough room for us to get through. We picked our way carefully among the fallen trees and shattered pavement for several miles, then out through another barricade. There we saw a hand-made sign of stick-on letters on plywood, pointing back the way we had come.

BLACK BROOK ROAD IS CLOSED
NO ACCESS TO RT 2

Later I learned that Hurricane Irene had washed away the road in August 2011, along with closing part of that nearby Route 2, the Mohawk Trail, for several months. (My paper map, dated 2012, still showed Black Brook Road, and the computer map, supposed to be dated "now," did, too.) It didn't look like that little road was ever coming back—but as Olivia likes to say, "You never know."

(Though she is usually referring to questions like whether mermaids have closets, or if aliens have eyes on stalks.)

The aforementioned Route 2, or Mohawk Trail, was one of the paved roads that had carried us along rivers and low mountains in twisting arcs, offering occasional "sporting" opportunities. But most gratifying in such a densely populated area as New England was

Drummer along the Mohawk
PHOTO BY MICHAEL MOSBACH

finding lots of unpaved roads and linking them together.

Some of the gravel tracks tunneled through the deep, shadowy woods, lined with overgrown, mossy stone walls (inevitably thought of New England's poet laureate, Robert Frost, and "Something there is that does not love a wall") and high along ridgecrests with sweeping views of distant peaks.

Once again that day I noted the "valedictory" feeling about these rides. "Farewell to all this," I wrote, then added, "Strange, and complicated."

Vermont Crest
PHOTO BY MICHAEL MOSBACH

Vermont Lane
PHOTO BY MICHAEL MOSBACH

COPS AND ROBBERS AND MORONS (OH MY!)

13

An extremely sharp-eyed reader might have noticed that starting in Martha's Vineyard the photographs show me riding a new motorcycle. Picked up in Toronto, "Cindy 2" was undergoing a careful break-in on these rides—their gentle pace and constant changes ideal for a new engine.

The bike I usually kept in Canada was an older generation than my U.S. bike, lacking its smoother and more powerful liquid-cooled engine and, more importantly, its electronic modes. Michael and I had found those *very* helpful in the widely varying conditions of our daily "commutes." For example, the Rain setting allowed no wheelspin, under braking or acceleration, which was reassuring in wet conditions. In contrast, the Enduro setting gave us the necessary wheelspin and rear-wheel locking on loose surfaces.

Another feature on the new bikes was something I never thought I cared about—cruise control. In my early years of riding I had tried various throttle-lock devices to ease the constant wrist pressure, but after a few hundred thousand miles I had refined my own technique to be relaxed and effortless. So it never bothered me, and I didn't think I cared about cruise control—until I had it. The unexpected advantage was in helping to avoid roadside conversations with LEOs.

On a stretch of straight, empty road on which you might tend to pick up speed unintentionally, you could set the cruise to a chosen margin—ten percent over the limit is usually fine. If you *really* need to make some time on such a road, a radar detector can be useful—to avoid surprises like an oncoming patrol car—but wiring it up every day and wearing the ear-piece is bothersome. We didn't bother with them this tour, and were lucky. And crafty.

In any case, even when I feel it's "safe" in every way to speed, like on a wide-open desert highway, I hold my velocity just under twenty over the limit—because that's the point at which LEOs can start to get *mad*.

Another Roadcraft rule I have refined lately in regard to both cops *and* robbers: "Don't Make It Easy for Them." Meaning strategies like the above, and why I always come to a full stop at signs and observe school zones. Good practice anyway, of course. And as for robbers, I never leave my computer in a car, for example, or the alarm off in the Hallowed Bubba Cave. Don't make it easy.

(On a bicycle trip in the Alps one time, about to cross from Switzerland over the Simplon Pass to Italy, I stopped in a hardware store to replace a failing bicycle lock. When I told the lady what I wanted, she gave me a stern look and said, "You don't need a lock here." When I told her I was headed for Italy, she shook her head and said, "No lock will help you there.")

Not that there are any guarantees anywhere, with robbers or cops. As a counterpoint to "Miracle in Colorado," I can offer the tale of "Entrapment in Ohio." A couple of tours ago Michael and I were riding into Columbus and for the "final approach" I accidentally led us onto the divided four-lane state highway rather than the interstate we wanted. We only had forty miles to go, so I decided to stay with it despite the annoyances I have cited before: low speed limit, frequent intersections, overeager law enforcement. After about twenty miles the putting along was getting to me, and when a pickup went speeding by us on the left, I thought, "Must be a local, probably knows what he's doing." So I led us in behind him as he cruised at about eighty. A mile or two later my heart froze at the sight of a row of black-and-whites at the side of the road and a line of troopers pointing us in.

The pickup pulled to the shoulder ahead of us, but I was surprised to see it driving away after less than a minute. Meanwhile Michael and I were written up "to the full extent of the law," and did not ride away until almost thirty minutes later. The burly officer finally returned with my paperwork and made a joke about my middle name, Ellwood: "Who gave you *that?*" I explained it had been my dad's middle name, but I didn't know why. Her good humor ended there and did not stretch to knocking one mile per hour off the speed clocked by the airplane pilot overhead. She handed me the ticket and said, "Have a good show"—so recognizing my name hadn't helped, either.

Looking back, no question it was a setup— aircraft circling above that cursèd road while an officer in a "civilian" vehicle lured outsiders into speeding. Both shameful and shameless—as the Ohio State Patrol has been known to be forever. I should have known better.

Another wrinkle of the "don't make it easy" advice covers the third kind of people who can ruin your day, if not your life: morons. Apparently most people are competent enough when sitting in a chair behind a desk or operating heavy machinery, but achieve sublime obliviousness behind the wheel. Others are scarred by the kind of territorial belligerence that ignites inside their moving capsules (motorcyclists call four-wheelers "cages"—often appropriate). Anger also makes people stupid, no question, so what it boils down to is that on a busy freeway, for example, you are largely surrounded by morons. Don't make it easy for them—to kill you.

Martha's Vineyard
PHOTO BY MICHAEL MOSBACH

You will have to think not only for yourself but for them, too. A motorcyclist survives by being hypervigilant, almost clairvoyant, scanning traffic in all directions, all the time. In highway traffic, for example, you might be thinking, "That brown car's driver doesn't yet see that his or her lane is ending, and they will be merging left at the last minute—putting it in *that* spot in my future. And in that same place in time, it will steer into the future of the driver of the blue van cruising steadily along in the middle lane. Blue van might avoid brown car by veering left into *my* lane." So you position your own future somewhere safe from theirs.

A tip I learned in bicycling continues to serve me. When passing a line of parked cars, or even moving ones, always look at the front wheel. Anything that's going to happen will start there.

I started riding motorcycles twenty years ago, after taking a motorcycle safety course at Humber College in Toronto. Two life-saving acronyms have stayed with me—indeed, become automatic parts of my mindset on the bike. One is ATGATT, for All the Gear All the Time

New England Lane
PHOTO BY MICHAEL MOSBACH

(we'll hear more about that one later in this story), and SIPDE, for Scan, Identify, Predict, Decide, Execute. Scan the traffic, identify potential hazards, predict other drivers' reactions, decide on a defensive strategy, and *do* it.

Another constant game is "What if?"—creating imaginary scenarios in surrounding traffic and considering alternatives. I say to myself, "Never let it be your fault," which is the same thing as saying "Don't make it easy."

Which brings us back to why I decided to trade the Canadian bike against a new one—it was safer—and made the switch in Toronto.

Olivia likes to name my machines (all of them are *girls*, even if their names are Guido or Sparky), and before this tour Olivia had christened my American bike Kate. "Good enough," I thought, and from then on she was Kate. Later I asked Olivia what to call the Canadian bike, and she thought for a minute then yelled out, "*Cindy!*"

Kate and Cindy are, of course, the singers from one of her favorite bands, the B-52s—perfect. (Later that year Olivia, Carrie, and I went to see them perform at the Hollywood Bowl, with the excellent Psychedelic Furs opening, and I had to wonder what the singers, Kate and Cindy, would think if they knew my motorcycles were named after them. I hope they'd see the coolness. It happened to be my sixty-third birthday, and thus the fiftieth anniversary of my starting to play drums—and I couldn't think of a finer way to celebrate it privately than watching *other* bands work—and watching Olivia and Carrie dance in the aisles to "Love Shack." Priceless.)

The following morning I awoke thinking only (almost wrote "solely") of my feet—two burning pain-generators, they were a wreck.

Simply getting out of bed, shifting my weight onto the soles of my feet, was like trying to stand on two raw wounds. Every step was groan-out-loud agony. I don't mind confessing a fantasy crossed my mind, one I have entertained for years—especially when I am feeling spent and miserable, and staying in a wonderful place.

What if, through no fault of mine, tonight's show was canceled?

Not anything *disastrous*, you understand, maybe a plumbing problem or something. Just so I could steal a day in a place like that, doing nothing and going nowhere—yet still ride to and from it. Once I remember having two days off in a row on a British tour, and Brutus and I purposely stayed an extra day in a wondrous country hotel in Devon.

But that call didn't come—it *never* had, despite my years of fervent prayers. (I actually sometimes entertain the same sort of fantasies on my way to the Y to force myself through my hated-but-necessary workout. I'll think, "Maybe the pipes exploded and they had to close the building." But that never happens either.)

Michael and I would face the 300-mile ride to Philadelphia, most of it on the New Jersey Turnpike. (A price I had accepted in return for the previous day's meanderings, and the opportunity to stay at the Wheatleigh.)

After Philly we would park the bikes for the last few days. With shows in New Jersey and New York City, I would stay in Manhattan and commute in a four-wheeler. Once again Carrie and Olivia were flying in, so we would have a few days to spend, then fly home together.

Our total motorcycle mileage for the second leg came to 3,406 miles, for over 10,000 in total already. And very few of those had been "easy" miles, on interstates and such. But right now *none* of my miles were easy.

I had to explain to Olivia that I wouldn't be able to go walking around, as we usually did, exploring Central Park and FAO Schwartz (the oldest toy store in America, closed that July, unfortunately—a victim of corporate downsizing). Olivia gave that problem some thought, then said, quite sincerely, "You could *hop!*" as she demonstrated a bunny-hop across the hotel room. I had to laugh.

Scuba-diving Genies in Ancient Egyptian Playground

Then I told her I couldn't even take her to the pool—another of our great hotel pleasures—because even walking that far was too painful. Once again she considered, then got down on her hands and knees and said, again quite seriously, "You could crawl!"

Don't think I wasn't tempted . . .

At least Olivia and I could continue working on art together in the hotel room. One was this remarkable composition of Olivia, Shimmer, and Shine—genies scuba diving past a mermaid god and goddess of Ancient Egypt, with a play structure including a pair of rings, swings for big kids and little kids, and a slide with a ladder. Oh, and the Zahramay Falls in the background.

Once again, she was my eternal mood-lifter.

In New York I saw yet *another* doctor, just to ask him if there wasn't something I could do for the pain. Unfortunately the only remedy would be some kind of numbing pads, and Bro-Doc—a sometime drummer himself—had asked me, "Do you really want to play drums with numb feet?"

Probably not—but the pain was truly becoming unbearable, and I had to do *something*.

Before one of those shows I said to the Guys at Work, "You don't know how much I would pay not to have to do this."

Madison Square Garden
PHOTO BY JOHN ARROWSMITH

Well, yes, they did, of course, and as always they were sympathetic. After those shows each of them sent me little notes congratulating me on having played so well despite the pain.

And again, yes, I could do it. But the cost.

At least I would have a break for a week at home, then twelve more shows to go . . .

14

PHOTO BY MICHAEL MOSBACH

EAST OF EDEN

In an earlier chapter I described my intention to visit the Mormon Garden of Eden at a later date, and now that time had come. Hence the chapter title, for the photo's location—in relation to the neighborhood (western Missouri), and referencing the Steinbeck novel and the quote from Genesis about Cain being exiled after he killed his brother Abel: "And Cain went out from the presence of the LORD, and dwelt in the land of Nod, on the east of Eden."

(In the interests of research, I did read the Book of Genesis to "check the geography"—similar to why I read the Book of Job a few years ago, thinking of our *Clockwork Angels* hero Owen Hardy. That time I was grappling with how much "punishment" a good soul could endure and still remain . . . good. This time I was grappling with even deeper issues of faith and forbearance.)

The first show in the third and final leg of the R40 tour was in Kansas City, and that day Michael and I did a "warm-up ride" through the area of Missouri northeast of Kansas City. The day was hazy and warm, the countryside rolling and green. Most of the roads that appeared on our GPS were the kind that have letters rather than numbers, rural routes like C, WW, Z, A, and so on.

During the short break I had been able to seek more medical attention for my feet, and they were somewhat improved, but not healed. The night before the show, Michael and I flew—not to Kansas City, but to St. Louis—to meet Dave and the bus. He drove us a few hours west and parked at the Château Walmart in Columbia, Missouri.

For that day's motorcycle ride I had two "attractions" in mind. The first was in the southwest corner of Missouri, "America's Sistine Chapel." Another traveling friend, Michael Cartellone (longtime drummer with Lynyrd Skynyrd, which would surprise you if you knew him—a sophisticated urbanite and fine-art painter), had told me about it, and here's how the attraction is described on the *Roadside America* website. (A useful resource if you want to find kitschy landmarks like "The World's Largest Fork"—Springfield, Missouri—or one that Michael and I actually stumbled upon, in Sumner, Missouri, "The World's Largest Goose.")

In 1985 the world's hottest figurine collectibles were Precious Moments. Their bulb-headed, anime-eyed, nearly mouthless children—many portrayed as baby angels with stubby wings—were in nearly every grandmother's curio cabinet. Founder and creator Samuel J. Butcher, a former janitor, was a newly minted multi-millionaire.

Then God spoke to Sam Butcher. He told him to rent a car and find a spot where Sam could create a masterpiece for the Lord.

The spot turned out to be just outside of Carthage, Missouri, and the masterpiece—inspired by the Sistine Chapel in Rome—is the Precious Moments Chapel. Its interior has been painted by Butcher with biblical murals and frescoes—not Michelangelo masterpieces, but cartoon art populated with bulb-headed Precious Moments children.

Well, of course I wanted to see *that*. Who wouldn't? However, the Precious Moments Chapel was in the southwest corner of the state, while the second attraction, the Mormon site near Eden, was quite far north. I soon realized that, alas, trying to visit both of them that day—a *show* day—would be too much. I would have to choose one—and my interest in Mormon history prevailed over Precious Moments. It is often difficult for me to scale back my ambitions, but in that respect I have learned the all-important difference between "compromise" and "limitations." (And oh, is that a First Principle of Roadcraft.) Obviously that day's *real* main event would always be our visit to the arena in Kansas City. You know—the *job*.

So—off we went on a roundabout loop of quiet country roads to Adam-ondi-Ahman. Like other Latter-Day Saints sites like Palmyra and Nauvoo, Illinois, it is spread over thousands of acres, much of it rented to local farmers (and all tax-free). According to Joseph Smith, it is the place where Adam and Eve lived after being kicked out of the Garden of Eden. (Which was just to the south-southwest, apparently, where Independence is now.) Smith visited the site in 1838 and proclaimed that at least two altars had been built there by Adam.

Joseph Smith was in his thirties then, and portraits show him to have been handsome, intense, and *poetic* looking. Believe him or not, there's no question he had a romantic literary spirit and a fantastic mind for names and legends. (Again, I wasn't there to judge or mock—merely to observe.)

I stopped for a moment beside a gravel road looking out over treetops and pastures, and pictured Joseph Smith and his followers wandering there. The revered prophet's fevered brain would have been afire with "revelations," as when he pointed to a pile of rocks and proclaimed, "Adam built that altar to the Lord!" All the while those around him dutifully wrote down every word.

From a Latter-Day Saints book of scripture, said to be a direct quote from Joseph Smith: "Spring Hill is named by the Lord Adam-ondi-Ahman, because, said he, it is the place where Adam shall come to visit his people, or the Ancient of Days shall sit, as spoken of by Daniel the prophet."

The phrasing makes clear that Joseph Smith believed, and his followers believed, that he actually, personally, *spoke with their god*. That is a huge amount of credibility and loyalty to command. Earlier I cited Wallace Stegner, a non-Mormon who had lived in Salt Lake City in his youth and later wrote two books about the Mormons. He described Joseph and his brother Hyrum riding their horses back to the area of Nauvoo, surrendering when they might have escaped: "Whatever else Joseph Smith was, he was at the end neither a scoundrel nor a coward." (A life-size bronze sculpture of the two brothers and their horses on that ride is a feature at the Mormon monument of Nauvoo.) The events leading up to this tragedy are confused and disputed, but no one argues that Joseph and Hyrum were murdered. After surrendering to the authorities at the nearby county seat of Carthage, Illinois, they were held in the jail above the courthouse. It was swarmed by a mob of men "with painted faces" who shot and killed Joseph and Hyrum.

The Saints do compare that courthouse (which Michael and I also visited on the way to Nauvoo, as described in "Shunpikin' It Old Skool" in *Far and Away*) to the "Calvary" of the crucifixion of Jesus Christ. They also believe that Adam-ondi-Ahman will be the site of the Second Coming—though all this is somewhat downplayed by the

Near Adam-ondi-Ahman
PHOTO BY MICHAEL MOSBACH

FairMormon apologists, who offer this official statement of . . . what do magicians call it? Misdirection?

> A common mistake is taking an obscure teaching that is peripheral to the Church's purpose and placing it at the very center. For example, the precise location of the Garden of Eden is far less important than doctrine about Jesus Christ and His atoning sacrifice.

Well yes, but . . . when you accept a prophet as the voice of your god, you can't really go cherry-picking the revelations that "work" for you, can you? Well, yes! Remember all that Old Testament stuff about smiting and stoning. Or setting aside the "revelation" of polygamy for the convenience of statehood. And how "Islam is a religion of peace"—if you overlook those 109 unfortunate verses in the Quran inciting holy murder.

Again, it's easy to satirize it all—and difficult to resist!—but that is not my intent. It is the *history* that is fascinating. The Precious Moments Chapel and Adam-ondi-Ahman are so American, so *peculiarly* American, you might say. I would rather avoid being derisive and "sacrilegious"—because people of faith are famously humorless about their beliefs. If you make fun of Islam, they'll kill you. If you make fun of Orthodox Jews (again, *so* easy!), they cry "persecution" and "anti-Semite"! If you make fun of atheists . . . well, nobody does, do they? (Went looking for "atheist jokes," didn't find any funny ones.)

The actual physical history of the Saints in the region was not funny—it was sad, and even sordid. It seems that at least some of their neighbors ganged up on them just so they could steal their hard-worked farms. In 1838, a conflict that became known as the Mormon War resulted in the immediate deaths of twenty-two people in various skirmishes, and further suffering when the Saints were driven from their homes. They were expelled from Missouri and moved to Nauvoo, Illinois—where after building up another prosperous and attractive community, they would again be persecuted and attacked by their neighbors.

For years it puzzled me why everywhere the Saints went their neighbors *hated* them so much—*why* they were hounded out of New York to Ohio to Missouri to Illinois. Only after Joseph Smith's death in 1844 did Brigham Young lead the Saints west on their long trek to the Great Salt Lake, where they could flourish on their own. I used to think the objectionable issue was *polygamy*—the puritanical Baptists and Lutherans around them got all riled up against such flagrant sinning.

But no, the multiple-wives "revelation" (for so Joseph Smith claimed it was, when God told him he should marry ever more and younger wives) didn't come to him until they were settled in Illinois. So the cause of such hatred had not been polygamy.

No, alas, it was both less and more than that—simply the familiar pattern of the Saints being industrious, prosperous, and setting themselves apart (thus unspokenly "superior"), perhaps comparable to the Jews in the early twentieth century.

The Saints' neighbors were made uneasy by Smith's claims that he talked directly *with* God, but the biggest factor was that as the Saints' numbers and prosperity grew, the neighbors feared their *political* power. The real worry was that as "gentiles" they would end up living in a Latter-Day Saints theocracy. And of course they *would* have. Any county in America in which the Saints settled and were allowed to achieve the majority would have been ruled by a Mormon Elder. It has to be said, no gentile would want that. There are probably Mormons who wouldn't want it either.

Western Kansas

Typically, after we've had even a short break, the three of us Guys at Work come back feeling like we've forgotten everything and won't be able to play. I always warm up a little more thoroughly on those first shows, and we do a few extra songs in our soundcheck. Then we get up there, and—surprise!—it all comes right back.

This time in Kansas City we were particularly honored to be picketed by the local maniacs—I mean people of faith—from the Westboro Baptist Church.

I will offer nothing but their own words, from their press release. It announced their intention to picket us, with a red sidebar reading "GOD HATES CANADA," plus a series of websites offering further divine wisdom like GodHatestheMedia, GodHatesIslam, BeastObama, JewsKilledJesus, and PriestsRapeBoys.

RUSH, the cursed God-haters who hail from the doomed land of Canada finally made the cover of *Rolling Stone* after forty-one years. Yes, that same sodomite-loving Canada that passed Draconian laws making it a crime to preach the gospel! What does this have to do with the rock band RUSH, you ask? Inasmuch that they have a platform—of any kind—they should have been boldly outspoken against the grievous, national sins of Canada: same-sex marriage, sex trafficking & the outlawing of gospel preaching. In addition, Toronto is their hometown, famously known for its rabidly proud fag community. Visit our website for more details about the sins of Canada [GodHatesTheWorld.com, with a special "slash" for Canada].

Neil Peart, Geddy Lee & Alex Lifeson should be known only for their protestations against the sins of the neighbors. So far from fulfilling that duty—they have been the chief proponent in the world of rock 'n' roll of the lying, antichristic doctrine of free will (and specifically against the Bible doctrine of predestination). These postmodern priests have a song called "Free Will" with these lyrics: "*All pre-ordained, a prisoner in chains, a victim of venomous fate, kicked in the face, you can't*" [should be can] "*pray for a place, in heaven's unearthly estate. . . . You can choose a ready guide in some celestial voice, if you choose not to decide, you still have made a choice, you can choose from phantom fears and kindness that can kill, I will choose a path that's clear, I will choose free will.*" These lyrics are in direct contradiction to God's word: "Nay but, O man, who art thou that repliest against God? Shall the thing formed say to him that formed it, Why has thou made me thus?" (Romans 9:20) & "For, lo, he that formeth the mountains, and createth the wind, and declareth unto man what is his thought, that maketh the morning darkness, and treadeth upon the high places of the earth, the LORD, The God of hosts, is his name." (Amos 4:13) There's still time—they still draw breath—so they ought to repent and beseech their fellow humans to fear and obey the Lord Jesus Christ. Will God have mercy on RUSH & their fans, giving them the gift of repentance? "Knowing therefore the terror of the Lord, we persuade men . . ." (2 Corinthians 5:11)

After a pretty good show, we drove west and south into Kansas, where Dave parked you-know-where in WaKeeney (the strange name from two early settlers named Warren and Keeney—I guess they rejected "Weeney").

That kind of "local knowledge" picked up in passing reminds me of a night drive early in the tour, when we had already crossed Nebraska

Words Fail
PHOTO BY MICHAEL MOSBACH

Fracking Truck
PHOTO BY MICHAEL MOSBACH

a couple of times, by bus and by motorcycle. Thus I had spent considerable time staring at the map of that state. As we roared down the dark interstate after the show in Lincoln, Michael wondered aloud where we were. I said, "Probably near Kearney." When Michael checked the GPS, he looked at me and said, "Wow—ten miles away."

We both agreed it was a little scary to know Nebraska so well . . .

In the morning Michael and I rode the Kansas backroads south toward a "mystery road" that had attracted me on the map—a long straight dotted line leading from Western Kansas into Eastern Colorado. Sure enough, it was a long stretch of gravel running almost perfectly straight for sixty-five miles. Must be one of the longest unpaved roads in the lower forty-eight—though online authorities argue the details.

Looking at the photos of the wide-open prairie, arid and flat, you can see how a drought and high winds could soon blow all the topsoil away, as in the Dust Bowl of the 1930s. One time we paused for a minute at the roadside and watched a cloud of dust gathering on the horizon, then approaching us. It was the kind of rough-hewn tanker rig used in fracking operations—familiar to me from North Dakota and Texas. Apparently Kansas pioneered "vertical fracking" in the

1940s, and is now adding "horizontal drills" as quickly as those operations can . . . pay for themselves . . .

Riding on loose surfaces is almost always less "serene" than on pavement, and this route had its challenges. Both Michael and I experienced a couple of "moments" when the gravel was suddenly deep and loose and the bikes started slewing around beneath us. "I thought I was going down for sure," said Michael, and I had the same experience once or twice—the electric chill of fear at your core.

The trick is to get on the gas and accelerate *out* of it, as counter-intuitive as that feels. Another important technique is to keep your speed down so you are *able* to safely accelerate, and stay in a lower gear for quicker engine response.

The nominal destination I had chosen for the day was Great Sand Dunes National Park, in southeastern Colorado. I had ridden nearby in the past, but never visited the actual park, so it was a worthy goal.

(Funny when I told Kevin Anderson I wouldn't be able to visit him and his wife, Rebecca, in their home this time, because I wanted to ride to Great Sand Dunes, Kevin, the serious high-country hiker, wrote back, "It's a nice park, but there's nothing really to *do* there." For Michael and me, as part of a day's ride of almost 500 miles, it was about getting there, *being* there, even for a moment, then moving on.)

Once again a journal note reflected my riding inspirations and reflections: "So often thinking, 'Nevermore.' About *so* many things. Bittersweet, but mostly sweet."

I knew that accommodations might be difficult to find near a remote national park in high summer, so I had taken the precaution of searching online the previous day. Everything in and around the park was full, so I asked Michael to go ahead and book the Best Western about twenty miles west of the park.

And oh, what a destination that Best Western turned out to be!

Called "Movie Manor," it was situated next door to a drive-in theater, the rooms lined up facing the screen, with an audio feed to your room! The whole scene was like something from fifty years ago, in a wonderful way. When the concrete forecourt was poured, it had been etched with the "autographs" of movie stars (my proofreader's eye catching errors in "Jim Carey" and "Russell Crow") and each room had a movie star's name on the door. (Mine was Paul Newman, Michael's was—oh yes!—Jessica Lange.) Inside, my room's walls were decorated with a couple of framed prints of semiprofessional copies of classic works—a Renoir painting, and the famous black-and-white photograph of a drive-in-movie with a passing locomotive by O. Winston Link, called *Hot Shot*

Eastbound, from 1956. (Having admired that image for *years*, I had just bought a print of it from a gallery in New Orleans.)

In both of these renderings, though, the original characters were all replaced by likenesses of movie stars like Marilyn, Elvis, James Dean, Brando (as in *The Wild One*, the motorcycle ruffian—like us—in his Perfecto leather jacket), Bogart, Mae West, Chaplin, Abbott and Costello, Judy Garland (as Dorothy), and so on.

With such a "characterful" destination, a decent restaurant next door, the day's high mileage ("not a speck of interstate"), and that record-length stretch of gravel, I made a journal note: "Perfect West Side Beemer Boyz day? Pretty much."

The following day we had a fair distance to travel to the show in Denver, 260 miles, with a couple of "mystery roads" along the way. So I roused Michael at 6:00 (it was *cold* that morning, at almost 8,000 feet) and we rode east to Fort Garland for breakfast at a nice little diner (another place filled with '50s style images of Elvis and Marilyn). Then north into the mountains on a gravel road.

The following photo conveys so much about the day—the clear high-elevation air, the wild-flowers, the characteristic barbed wire staked with unfinished tree limbs, the distant peaks with avalanche tracks down their sides and patches of snow on bare gray peaks. Sing it, John Denver—"*Colorado Rocky Mountain high!*"

Great Sand Dunes National Park

Movie Manor
PHOTO BY MICHAEL MOSBACH

PHOTO BY MICHAEL MOSBACH

That mystery road was quite a remote and somewhat worrying route that morning, as it continually diminished into sandy tracks across high meadows, or rutted single-tracks through gullies of mud and boulders. It was as we emerged from this road that I snapped a photo of the sign that would adorn the back of our tour T-shirt: "CAUTION/ROADENDS." Not for us!

The history of my touring by motorcycle over eighteen years can be readily sketched by the T-shirts I had commissioned along the way—starting with the one for this tour, the front shown here. It was an early example of the cover-image theme—this one in Western Kansas rather than Nevada—and it remains a good scene-setter.

The pose and setting were inspired by a failed experiment a few years ago on the *Time Machine* tour. Just at sunrise Michael and I rode out of Seymour, Texas, making an early start because those days were fiercely hot, and we had far to go to the next show. As we rode along with the sun just creeping over the horizon, I pulled my camera out of the tankbag and snapped a few "action self-portraits." Once I stretched out my left arm to aim the camera forward and Michael spread his arms wide like that as he coasted along. But unfortunately, in that dim light on a bouncy two-lane, the result was too blurry to use. Still, I loved its message.

When I showed it to Michael later, he laughed and bellowed in a theatrical voice, "*Bring the horizon to me!*" I laughed along and asked him where he had picked that up. He didn't remember, but I eventually traced it to one of the *Pirates of the Caribbean* (*please* say "Cari-BE-an") movies. The context, though, is quite different from my imagining—at the end of the film the perpetually swizzled Captain Jack Sparrow merely caresses the spokes of the ship's wheel rather erotically then mumbles in a lifeless deadpan, "Now, bring me that horizon . . . " [tuneless humming] "and really bad eggs. Drink up me hearties, yo-ho."

Rather less "scenery-chewing" than Michael's interpretation—so I'll stick with his.

In early summer of 2015, as Michael and I began our travels on the R40 tour, I was determined to restage that photograph in better light and with more care. Once we got to open country (the West), we set it up a couple of times. When the all-important horizon stretched wide from the road's vanishing point, I waved Michael to park at the roadside. I circled back and passed at moderate speed, cruise control on, then he stepped out behind me and snapped the shot.

A longstanding tradition on rock tours is that toward the end each independent contractor or "vendor" (sound company, lighting, lasers, pyro, trucks, buses) will produce a tour T-shirt. Not the ones for sale at the merchandising stands, but commemorative gifts, "swag," for band and crew. Sometimes we receive more useful swag, like laundry bags or luggage cases—or a more permanent remembrance, like the cool TAG watches we got for our crew after R40. In light of how long some of those people have been with us—many for *decades*—I like the engraving we chose: "Thanks for the memories."

BRING THAT HORIZON TO ME!

PHOTOGRAPH ON T-SHIRT BY MICHAEL MOSBACH
T-SHIRTS PHOTOGRAPHED BY CRAIG M. RENWICK

First Scooter Trash Shirt, Front, Back, 1997

Ghost Rider, Back

Since the *Test for Echo* tour in 1996–97, when I first traveled by motorcycle with longtime riding partner Brutus, we have often played with that tradition. Second-generation merch guy Patrick McLoughlin always helps with the designs. For that first one Brutus and I commissioned the "Scooter Trash" logo from Hugh Syme. (I think the bike image was lifted from BMW.) For the lettering I asked Hugh for something along the lines of what he used on *A Show of Hands* (which Geddy once described as "like something scrawled by a murderer"). On the back, rather than the usual tour dates, we listed some of our favorite day-off destinations.

Some names were chosen solely for their humor (however childish—actually, I like the word "puerile," because it includes a snide twist beyond boyish or childish), others for their history, and some for the beauty of their surroundings (Death Valley, Sun Valley, Grand Canyon). At least one, Mexican Hat, represents all three. The last two, of course, were our nicknames. (*One* of them, in my case; see "Bubba and the Professor" in *Far and Near*.)

A few years later, a shirt was produced to promote *Ghost Rider*. The front was the book's cover and on the back I listed some of the destinations that had been important in that journey. What a travelogue they make, and there is even a happy ending with the last place name—Santa Monica, California, where I settled with Carrie after that desperate and lonely journey.

Toward the end of the *Vapor Trails* tour in 2002, Michael and I made a similar list of place names, once again chosen for both silliness and splendor. We included a new gang name, the West Side Beemer Boyz, framed by pop culture references from Limp Bizkit and Dave Eggers. The last destination once again represents a happy ending, while the penultimate two are locations where Michael crashed (without injury except to bike and pride—he was green then but well armored).

That tour I had my own "get-off" near Teec Nos Pos, a dot in the desert of northeast Arizona near Monument Valley. During the *Vapor Trails* tour in summer 2002, Michael and Brian Catterson and I were lost and bushwhacking through the vast Navajo reservation on impossibly rugged 4x4 tracks. In one sandy stretch, Michael's rear tire spun helplessly until it was buried to the hub, and we were able to try a technique that until then I had only read about. Rather than try to dig it out, we laid the bike on its side, slid it over a little, then stood it up outside the rut. Worked like a charm.

A few minutes later I came bucking up the hump of a rise in

slippery dust and gravel, lost the front wheel, and the bike went over sideways. I did a neat little somersault on the ground, then quickly got up to be sure everything "worked." After assuring Brian that I was fine, I posed for a photo with my foot atop the fallen beast, as if on a hunting trophy.

This list of "attractions" on the *Vapor Trails* tour includes Verona, Kentucky, just south of Cincinnati, because part of Michael's boyhood was spent there. He made us stop and look at where the house *used* to be—a former funeral home, now demolished and replaced by a car repair shop. After we marveled at that sight for a while . . . we rode on past Big Bone Lick State Park. I swear. Because they found dinosaur bones there. And because a lick is what would be locally pronounced as a "crick." (And because we are . . . puerile.)

At the end of the *Snakes and Arrows* tour in 2007–08 Michael and I came up with a shirt that introduced one of my new themes, "Shunpiking." On the back we listed all of the *cheap* places we had stayed—all perfectly fine havens on the backroads of America, and all memorable enough that I can still picture each one. A number of them we've even been back to, because . . . location.

"Camp Brutus" was a reference to our bus, on which we slept every show night, as we continued to do right up to the R40 tour.

"THAT'S THE WAY WE ROLL" was a sly comment on the contrast between my accommodations (and expenses) on the road compared to my bandmates' on their private jet between twelve-star hotels. (Not complaining, understand—I made my choice and wouldn't change it.)

For the *Clockwork Angels* tour, Michael and I went with something simpler: a riding photo on the front showing your correspondent threading a series of curves in Kentucky.

Vapor Trails, Back

Snakes and Arrows, Back

On the back was a phrase that has continued to reveal its truth every tour:

"The best roads are the ones no one travels unless they live on them."

This time, for the R40 tour shirt, I thought I'd like to use that "horizon" theme on the front. Because it amused me. (Multiple levels of meaning in image and text, I think.) For the back I chose that sign from our ride in the Colorado mountains.

Again, I like the way the two images and texts comment on each other—though my mother, for one, thinks it's "kind of sad." But she is a sentimentalist. Perhaps not everyone shares my feeling (and frequent experience) that even if the road ends, there's still another horizon . . .

Clockwork Angels, Front

R40, Back

Utah Backcountry
PHOTO BY MICHAEL MOSBACH

WESTBOUND
AND DOWN

In Denver we were joined by Brian Catterson, the veteran moto-journalist who had accompanied us for a ride on every tour since *Vapor Trails*. This time we managed to avoid the thunderstorms and snowshowers that usually shadowed his travels with us, and in fact gifted Brian with probably the greatest ride of the tour. Not just the scenery of Western Colorado and Eastern Utah on a cool and sunny day, but some of the most adventurous routes we had ever encountered—and conquered.

But first, there was a tragedy. The day had grown hot in Denver, and as we sat around the front lounge of the bus that afternoon in a parking lot outside the venue, the generator suddenly shuddered and died. Dave got out and went to check on it, and after a few minutes he came back in—soaking wet, and with a fraught look on his face. At first I thought he must be dripping with sweat from the hot generator bay, but then he quietly asked Michael to call a medic.

He had tried to remove the radiator cap—knowing and even thinking at the time, "This is a bad idea." Steam and boiling water had exploded out on his hand and face, scalding him badly. Hard to say if the work gloves he wore helped or just kept the boiling water on his skin longer, but certainly his glasses had saved his eyes. Kevin

Dave and Me—L.A. Forum
PHOTO BY CRAIG M. RENWICK

on our crew, a trained paramedic (former Canadian soldier and firefighter), arrived on our bus first. He urged Dave to put his hand in lukewarm water, and Dave complied. Kevin began asking him "skill-testing questions," like "What is your birthdate?" and "Who is the president of the United States?" to check for shock. The Denver paramedics arrived soon after, ran some of the same tests, then urged Dave to go to the hospital in an ambulance.

Dave said, "How about if I just go on my own?"

One of the paramedics explained that he was likely to get faster service if he went by ambulance. I said, "Dave—take the ride."

Dave took the ride and came back an hour or so later with a big white bandage over his hand. "Like I'm holding a pineapple," Dave said. It had already been obvious that Dave wouldn't be driving that night (the wound plus the painkillers), and maybe for a longer period. (It turned out he didn't return until the end of the tour, for the party.)

Tour manager Liam came aboard the bus to discuss our options, and suggested Michael, Brian, and I book a hotel in Denver and stay there for the night. My heart sank.

Oh, I *really* didn't want to do that and miss the prospect of the next day's ride. Again, I knew all of these days, and every single ride, represented a kind of "last opportunity." I couldn't stand to lose one—especially a ride as great as I hoped the next day's would be. And the prospect of packing everything to move into a hotel, getting the bikes parked there, then checking in after the show instead of sleeping on the bus, only to rise and face a straight-shot interstate slog to Salt Lake City the next day (as we'd pretty much have to do, with over 500 miles between)—it was all too grim.

It occurred to me that at worst, now that the generator had cooled and was working again, I would even rather have the bus moved to a truck stop outside Denver. Then I could sleep aboard before riding *some where* the next day. ("Could still make Moab," I know I was thinking.)

That, at least, would be doable—then I had another thought. I asked Liam, "Couldn't I steal one of the other drivers?"

He protested about leaving nine other people "stranded," but it didn't seem that way to me. I didn't imagine it would matter to the crew guys where they spent their day off, and they would have to make the drive no matter what. In any case, a replacement driver was on his way later that night, so no one would be stuck anywhere for *too* long.

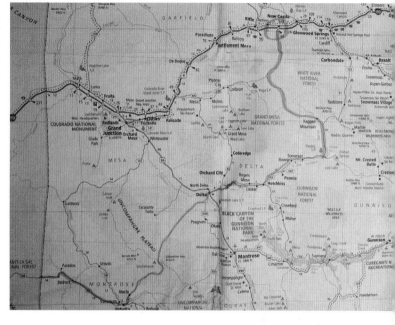

In the end, that's what we did—we stole "Papa John" from the sound crew, and never gave him back for the rest of the tour.

The best way to introduce this day is by the map—to show my intentions, explain the challenges, and better understand the scale of the accomplishment.

The blue highlighter line leads down from the interstate at Silt, Colorado, over a dotted line (unpaved) to Ragged Mountain and Highway 133. Michael couldn't find that road anywhere on the computer map, Mother. Nor could he find the next long dotted line, from Delta to Nucla. So he didn't put *anything* on Doofus and Dingus—I was left to navigate from map, compass, and instinct.

The previous day I had ridden Kate, just to make sure she was ready for Brian on the next ride. But once I had all my tools and such packed on her, I just left it like that and put Brian on Cindy. (Actually Cindy 2, the new bike from Toronto, was pretty well broken in by then, with a few thousand miles and, in any case, Brian wouldn't lug or over-rev the engine to hurt her.) Up at 7:00 and riding out from a Château Walmart, we set off south to look for that first road. However, Papa John had parked us nearer to the town of Rifle exit than I had thought, so it was a dead-end search—through a large fracking zone, apparently.

Determination undiminished, I led us east on the interstate to Silt, where I remembered the map had shown that road beginning. After a bit of scouting around, we found it—though couldn't be sure until we encountered a *sign*. As so often happened on such roads, seeing

a National Forest sign with a number on it was all the reassurance I needed. "I'm on a road with a number, so I am not lost."

Indeed, there is a lot of information in this static image in addition to the road number. The ATV sign shows you the kind of use the road normally gets, and the distances on the big sign told me exactly where we were. Because those places were all on the map! (Why that road wasn't on Mother I will never understand—it was graded and maintained all the way through, and well traveled by pickups and ATVs on that summer Sunday.)

My confidence at that junction was high enough that I led us on the longer of the two unpaved routes, twenty-three miles to Paonia. Ranchers obviously used the area as summer rangeland, because cattle roamed free on many of those high-elevation meadows (and on the road—you had to keep your eyes open).

The surface was dependable graded gravel, and we made good time. The scenery around us was simply majestic, and as we crossed an open ridge at about 7,000 feet, I parked my bike at the roadside and climbed a little higher to snap this photo of Brian riding by on Cindy 2.

Emerging at pavement right

Brian at 7,000 Feet

where the map said we would (hurrah!), we traveled west to Delta and stopped to refuel for the next "mystery road." Michael had been feeling poorly with stomach troubles, so left us there to take the smoother paved route to the night's destination, Moab, Utah. Delta was a big enough crossroads town that I was concerned about trying to find that one unpaved road that would lead over the Columbine Pass (9,120 feet—pretty high for the rest of the country, but Colorado has many 11,000- and 12,000-foot passes).

I asked around the gas station—the cashier and a motorcyclist lounging by his cruiser—but they didn't know of it. I tried setting Dingus for the town of Nucla, but it wanted to send us way around by the *paved* route. No, no, no. So off we went, armed only with the evidence of that dotted line on the paper map, the GPS set to compass bearing, and eventually we found ourselves on a gravel road that at least *led* toward the Uncompahgre Plateau. (Always liked that name—apparently it means "rocks that make water red.")

And oh look—here's some of that red water now!

Photogenic, of course, but this little mud puddle was far from the worst of our obstacles. If I couldn't understand why that previous gravel road wasn't on Mother—this one should never have been on *any* map. There were sand and ruts and boulders and washes and mud, all of them trying to knock us down. One time my front wheel was deflected violently sideways by an unseen boulder and the bike fell over—the rider, too, of course. I was unhurt, but was glad when Brian came back to help me pick it up.

Bubba's Big Splash
PHOTO BY BRIAN CATTERSON

As the miles go by on a rough, remote road with no signs of any kind, you have no idea if it's *really* the right road, or if you will get through. And you do not want to turn around and go back over all that. I kept an eye on time, distance, and our fuel range the whole time, figuring when the point-of-no-return might come.

There were still a lot of free-range cattle on their summer pastures, and Brian told me later that on a narrow part of the trail, with trees on both sides, he had hit a calf—a glancing blow. Then later a big cow had stepped out of the bush beside him and basically body-checked him. His ribs hurt for a couple of days after that.

We also saw elk here and there, and at one point my heart skipped a beat (I think literally) when I looked ahead and saw a bear in the road. As I slowed in alarm, it stopped and looked at me, huge and

Brian—Way Out There,
and Way Up There

dark and powerful looking. Its ears perked up as it paused and stared at me for a long moment, then it turned and ambled away. You can bet I was glad about that.

The alpine meadows were brightened by a few woodpecker-like flickers and quite a number of mountain bluebirds—a longer-winged, brighter blue species, emblematic of the high country. (It seems strange that the mountain bluebird is the state bird of both Idaho *and* Nevada. You wouldn't think that would be allowed—like, *wars* would be fought over it . . .)

One technique I had been watching Brian do, and learning to imitate myself, was banking the motorcycle over in corners on gravel and spinning the rear wheel to make the turn. Following behind him for a while, I saw those skid marks arcing through every corner—a typical dirt-bike technique, steering with the throttle and using the rear wheelspin to keep up your cornering speed. It was fun and effective, and I was soon doing it fairly well, but it took me into a zone where I needed new braking techniques, too.

That I learned the hard way, powering into a bend a little too quickly then trying to slow by using only the rear brake, as you would usually do on a loose surface. However, at speed, with the wheel already deliberately breaking traction, it was a bad idea. Because the back tire was no longer "hooked up," it only skittered over the surface, and the bike began to slew around, out of control. The edge of the road and the wall of pine trunks suddenly seemed *very* close, and I was sure I wasn't going to make it. Fear lit me up inside like electricity. Eventually I regained my balance and got back on the throttle, and managed to *just* slip along the edge of the gravel. That sense of imminent death shook me up for a while.

Ian Fleming's James Bond novel *You Only Live Twice* takes its title from a haiku-like verse. "You only live twice/ Once when you are born/ And once when you look death in the face."

As this man had just done. Finally I can tell about the worst crash I ever had—a "Now It Can Be Told" kind of story, after keeping it quiet for more than five years. Witness the biggest smile any camera has ever seen on this Bubba's face, also reflecting Sir Winston Churchill's statement, "Nothing in life is so exhilarating as to be shot at without result."

Man . . . Alive!
PHOTO BY MICHAEL MOSBACH

It was September 15, 2010, cool with mixed sun and clouds, a day off after a show in Boston on our *Time Machine* tour. Dave had dropped us in New York State near Albany, and in the morning Michael and I worked our way over to the Delaware River and started west across the backroads of northeastern Pennsylvania. We were riding in the general direction of the next show, in Pittsburgh, planning an overnight stop somewhere along the way.

The narrow paved two-lane wound along creeks and low ridges, through farmland and leafy woods, with many blind hills and corners. So our speed was "careful." I came around a right turn to see a sharp left ahead, so was aligning the bike for that next corner entry, when suddenly the whole machine started shimmying below me. It oscillated side to side a few times, then went down. In a snap I was off and sliding across the pavement on my left side. What a universe of fear and helplessness opens inside you during split seconds like that. And no wonder time seems to slow, because it is so *full*—of raw, existential terror.

Michael came around that corner behind me to face a scene no riding partner ever wants to see—me curled in the fetal position in the ditch on the right side of the road, and my bike down on its right side a little farther on. Instantly alarmed, to put it mildly, Michael slowed and parked his bike across the road, where there was room. I got to my hands and knees, then stood up, seeing if everything "worked." Then I stumbled down the roadside to hit the "kill" switch on the bike—still idling away on its side.

If my first thought was about myself, and my second thought about the bike, my *third* thought was "What happened?" I looked up the sloping road behind me and saw a large rectangular patch of tar and gravel about five feet wide and twenty feet long. The patch and the loose gravel scattered from it took up most of the road, so there was no way I could have avoided it, even if I had been able to see it around the corner. Other passing vehicles had spread the gravel downhill on that lightly traveled backroad, so my best guess was that it had been patched a few days before. It was a Wednesday, so maybe on the Friday afternoon a repair crew had decided that was "good enough," and left it like that. Presumably there were no motorcyclists on that crew to notice how potentially *deadly* it was.

Ironically, though, even as the loose gravel knocked me down, it might have saved me from worse injury. As my body fell and slid along the pavement the gravel was like ball bearings, and later I noticed that even my plastic rain jacket wasn't torn. Greater friction might have bent my limbs in different directions, making for more pain. Though on the other hand, that gravel meant I slid *farther*, closer to a roadside banked with limestone ledges and trees. Or there could have been a guardrail that would have brought me to a quick, painful stop.

The guardrail behind me in the previous photo was at the next corner, where we could get both bikes safely off the road. Already I was imagining so many other possible outcomes to that grim moment—like the bike suddenly catching traction and pitching me across the road in what is called a "high-side," maybe into the path of an oncoming truck.

So on balance I had been lucky. I would never deny that motorcycling is dangerous, and it even seems that way to me—"from a distance"—though not when I am *doing* it. Then I feel in "command and control" mode, as much master of my destiny as in any other situation. One longtime rider I read about spoke with wry wisdom, "If you love motorcycling enough, and you do it enough, it's going to kill you. The trick is to survive long enough that something else kills you first." To me that "trick" lies in being as safe and observant on the motorcycle as I can possibly be. The excitement and experience of motorcycling seem worth the risk—but a telling principle is that I would never encourage anyone else I cared about to take it up . . .

My armored suit, heavy boots and gloves, and full-face helmet all played their part in protecting me. (Imagine taking that fall and slide wearing running shoes, shorts, tank top, and bandana—maybe mirrored shades for "eye protection"—the way too many riders in America dress. It might not kill you, but it sure would hurt—and the results would not be attractive.)

Battered Brain Bucket

In any case, I was still well shook up, and a little battered about the ribs and hips, limping already. We noticed a scrape on the side of my helmet, so had to worry about concussion. I thought I was okay, but just in case Michael was checking on the location of the nearest hospital.

The poor motorcycle was an utter mess, the entire front section of fender and windscreen smashed away, and the right-side luggage case and frame askew. The front brake reservoir was torn off, so I would not be riding that motorcycle away—which was good, because later it was discovered that both front and rear subframes were bent.

Michael got on the phone to Dave and asked him to come and pick us up. Without telling him exactly what had happened, Michael assured him, "We're okay." Later Dave told me, "The way he said it I figured you'd gone down."

With my wrecked GS only fit to be rolled on its wheels, Dave had to stop the bus and trailer across that whole turn to load it. Michael and I stood on the opposite hilltops holding T-shirts, ready to wave down and warn any oncoming drivers. (It says something about the road that, in midafternoon, there were none.)

With the wreckage in the trailer, Dave and I drove up the road to a nearby ski resort parking lot. Michael followed on his bike, then, in that safer spot, loaded it into the trailer. We drove south and west to Williamsport, Pennsylvania ("Billtown"), where Michael and I had often stopped in that part of the state. We took Dave to a restaurant we had enjoyed before, 33 East, and I limped my way inside. I was already worrying, "Hope I can play tomorrow." After a good dinner (though I was conscious of Michael and Dave watching me for any suspicious symptoms of concussion), we slept on the bus near there.

Talking to Carrie on the phone that night, I gave her a mild version of the events—just saying I'd had a crash, but was fine.

The following day we had to ride over 200 miles, much of it in the rain, to the arena in Pittsburgh. I was on the spare bike, of course, and was glad to feel I hadn't been made *fearful* by the accident. Down deep I believed there was nothing I had done "wrong," and that has always made all the difference to me. ("Whatever happens, it must never be *my fault*." Though I still wonder about the highway worker who walked away from that gravel patch thinking it was all right.)

Dave and Michael,
September 16, 2010

Michael, Dave, and I agreed not to tell anyone else until after the Pittsburgh show—until I knew I could *play*. My journal note in all-caps advised myself: "PLEASE—TRY NOT TO TELL THIS STORY. FOR ALL GOOD REASONS."

Because I knew I would *want* to write about it—for equally good reasons. Michael also chimed in and said I should *never* write about that crash. He shook his finger and said, "They'll take away your fun license."

We were both talking about, of all things, *insurance*—referring to the medical affidavit each band member had to sign to insure the tour against . . . any interruption to the flow of commerce. That affidavit included this question: "Do you participate in any hazardous activities or pastimes (e.g., motor racing, flying other than as a fare-paying passenger, hang-gliding, etc.)?" The list did not yet include motorcycling, but I knew that actors, like keen motorcyclist Ewan McGregor, were not allowed to ride while filming. If news like this got out to the actuaries and "cover your ass" people, motorcycling might well be added to that "forbidden" list. I couldn't imagine touring without motorcycling, but figured it was probably impossible without *insurance*, too.

So I kept it quiet and had the totaled motorcycle repaired at my own expense. (It was only a few weeks before the South American tour, when I would need it for Brutus to ride, so there was a bit of worry there, too—I didn't tell Brutus until later. Funny that Brutus now *owns* that motorcycle, Geezer IV, having bought it from me when I retired it.)

That night in Pittsburgh I got through the show okay, limping on and off stage but able to play "properly," so that no one else would know. A few days later I shared the story with the Guys at Work, but still for the next five years I kept my resolve never to write about that crash. Until the time might come when I no longer worried about anybody taking away my "fun license."

Fast forward to 2015 again, almost five years (and tens of thousands of miles) later. The dust-eating photograph was taken on yet another fantastic ride, from Moab to the show in Salt Lake City. Our evening in Moab had been traveler's perfection, staying at a Best Western on the main street and dining at a fine steakhouse. Moab was highly praised in *Ghost Rider* as one of the great destinations in the West, and for me its high ranking (probably top five) endures.

I was feeling pretty high that night after having, as I noted, "Defeated Mother big-time—on TWO big routes. First route must have been 50 miles off-pavement, and the second one 75 miles. Almost half the day's ride." By "defeating" Mother I meant that I had led us through where she said we could not go. It really *was* a sense of triumph.

On the show day ride, we had a couple more "mystery roads" ahead of us, so I got us up at 6:00 for an early start. We began with a sunrise-shadowed ride to the Canyonlands National Park Visitor Center (too early for a passport stamp, unfortunately—but that road is always worth the riding), then striking off on a long unpaved route north toward Green River. There we paused to enjoy a big breakfast at a good diner called Tamarisk.

I shared with Brian and Michael that tamarisk was a tree from Eurasia brought to the American West to plant as windbreaks. "They are pretty, delicate, and green in the desert, but are now considered an invasive pest."

Michael gave me *such* a look. "How can a person claim to have had any kind of a normal sex life and *know* stuff like that?"

I told him what to do with *his* sex life.

Fed and fueled, we headed a little farther north to another long unpaved stretch, running (I hoped) about fifty miles west to a dot called Castle Dale. One of the landmarks along the way was named Chimney Rock, a round eroded tower in the distance.

A curvaceous stretch of pavement, Highway 31, brought us out to Interstate 15 at Spanish Fork, and on to the arena in Salt Lake City. Every city we play in is full of memories, but Salt Lake has some

ATGATT: "All The Gear All The Time" (Even to the Grocery Store)
PHOTO BY JUAN D. LOPEZ

Michael Eats Bubba's Dust
PHOTO BY BRIAN CATTERSON

special ones for me. Even thinking of an earlier tour when Michael and I had ridden in from west of the city, coming from Nevada (and Great Basin National Park!). Coming into the city we had been challenged by a particularly rough unpaved track (couldn't call it a road) called Butterfield Canyon. It had been one of those "mystery roads" that had me wondering if we would even get through, or if we would have to backtrack and go around another way. Onstage that night

Michael Passing Chimney Rock

I looked out at the audience and thought, "If they only knew what I went through to get to work today!" A new impossible dream was born—that every night before the show the audience could watch a beautifully shot and edited film of my commute that day (but not by having a camera crew to disrupt that actual ride—the futuristic kind of film I described in the introduction that could be made from pure memory).

Back in 1984, Salt Lake City is where I first started bicycling on tour. On a day off I was feeling restless and went out and bought a bicycle and, oh, what a "road," so to speak, that started me riding. (Many of this book's bicycling photos show me carrying luggage cases, or panniers, from a company called Lone Peak, still in business in Salt Lake City.) Soon I was on that bicycle every day, building up my mileages until I was riding between cities on days off, if they were anything under 150 miles. (Once I tried 175 miles, between Augusta and Atlanta, Georgia, but that was . . . too much.) Twice I rode into Salt Lake from Evanston, Wyoming (where the bus dropped me on the way from Denver), a mountainous ride of 150 miles and two 10,000-foot passes, over the Uinta and Wasatch mountains. That was too much, too, but beautiful, challenging, and worth doing—twice.

Just a year later, in 1985, during a break between touring and recording, I signed up for my first "adventure tour," a guided bicycle trip in China from Shanghai to Beijing. That was of course another life-changing experience. For that trip I was inspired not even to bring a camera and instead carry a journal and try to record what I saw

Sunrise at the Truck Stop,
Evanston, Wyoming, circa 1990
PHOTO BY ANDREW MACNAUGHTAN

and felt in words. That was the beginning of a permanent mindset, a writer's exercise of looking around, or inside at my feelings, and thinking, "How would I put this into *words*?"

When I got home from China I expanded my journal notes into a first attempt at travel writing, *Riding the Golden Lion* (the brand of my rented bicycle). Although the beginner's prose was amateurish (read "terrible"), it was the true beginning of . . . another kind of journey.

(In prose writing I was fortunate to be able to write about six unpublished books, learning all the way, over the next ten years. Not until 1996 did I publish my first book, *The Masked Rider*, and I often say I wish I'd had that advantage in music!)

In Salt Lake City we said goodbye to Brian, and hello to Chris Stankee, who would join us on the next ride up to Calgary.

Of course all of my riding friends had been lobbying me to join

Forbidden City, 1985
PHOTO BY JOHN CHRISTIE

us on one of the western rides, and from here on out we would have somebody joining us at nearly every show. Chris had "reserved" this one months ago, but like many of our guest riders, he was going to get more than he probably bargained for. (I'm sure Brian would agree with what I had told Richard Moore back on the first leg: "You're going to get a week-long motorcycle tour—in three days.")

Our accommodations for the next night were the only destination. on the entire tour booked in advance—six months in advance, in fact. First seeing the itinerary back in January, with a day off between Salt Lake City and Calgary, I immediately thought, "Glacier National Park." Right that day I asked Michael to book us at the little place we had stayed just outside Glacier last time. (Roadcraft tip: When visiting a national park in summer, arrive just outside it the previous night and ride through early in the morning.)

Backstage in Salt Lake City me 'n' my gang happened to pass the meet and greet backdrop, and posed for my only appearance in that setting— well, *ever*.

Every night between dinner and showtime the Guys at Work stood there and posed for photos with thirty or so people, one or two at a time, all handled efficiently by Kevin and Donovan. It was one of those unbridgeable chasms to me—in that setting I would be embarrassed, self-conscious, and uncomfortable, while for the two of them it was just a small "duty" they didn't mind—most of the time. Michael would often warn me not to travel from the bus to the Bubba Gump Room, or vice versa, at a certain time, or I would run right into "all that." Even at a distance, in another room, when I heard the people roar as the Guys made their entrance I got an uncomfortable feeling. As I said at the outset, we have always been different—and one is always the misfit.

A happy misfit, though, most of the time.

Chris, Bubba, Brian
PHOTO BY MICHAEL MOSBACH

PHOTO BY MICHAEL MOSBACH

16

Going-to-the-Sun Road
PHOTO BY MICHAEL MOSBACH

IN A BIG COUNTRY

A documentary filmmaker named Miller had been traveling with us all tour, shooting backstage scenes of us and the crew. He had filmed Michael and me arriving a few times in different cities, and back in Greensboro, North Carolina, he captured the exciting event of me changing my oil. Before the tour was over he wanted to come aboard the bus in the afternoon and shoot me drawing a route. I had told him we should do that in the West, where the routes would be more spectacular.

In Salt Lake City I invited him and his camera to the bus and he filmed me on the floor of the bus's front lounge, among the paper map of the western United States, state maps of Idaho and Montana, and my trusty blue highlighter. I deliberately hadn't looked in advance, wanting to "make it real." Starting with the big map, then to

Going-to-the-Sun Road

the states, I sought those revelations of good routes toward Glacier National Park and Calgary. Measuring my fingertips with the map's scale (three fingers equals twenty miles, say), I estimated distances to Glacier and saw that we would have to start from somewhere on the interstate in Idaho. Blackfoot looked (and sounded) good. So I started working north from there, discussing it aloud as I drew.

Along the way, it turned out I had some stories to tell. Tracing a thin gray line northwest from Blackfoot, I noticed a dot called Atomic City. From a previous journey I remembered the nearby town of Arco—the first town in the world to be powered by atomic energy, in 1955.

As told in "A Little Yellow Cabin on Yellowstone Lake" in *Far and Away*, in the late 1940s the U.S. government set out to develop peacetime uses for the terrible power they had unleashed on Hiroshima and Nagasaki to end that war. A massive area of Southern Idaho, almost 900 square miles, was set aside as the Nuclear Reactor Testing Station, now known as the Idaho National Laboratory. For complicated reasons, the development of nuclear energy's potential has since been stymied. Unfortunately, not by "scientific limitations," but in a couple of senses by "human limitations."

Three soldiers died at the site in 1961, in the world's first reactor accident. It had been their own human mistake, as every accident since has been—and that is a serious concern. I used to believe in the eventual perfectability of machines, but when the shuttle disasters occurred, I saw that even NASA couldn't do it. So I figured nobody could.

Still, the other human factor was know-nothings like Jane Fonda and Ralph Nader preaching with and to ignorance and fear. Few would argue that it was short-sighted to turn back to burning coal and oil to generate electricity. Those fuels—getting them and burning them—are phenomenally deadly, too. A couple of scientific facts suggest a world that could have been quite different, ecologically and politically.

One ton of natural uranium can produce more than 40 million kilowatt-hours of electricity—equivalent to burning 16,000 tons of coal or 80,000 barrels of oil. So that would have reduced greenhouse gases enormously, and eliminated the necessity to "make nice" with abhorrent regimes who happen to possess oil.

An article in *Scientific American* described how a so-called breeder reactor could create more nuclear fuel as a byproduct than it consumed during operation. Truly free energy, and self-perpetuating. The stuff of science fiction. One project underway at the Idaho National Laboratory is the development of "radioisotope thermoelectric generators," extremely long-lasting power sources to be used as batteries on space probes to Jupiter and Pluto. Perhaps one day those batteries will do their magic . . . closer to home.

This "big country" setting is the Bannock Pass, an unpaved route between Idaho and Montana, through a treeless expanse of sagebrush and grasses rising to 7,684 feet. A closer look at the photo shows two tiny motorcyclists, Chris and Michael, riding across the lower middle. It was indeed a big country. Just to the north, the Lemhi Pass had been the route of the Lewis and Clark expedition in 1805—and until 1846 that very spot marked the western border of the United States. Stories and history everywhere.

Not long after crossing into Montana, I led us off-pavement again, and right away Dingus started—well, freaking out. No other way to put it. One minute he would know what road I was on, and where we were headed, the next he'd be "recalculating," then suggesting I make a U-turn. As usual, I just pressed on in the general compass direction I wanted, ignoring Dingus until he came up with some *useful* information.

The style of fencing in the background is called buck-and-rail (that was *not* easy to find out!), and seems characteristic of the Idaho-Montana region. I learned that it is often preferred in western areas because it doesn't require post-holes— useful if the ground is rocky. In any case, buck-and-rail fences are pretty against the grasslands and distant peaks.

Shortly after this photo was taken the three of us were pootling along single-track trails through sagebrush and tall

Chris and Michael, Montana

grasses. Sometimes the track led down a steep ravine, often with a rocky wash at the bottom, then a steep, rutted climb uphill. It was hard, sometimes tricky riding, especially for Chris, who was well experienced on pavement, but not this kind of terrain. Free-range livestock were a threat once again, and several times I had to stop and open a series of barbed-wire gates, then close them behind us. At one I paused for a minute or two, because a huge black bull, with a massive pendulous scrotum, was standing on the other side, regarding me. I parked, turned off the engine, and stood at the rail, but the bull didn't seem disturbed. I opened the gate and waved the other guys through. "Michael, you go first!"

And still, as the "responsible leader" of this little expedition, I had no clue if we were on the "right" route or not. Or any kind of route at all, really. A lot of times it was just tracks through the grass, or ruts through dried mud and rocks. After meandering around for a couple of hours, as close to north and east as I could keep us, I saw windpumps and water tanks, then a more well-traveled track leading toward distant ranch buildings. Figuring it was time to cut our losses and get back on a *road*, I led us that way.

Out through the ranch's driveway we rode, triumphant—we had conquered the wilderness! We reached an intersection with a paved road and I waved us to a stop at the roadside. Time to figure out

"It is *SO* a road!"

where we were, where *gas* was, and where to go from there.

I looked over at the street sign, Mansfield Lane, and my jaw fell open. The name had stuck because a friend used to live near Mansfield, Ohio, and I remembered it—though with disbelief. It was

exactly where we had turned *off* the pavement, two hours and all that struggle ago.

So now I also had to figure how we might make up some of those lost miles, and the lost time. We had the entire south-to-north expanse of Montana to cross—three or four hundred miles, I guessed.

Looking at the satellite map now, trying to figure out where we went wrong, I see it clearly. We had left pavement at Mansfield Lane, wandered over the Crossranch Road to Bannack Bench Road (yes, spelled differently from the pass), and somehow back to Mansfield Lane. The route we had wanted was clear, too, though several miles away. The satellite map shows a continuous track with the unfortunate name of Bloody Dick Road running for miles up past Reservoir Lake to the Big Hole Pass, near Wisdom, and on to Wise River. Just where I wanted to go!

So alas, it was operator error. Michael, not Mother.

I could only guess he had grown *tired* of all this—or just tired—or was waging passive-aggressive war against me. Because nearly every single route from then to the end had some major error in it. (No

Fear Knows Michael –
In the Biblical Sense

matter how many times I scolded him like a schoolteacher, "Check your work!")

A passage from *Far and Near*'s "It's Not Over When It's Over," toward the end of the previous tour, *Clockwork Angels*, describes a similar scene.

All urgent and confident, he said, "This isn't the right way—I remember from Mother. We were supposed to turn left back at that highway. We have to turn around."

At first I could only look at him. Then I said, "Why do you always get like this near the end of a tour?"

"Like what?"

"All argumentative, all stroppy, all negative, all . . . insubordinate. All your 'cognitive dissonance.'"

(One prime example of that psychological mechanism that Michael and I always refer to is when someone is about to be separated from a loved one, and picks a fight—so they can go away mad instead of sad.)

I impugned his masculinity, and said, "We have lots of time, and lots of gas—just man up for a few minutes and let's check it out."

That prompted Michael to laugh and add one (actually two) more items: "We have time." "We have gas." "And we have . . ."

Let's say "fortitude." (Michael is so often unprintable, while I strive to keep my contribution to our discourse to the highest standards of decency.)

In any case . . . we still had over 300 miles to cover, even by "Quickest Way" (which Allah forfend I should ever have to take on a day off in Montana), and it was midday.

(In the Islamophobic days of 2015 it occurred to me that in recent emails I was using Islamic references like that, or my favorite qualifier "inshallah"—God willing—and actually wondered if I was being "flagged." Like the old woman in Wisconsin who called 911 and claimed her female neighbor was chanting "ISIS is great!" during sex.)

Time to hop on the interstate, find a gas station, and make up some time on the Mileage-Disposal Unit. That zoomed us 100 miles or so up to Garrison pretty quickly. There we turned off to work our way over to Highway 83, a pretty two-lane up the long Clearwater Valley, the Chain of Lakes, between ponderosa pines and the craggy peaks of the Rocky Mountains. (Something novelist Richard Ford said comes to mind, "When I write sentences set in Montana, I write different kinds of sentences.") The vast expanse of Flathead Lake glittered in the lowering sun, and we . . . grew wearier . . .

Storm clouds were looming in from the west, and the temperature dropped sharply. Well in front of the other two, in a fever of "Get There," I felt the chill and pulled off the road to put on my plastic jacket and heavier gloves. A few brief showers came and went as I navigated the busy tourist area west of Glacier National Park, then made my way to Apgar, just inside the park. We had stayed there in a nice cabin-style motel the previous time, and I had asked Michael, back in January, to book us there again. The plan would be to rise early the following morning and ride through the park at sunrise, when we would largely have it to ourselves.

So I pulled up to those cabins and waited, but they didn't show. I

Going-to-the-Sun Road
PHOTO BY MICHAEL MOSBACH

Bubba Approaching,
Glacier National Park
PHOTO BY CHRIS STANKEE

backtracked a little to the park entrance and saw them riding away, in the opposite—wrong—direction. Short version: I waved them down, and Michael showed me some piece of paper, saying, "It's this way—only twenty-eight miles."

But I saw the name on the paper, Rising Sun, and was doubly crushed. First, it was not the place we had stayed last time and, second, it was on the opposite side of the park—the *eastern* side, as you might guess from the name—at the other end of a *serious* stretch of crowded, serpentine pavement, the Going-to-the-Sun Road.

Well. If I was disappointed to have missed Bloody Dick Road—not the name, the failure to make it to the Lemhi Pass that way—imagine my feelings now. Knowing with a sinking sensation inside what that "only twenty-eight miles" meant. Especially after over more than 550 hard miles already. "Furious" would be about right—even "desperately furious," because I knew there was no choice.

Seeing my expression, Michael chirped encouragingly, "It's right inside the park!" I just growled low, "At the other *end* of the park." Possibly there were several expletives, for emphasis.

Because I had visited Glacier National Park five or six times since 1998, and I knew what this situation meant in a way that Michael and poor innocent victim Chris did not. The Going-to-the-Sun Road is a scenic two-lane that winds and loops high enough into the mountains to be closed in winter. (Logan Pass, at 6,646 feet, can get up to one hundred feet of snow!) It was then late afternoon shading into early evening, and the little road was at its busiest, packed with cars, national park tour buses (pretty retro models from the 1930s), campers, and slow parades of two-wheeled cruisers. The speed limits were low, for the safety of such vehicles, and there were very few places to pass—even illegally. (Because obviously a motorcycle can zip around slower traffic much quicker than any car. Yet national parks are strict, well-patrolled with ranger vehicles, and—frankly—need the money. So you don't get away with anything.)

From Chris, to Michael, to Bubba
PHOTO BY CHRIS STANKEE

I rode away alone, with steely determination, at what pace I could. Finally, exactly twelve hours after we'd left the bus, at 7:30, and after almost 600 miles, we arrived. Of course it was all "worth it," but . . . it could have been nicer. That's all I'm saying.

Naturally I still wanted the early morning ride through the park, as well as the photos, so there was no choice but to get up early, go back, and start over. Thus I had my revenge on Michael, but unfortunately Chris had to suffer, too—meaning the 6:00 a.m. departure, on a *bitterly* cold morning, near freezing. I put on a few extra layers, including the balaclava under my helmet, usually

Bubba and the Waterfall, Glacier
PHOTO BY MICHAEL MOSBACH

"No, Michael, It's Not about Tulsa"
PHOTO BY MICHAEL MOSBACH

Aurora Smiles at Daddy and Olivia
PHOTO BY DANIEL GLEN LINDLEY-PEART

reserved for truly Arctic riding conditions. Temperatures in the mid-thirties had the "frost" warnings lighting up on our bikes.

Traffic was light, but the road workers were already at it, shutting down one lane in each direction for several minutes at a time. At first only the highest mountains were lighted by the sun, gradually creeping down the snow-dappled peaks and radiating into the valleys.

After Angry Bubba was satisfied with the number and quality of the photographs we had taken, we turned back and made our return to Rising Sun for breakfast. There were still a couple of hundred miles to go, and a border crossing into Canada, so we kept our pace "determined."

In Calgary and Vancouver there would be some warm reunions. Brutus had lived there for several years, and my dear West Coast friend Matt Scannell was flying in for the show—the first time two of my best friends had ever met. That night Matt and Brutus would ride on the bus with Michael and me, and in the morning Brutus and Michael and I would get off in Kamloops and ride the rest of the way into Vancouver, while Matt rode in with Dave. There we would be met by Carrie and Olivia, with Craiggie flying in from his South Pasadena home to photograph the show. All of us would meet that evening to visit brother Danny and his wife Janette at their house. What a gathering *that* promised to be.

That night Brutus orchestrated a fantastic dinner at Danny and Janette's house—though typically Danny took credit as Le Grand Chef on his handwritten menu, relegating Brutus to "sous chef."

Next morning Olivia and I were up early (or she was— and if she is, Daddy is!) and we carried our sketchbook and markers to the hotel restaurant. The second morning, though, the atrium lobby was full of conventioneers— throngs of suits with nametags and permasmiles waiting for tables. Asking at the front desk, we walked a couple of blocks down the street to a perfectly cute little restaurant, Scoozis. We liked their comfortable banquettes and friendly staff so much that we went back again on the third morning. The show there went well, with Ben Mink once again appearing for "Losing It."

After breakfast on the day off, Danny and Janette picked up Olivia

Hard Labor, Vancouver
PHOTO BY JOHN ARROWSMITH

and me and took us to the aquarium. (A Saturday morning, so had to go early—too early for Mom!) That evening our family hosted Danny, Janette, Brutus, and Craiggie at a fine restaurant, amid much laughter and raillery. (And Olivia and me doing art.)

Early on the day of the Seattle show, Papa John picked up Michael and me at our hotel, and we headed south. The border crossing was slow, but painless, and when we parked at the arena I started working on the next day's route. Near soundcheck I had a pleasant reunion with Michael Shrieve, early drummer with Santana (including a solo at Woodstock that had influenced me greatly—funny to think he was nineteen then, and I was going on seventeen; he was just old enough to manifest the Gift, and I was just old enough to be inspired by it). Michael also played in a couple of other influential groupings, like

Last Note and Stick Toss, Seattle
PHOTO BY JOHN ARROWSMITH

Go! and Automatic Man. However, even with that sterling history I knew his career had not been easy—but his passion for the music remained strong.

A month or so later, as I looked through my photos from those few days, at first I was puzzled about why there didn't seem to be any of the following day. Where did we ride after Seattle and before Portland?

Then I looked at my notes—and remembered. Ach. A day I would rather forget—and Michael would rather I forgot it even more. When he saw that this time I wasn't *angry* about it, but sad, he said, "I'd much rather make you mad than sad."

I had to smile and nod at that—it tells a lot.

But the girl can't help it.

(Perfect song reference—"The Girl Can't Help It" was written by the composer of "Route 66," Bobby Troup, about the character played by Jayne Mansfield in the movie of the same name from 1956. It was perhaps *the* seminal and influential rock 'n' roll movie, with riveting performances from pioneers like Little Richard, Gene Vincent, and Eddie Cochran. Teenagers at the time, like John Lennon and Paul McCartney, were transformed.)

On a couple of tours in the mid-1980s, the Guys at Work and I took French lessons on the road. Our office would arrange with the local Berlitz school to send a teacher to the arena to converse with us for an hour before the show. One memorable character always taught us in the New York City area, Jean Gallia—a classic *bon vivant* French sexagenarian, both playful and wise. One phrase he taught us comes back to me often: *Ne jugez jamais personne pour quelque chose qu'ils ne peuvent pas changer.* "Never judge anyone for something they can't change."

Well, yes. I have been thinking about that concept for years, and trying to live by it. It has obvious applications to race, gender, and orientation, and raises interesting questions about faith, ignorance, and feeble-mindedness. As I think about and observe human judgmentalism in this light, I notice people are judged more for their "apparent" *stupidity* than any other quality. I confess I'm not sure what to *do* with that information—nor with what is called the Dunning-Kruger Effect, which finds that some people are too stupid to know how stupid they are. If that isn't scary, I don't know what is.

But, you have to wonder, is a person's character and personality "something they can't change?"

Almost always it is, I concluded after long miles (years, really) of in-depth reflection. Sometimes it's the way people are wired, sometimes the way they have been *warped* (usually by parents, with faith, ignorance, and feeble-mindedness). Sometimes character and determination can help us "behave better than we are," and try to improve—be "progressive," ha ha. But with some wounded souls there isn't enough therapy in all the world that could save them.

In my everyday domestic and professional life I have truly been liberated from worthwhile amounts of anger and frustration with others by simply accepting another version of "It is what it is."

I just shake my head and think, "He can't *help* it." Or she.

Michael will protest—and he can't help that, either—but he can be scatterbrained, easily distracted ("Oh look—a chicken!"), and, probably the worst handicap of all in the Book of Bubba, he is fundamentally uninterested in roads and destinations. You know, "scenery and that." That does cause conflicts of interest, you might say.

The two of us have long shared rueful laughs of recognition at the two characters in the movie *In Bruges*. After a killing goes wrong,

Irish hitmen Ken and Ray (Brendan Gleeson and Colin Farrell) are exiled from London to hide out in the quaintly picturesque Belgian city of Bruges. They each react to its "fairytale atmosphere" in opposite ways, as the proverbial odd couple in an obscenity-laced, darkly comic pageant. To Michael and me, the relationship between Ken and Ray is . . . let's say "familiar."

In one scene they are standing outside the 300-foot bell tower in the middle of Bruges, and Ken says, "Coming up?"

Michael: "Look at me! Look at me!"

Ray replies, "What's up there?"

Ken says, "The view."

"The view of what? The view of down here? I can see that from down here."

"Ray, you're about the worst tourist in the whole world."

"Ken, I grew up in Dublin. I love Dublin. If I'd grown up on a farm, and was retarded, Bruges might impress me, but I didn't, so it doesn't."

That's our Michael, all right, and what it says in my journal about the ride between Seattle and Portland is simply, "Heartbreak day."

Then the reason, "He forgot. To turn over. The map."

I will just leave it right there, with the heartbreak, and "The Girl Can't Help It," and move on to the following ride, out of Portland. As Gord Downie wrote for the Tragically Hip in "Wheat Kings," "Besides, no one's interested in something you didn't do."

17

Crater Lake National Park, Oregon

BINGE RIDING

On the afternoon of the Portland show we were joined by Tom Marinelli—pictured here in the vivid yellow helmet he insists was an emergency purchase: "The only one that fit." A few degrees of separation brought Tom and me together on the R30 tour, ten years before, when he joined us on a ride from Ann Arbor, near his home in the Detroit area, through Indiana and Ohio to Cuyahoga Falls. Tom and I were drawn together by a shared dark fate—Tom lost his daughter Jenn in 1997 when she was about the same age as Selena had been, and within a month of my loss. People who live with that permanent black hole in their lives often complain that there's no *name* for us— you can be an orphan, a widow, or a widower, but we're just . . . losers.

Sometimes it can be helpful for us losers to know each other and share what only we are unfortunate enough to understand—what one

Crater Lake, Wizard Island
PHOTO BY TOM MARINELLI

of the grief books called "The Greatest Loss." Tom is also a serious and highly competent motorcyclist and a good travel companion, and after he moved to St. Louis we rode together around Missouri, Arkansas, and Nebraska. These days Tom also lives part-time in Oregon, so on the past couple of tours he joined us there.

That night Tom rode with us on the bus out of Portland, with his BMW GS in the trailer, and Papa John parked us in the quaintly named Cottage Grove, Oregon. We must have liked it there pretty well because, an hour after leaving, we were right back there again. But only to get gas. Our first sortie into the nearby unpaved roads had ended where an active logging site blocked our way, and searching around and ahead of us, I decided it was wisest to head back to where I *knew* we could get gas. Wise, but . . . frustrating.

Perhaps my major ambition for that day was to get riding photos of Crater Lake. After five or six visits over the years, I had never managed to capture the "sense of place" in a single image—and if I could do that with a motorcycle passing through, that would be the ultimate. (We have ridden through and photographed some impressive walls of snow around there, towering above the plowed road even in early summer. The area gets forty-five feet of snow, so it takes a while to melt—but was all gone by July 22.)

The larger and more spectacular a place is, the harder it is to convey to others—in words or in photographs. I believe the opening image does a pretty good job (thank you, thank you), but some places you just have to see for yourself. A few examples would be Lake Louise, Grand Canyon, Bryce Canyon, Death Valley, and Crater Lake.

Long Shadows in the Pines

In the center of this frame, and the background of the previous one, is Wizard Island, actually the cinder cone from the original volcano. The caldera-lake is almost 2,000 feet deep, the deepest in the United States, and lies at an elevation around 6,000 feet. Story-wise, I was particularly taken with the lake's native midge fly, which lays its eggs on the water's surface. They sink to the deepest bottom, hatch and feed as larvae in that frigid darkness 2,000 feet down, then change to pupae, which float to the top and emerge as adults. The adults live only a few days, not even getting a meal before they mate and die, and the cycle repeats again. Nature can be so . . . visionary.

Journal notes from that 431-mile day:

> Definitely "going big" on these last few rides. "Bingeing," I guess.
>> New disorder: "binge riding."
>> Up at 6:30 again on bus—after show, and 1:00 a.m. bedtime.
>> Because . . . won't be doing this anymore.
>> Gone slackjaw again.

[Once again I reach up, push it closed, and say, "Don't be like that."]

> After morning's flailing loop, had to give up Lassen [Mount Lassen Volcanic National Park], but . . . is what it is.
>> Now to reconsider tomorrow . . .

Yes, tomorrow was going to require some reconsidering. We had fetched up in Susanville, California, that night, because the previous day's online search around Lake Almanor, where I'd hoped to stay, had come up empty. Or full. (Skilled amateur travel agent Brutus, whose talents are frequently requested when I have a "challenging" destination, tells me the trade code for a fully booked hotel is "solid.") Our Susanville stop would add an extra distance to the show-day's ride, making it over 300 miles even by the quickest way.

Riding Off in a Huff

This photo's two long morning shadows suggest that Michael and I had paused to confer about the road ahead. In fact I had just waved him alongside to send him ahead to take a photo of me, shooting back toward the rising sun. At this moment Michael had just put away his big camera after snapping a photo of this scene while I had scoffed and jeered at his whimsy—even as I pulled out my own little camera to take this shot. You can see his helmeted profile looking over at me as he acts all shocked and hurt.

"But you just made fun of *me*!"

"Yeah, I did."

"Why do you always have to *hurt* me?"

"That's what I do." Then a second later, "You really oughta be used to it by now."

He spat out, "I'll *never* get used to your abuse. And . . . and—you're not my *real* dad!"

That one always gets me, and I laughed aloud as Michael rode off with a flounce of his helmet.

Tom had been reconsidering his future, too. The previous night he asked me if I thought we would hit Lassen National Park in the morning. I shook my head regretfully, "No, I'm afraid not—we'll have to make some time."

Tom said, "Well, if I follow you into San Jose I'll just have to turn around and ride back through all that. I thought I might run over and have a look at Lassen, then head home from there."

I nodded with a wry smile and said, "That's what I would do all right!" But I had to consider the barricade of sheer *distance* between where we were and where the San Jose arena was. Many miles of congested areas and freeways—no fun. And it makes me nervous when I'm too far away on a show day.

Though I did start us off with a "mystery road" (because it was there) a stretch of dotted line bridging from Lake Almanor down to the Central Valley. The lake is a large manmade reservoir—named for the power-company president's daughters, Alice, Martha, and Eleanor—on the Feather River. Around the region I saw cryptic signs reading "STOP THE THERMAL CURTAIN." Curious, I looked into it, and realized that, although the issue was local, it relates to many other water projects in the West, and seems worth citing as an example.

Like other dams on other rivers—the mighty Colorado being most emblematic—the dam that created Lake Almanor changes the downstream seasonal flows, siltiness, and water temperature. Those changes are thought to be harmful to wildlife, especially spawning

Sunrise Road to Humbug Summit
PHOTO BY MICHAEL MOSBACH

fish. The Thermal Curtain is a proposed structure that would hang underwater and attempt to cool the water temperature downstream—how much is debated, as well as its effect on the lakewater's temperature (too warm would cause algae blooms) and its fish. The enormous cost would be borne by the power company's customers, so there was organized resistance, and the conflict stands as a fine example of endless water issues in the West. A quote often attributed to Mark Twain remains true today: "Whisky is for drinking; water is for fighting over."

We rode around Lake Almanor to a gravel road and turned off into the mountains. This time Mother had "allowed" that route, but we soon found that the Boys were having their problems. Or really, it was just that Mother had decided on her *own* interpretation of the route. Many a long established but remote road exists but is not properly logged in her software, thus she instead chooses the roads really, *really* less traveled. Or like what happened to us in Montana, sending us deep into hell's half-acre, then "recalculating," and directing a U-turn.

The *proper* unpaved route had the fetching name of Humbug Summit, but I noticed that we were often on much smaller, completely unmaintained logging roads. And there was a *lot* of logging going on around there. Even that early in the morning we had to be watchful for oncoming trucks, gigantic roadhogs heaped with logs of ponderosa pine. Only occasionally did we encounter a few remote campgrounds, or occasional rickety cabins and parked trailers back in the woods.

One time the purple line led us past an imposing barricade—a gate of heavy iron tubes painted yellow. Fatefully, it happened to be open just then, with a corporate pickup parked just on the other side. Probably a logging company surveyor, I realized later. Dingus pointed onward, so onward I led us. However, a considerable time and distance later, we came upon a similar barricade—only this one was *closed*.

I checked the padlock—it was hefty, and shackled. I scanned the woods to either side, but boulders had been placed at each end of the barricade to stop people like us getting around them. Any other way out would be a *long* way back—and even that open gate we'd passed through might be locked again now.

Michael said, "Are you thinking what I'm thinking?"

I said, "I'm readin' your mail."

This image, for once, looks worse than it was. We decided to lay the bikes down, remove one of the luggage cases and a mirror, then slide them *under* the barricade. We did it, and it was good. A fist-bump celebrated our triumph against The Man.

However, once again, all that rambling around had eaten up a lot of time, and I would have to "reconsider" a

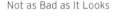

Not as Bad as It Looks

little further. There would be no time to stop at the Black Bear Diner in Willows (familiar from track days and races at nearby Thunderhill Raceway), or to take the meandering route along the foothills of the Coast Ranges we had explored once before—a series of unpaved roads through ranchland that had been scenic, deserted, and adventurous. No, we would have to get to Interstate 5 and get *moving*.

Hence my journal note later that day, on the bus, when I had called ahead to ask Frenchie to make us a couple of omelettes for around 2:00 that afternoon.

8 hours, 300 miles, not even a cup o' coffee.

Passing on the morning coffee had been deliberate rather than "negligent." On past tours if I wanted to make an early start I would set up the in-room coffee the night before, then just press the button in the morning. Lately I had even given that up—not worth the trouble, and I found I felt fine without it.

(Roadcraft: It is troublesome enough having to figure out a completely different shower every day, never mind another coffee machine.)

In any case, finally settling at the bus's table and tucking into Frenchie's wonderful omelettes was rendered even more superb by our long fast. The day was truly reborn, and being fueled and refreshed, I would summon the energy to face the next part of the day: route planning, soundcheck, dinner with the Guys at Work, warm-up, and show number thirty-one.

Just five more to go, as we headed into the Southwest and the home stretch—*literally* home, for me.

18

The Loneliest Road
in America, 2015

THE LONELIEST ROAD IN AMERICA

In San Jose we were joined by yet another guest rider, Greg Russell—
the Master of All Things Creative, including the design of my website,
and the steampunk drum riser on our *Time Machine* and *Clockwork
Angels* tours.

Like the other guests, Greg had ridden with us several times before
on his Halloween-colored KTM. And like the others, he would get
more than he likely bargained for—the next day's route took "binge-
riding" to new extremes.

Once again starting with the big map of the western United States,
I thought I would like to start with Yosemite National Park (though
on a midsummer Friday, we would have to get in and out early), then
cross a big stretch of Nevada's vast emptiness, including Highway

50, The Loneliest Road in America. (Funny that it's repeatedly misspelled on the Rand McNally map.)

"The Loneliest Road in America" became a chapter title in *Ghost Rider* and, in a way, also contributed to its title and cover. Back in 1998 I rode west on that arrow-straight two-lane across the high desert for most of a day, and hardly saw another vehicle. On a whim I stopped my bike in the middle of the road and pulled it back on its centerstand. I walked around, had a smoke, watered the roadside gravel, and finally decided I ought to take a photograph of that sight—looking from behind at the motorcycle in the middle of an empty road. I smiled and thought, "Ghost Rider."

Even in a day that promised to be very long—about 500 miles—I chose one tempting off-pavement excursion (mystery road) along the way. Despite Mother's and Michael's intention to cheat me of it by keeping our route to the pavement, I remembered the (obviously memorable) town name of Gabbs, and that we were supposed to turn off there. (It was named after a nineteenth-century paleontologist who worked in the area, seeking bones rather than ore.) I stopped beside the town sign and asked Michael why that turn wasn't on our route now. He shrugged and looked away, "Mother couldn't find it."

Michael at Yosemite

Well, maybe—right then I certainly had no way to prove him wrong. But I do now. The road I wanted seems well charted on every kind of map. But never mind—fortunately I remembered Gabbs, and the road turned out not to be too hard to find. In fact the decently (and recently) graded gravel was modestly well traveled—to the

Berlin-Ichthyosaur State Park (another memorable name I recalled from a previous trek through there, in the opposite direction), then through the Shoshone Mountains to the Yomba Shoshone Tribal Lands, and on up to Austin, Nevada.

In searching for that road "on the ground," as it were, I first led us up a gravel track that led into the middle of a gigantic mine—"The Oldest Continuously Operated Mine in Nevada," which had been processing magnesium since World War II. Circling around the grim mountains of slag ("overburden," miners call it) and crude metal buildings, just seeing if there was a way to continue east, I saw hard-hatted, dust-grimed workers looking at us curiously. I stopped and asked one of them if there was a way to ride east, and he said there was a road across the mountains just to the north. As we turned around and headed back down to the main road, official-looking white pickups were converging with seeming "security" intentions. I waved to them and pointed that we were leaving, and they returned my wave as they turned back.

Gabbs itself grew up around the mine, of course. It is one of those desert towns sited just off the highway, rather than around it, so you don't actually ride through it, but beside it. Even then, I could see it was fairly sizeable and "established." It occurred to me that maybe Gabbs was in the middle of nowhere, but the *town* wouldn't be nowhere—not to the people who lived there. In fact, I might say that *nowhere* is nowhere, really. Not if someone lives there—or even if *stories* live there.

And after all, Gabbs has one vital sign of any living town: a website! It says they have 269 residents, and "the Town of Gabbs boasts a k-12 public school, grocery, café, bar, gas station, motel, propane utility company, library, a volunteer fire and ambulance service, VFW and ladies auxiliary, senior center, women's Club, LDS church, community church, community swimming pool, homes, and a progressive mine."

So that's not nowhere, is it?

About twenty miles east on that gravel road (it had a *number*, Michael—Nye County Road 844), the virtual ghost town of Ione, Nevada, brought us a little closer to nowhere. "The Town That Would Not Die," they proclaim on the sign, along with "Elevation 6,782 feet," "Founded 1863," and a claimed population of forty-one—though no one was in evidence as we rode through. Plenty of stories live on, though, dating back 5,000 years to Shoshone and northern Paiute settlements and livening up in the prospecting era in the late nineteenth and early twentieth centuries. Mining booms had been brief, silver first, then later cinnabar (mercury). The population once reached about 600

Ione, Nevada

people, but it was all over by the 1930s. (A holographic time projector would be a great attraction in a place like that. Someday, I'm sure . . .)

I was still setting my sights on overnighting in Ely, Nevada. (Not that there are a myriad of choices in that desolate state. For which we love it all the more.) I had stayed in Ely a couple of times before, including on the *Ghost Rider* travels—when I learned it was pronounced "Elee." In 2002 the Jailhouse Motel in Ely hosted Michael and me, and was featured on the West Side Beemer Boyz T-shirt among the lower-priced accommodations.

($89.95 then, and only $70.00 now. That's probably not a good sign.)

Storm Chasing
PHOTO BY MICHAEL MOSBACH

The rainshower in the distance was rare in the high desert at any time of year, but especially so in July. However, in our time of global weirding, just a few days before heavy downpours had swept across California and Nevada. We managed to avoid all but a few drops that day, but saw plenty of evidence of recent flash flooding. Scatterings of debris and mud were strewn in ragged lines across the roads in low-lying areas, and even the day before we might not have got through on the gravel tracks. Stretching out beside us between distant dark mountains were tremendous expanses of sage and grasses, all suddenly vividly green. Wildflowers had popped up at the roadside, where extra moisture drains off the pavement after a rain and gives nearby plants a noticeable boost. Opportunist as all desert life must be, seeds and plants had stood ready for the slightest hint of moisture to bloom and reproduce.

One prominent roadside flower grew in large green spiky clumps, the petals white and papery around yellow centers (the reason for one nickname, "cowboy's fried egg"). A simple wish to know that plant's name (easy search under "white flower Mojave," because there aren't that many) led me to the prickly poppy—but as always, there was so much *more*. (One detail: "fairly common because even cows won't eat them.")

Looking at the list of search results for prickly poppy, I noticed a website called *Shaman's Garden*. There I learned that the Aztecs called prickly poppy "nourishment of the dead," and that *all* parts of the plant have psychoactive properties. You could mail-order prickly poppy resin, seeds, powder, and even something called "dried latex (summer only)." I also learned about a . . . "thing," I guess? a subject? . . . called "entheology." It is defined as "a branch of theology that addresses the experience and/or knowledge of the divine, and of the revelation of the divine, through the ritual use of psychoactive substances."

Little did I know all these years I had been an entheologist . . .

Revelations of the divine may be achieved through psychoactive substances, yes, but one learns in time that ordinary life requires more *practical* illumination. A "worklight," for example. As I consider the unlikelihood of having reached my seventh decade, I discover that my life's driving forces are pretty basic. Two simple commandments, really.

1) Try to be a good person.
2) Try to be your own hero.

Both are full-time occupations (ones you can't retire from) and ultimately unachievable—but such realities never held back anyone lofted by ideals (or entheology) or spurred by hyperthymia. Hyperthymic people are haunted by that very desire: to live up to their own expectations, to be their own heroes.

No man really knows about other human beings. The best he can do is to suppose that they are like himself.

That profound thought is from *The Winter of Our Discontent,* John Steinbeck's last novel, published in 1961, when he was fifty-nine. (He

Prickly Poppy

Greg Roosts Past a Psychoactive Flower

died in 1968.) Alongside his masterworks like *The Grapes of Wrath* and *East of Eden*, this little novel seems overshadowed and underrated, but on closer reflection it quietly offers the wisdom of a lifetime. The main character Ethan Hawley is an old-line New Englander, described as going through life with a judge on his shoulder. Like trying to please *any* kind of "imaginary friend," human or supernatural, that would be a life sentence. That omniscient judge certainly inclined Ethan Hawley *toward* being a hero, though he would ultimately fail and be broken on that wheel. As Hemingway wrote in *A Farewell to Arms*,

The world breaks everyone and afterward many are strong at the broken places. But those that will not break it kills. It kills the very good and the very gentle and the very brave impartially. If you are none of these you can be sure that it will kill you too, but there will be no special hurry.

The idea of aiming to be one's own hero is a recent revelation to me, first encountered in a book called *Hemingway's Boat*, by Paul Hendrickson. A friend gave it to me a few years ago, and at first I was doubtful. I greatly admire the best of Ernest Hemingway's prose, the stories and some of the novels, and his life was quite epic—from the Michigan woods to World War I battlefields in Italy, Paris between the wars, the Spanish Civil War, East Africa, Key West, Cuba, and Idaho. He was inarguably a paradigm-shifting artist of the twentieth century, like Picasso, Stravinsky, or Frank Lloyd Wright, and sometimes a boor and a bully. Since his suicide in 1961 there has been a steady stream of "Papa fetish" books, filled with riffs about Hemingway's women, food, drink, dead animals, guys who fished with him a couple of times—you name it.

So I opened *Hemingway's Boat* with trepidation, but was soon won over by its depth and insight. The book's subtitle is *Everything He Loved in Life, and Lost*, and his beloved fishing boat *Pilar* symbolizes the period of Hemingway's life that was happiest and most artistically successful, from the middle 1930s to the early 1950s. Toward the end of the book I was dumbstruck by the author's illumination of Ernest Hemingway's one essential truth, and perhaps fatal flaw. His life was a constant struggle to be his own hero. From boyhood on he lived every day trying to be the man he had visualized becoming as a boy—the writer, hunter, fisherman, naturalist, and all-round he-man. Out of the same idealism and imagination that ignited his prose, Hemingway created this persona, and tried to live it—*be* it.

With a start of recognition, I saw how similar that was to how my life has felt to me—always trying to be the guy I would have admired at age sixteen. My own hero. After six decades of being driven by that force, having words for it was like a sudden mirror—or better, a *lens*—appearing before me, just as it was when I read about hyperthymia.

Though both qualities have their dark sides, naturally. *Hemingway's Boat* sketches harrowing portraits of the fates of Hemingway's three sons, Jack, Gregory, and Patrick—each in turn damaged by another psychological twist: the hopeless struggle to become their *father's* hero. That would be unlikely to impossible in any family, a generational battle right out of the bible, Greek myth, or Shakespearean tragedy. It makes a fascinating twist on *King Lear*, for example, in which the king's daughters, Regan, Goneril, and Cordelia, were judged by him on how much they *appeared* to love him. The sons of Ernest Hemingway judged *themselves*, and by how they measured up to the father's *ideal* of himself. That is one complicated chain.

As for the collateral damage in an artist's life—another great American writer, William Faulkner, gives one opinion.

> The writer's only responsibility is to his art. He will be completely ruthless if he is a good one. He has a dream. It anguishes him so much he must get rid of it. He has no peace until then. Everything goes by the board: honor, pride, decency, security, happiness, all, to get the book written. If a writer has to rob his mother, he will not hesitate; the "Ode on a Grecian Urn" is worth any number of old ladies.

Funny, yes—but true? Probably not to the old ladies. And how many *children* is it worth?

From "Ode on a Grecian Urn" (1819) by John Keats:

> Beauty is truth, truth beauty—that is all
> Ye know on earth, and all ye need to know.

For almost 200 years that zen-like statement has caused much debate, and will continue to be challenged not for its poetry, but for its *meaning*. Beauty may be truth, all right, but truth is certainly not always beautiful.

Another literary character comes to mind from the 1965 novel *Stoner*, by John Williams. (Modern reviewers feel compelled to point out that the title is the main character's name, not his entheolog-

PHOTO BY MICHAEL MOSBACH

ical lifestyle.) William Stoner is a farm boy who becomes a teacher at a Midwestern university, where he lives and dies without apparently doing much—yet the author defined him as "a true hero." And yes, in circumstances both mundane and achingly tragic (*Stoner* is perhaps the saddest novel I have ever read, so I have trouble recommending it to others), Bill Stoner always did what he *ought* to have done.

In his case, and so many others—maybe most everyone—being a hero may consist only of doing the right thing every day, every way you possibly can—in the face of those who don't notice, don't care, or deliberately set out to trip you up, through envy or sheer malice. Such a day-to-day integrity in one person's life needn't be spectacular in any way—probably won't be—but it will be truly heroic.

Could it be that introverts look inward for approval and extroverts cast around for it? Too simplistic, of course, but there's something in it. The word "authentic" means self-authored, or self-invented, and people can invent themselves in varied ways. Some decide how they wish to be *perceived*, then act that role until they even fool themselves, and maybe others. Wanting to be one's own hero is another step removed: an obsession with how one appears—but only to others who are exactly like oneself. Or to the sixteen-year-old judge on your shoulder.

In the early '90s I struggled with the lyrics for a song called "Nobody's Hero." Typically my lyrics would grow not from one idea, but from blending two or more seemingly separate themes that raised each other into another realm. "Nobody's Hero," alas, took that to extremes—I guess I simply tried to get too much in there.

The single notion I began with was *me* insisting I was "nobody's hero." When a stranger comes up and tells me I am their "hero" or "idol," I am taken aback—what can you say to that? "Thank you" is all I can manage, and there's nowhere that conversation can go. A true answer, I see now, would be "Thanks, but I'm still busy trying to be my own!"

From that notion, I cast my net wider and built the choruses around ideas of true and false heroes.

[Chorus 1]
Hero—saves a drowning child
Cures a wasting disease
Hero—lands the crippled airplane
Solves great mysteries

Hero—not the handsome actor
Who plays a hero's role
Hero—not the glamor girl
Who'd love to sell her soul
If anybody's buying, nobody's hero

That would make about enough Deep Thoughts for one song, right? But onward soldiered the overambitious hyperthymic, grafting on a sad verse about my first gay friend, Ellis Booth, an early casualty of AIDS, and one about a tragedy in a childhood friend's family. Those

The Loneliest Road
PHOTO BY MICHAEL MOSBACH

were intended as counter-examples of good people who hadn't *lived* to be any kind of hero.

Then I added a little bridge, or pre-chorus, to express regret for falling out of touch with dear ones, and sorrow for their losses.

As the years went by, we drifted apart
When I heard that you were gone
I felt a shadow cross my heart

Counterparts cover art

But, the way things worked out, I felt those meanings all got mashed into mixed and unclear messages. Too much adding up to too little. Geddy's vocal is great, and the musical and vocal arrangement is beautiful in itself, but it elides the verse into the chorus confusingly. At that point you don't know if he's singing about nobody's hero, or *somebody's* hero. The orchestrations are rich and passionate, and Alex's guitar work is sublime as always. I like the *composition* of the drum part, but the execution felt stiff to me then, and still does—a feeling that drove me to study with Freddie Gruber, a master of movement and rhythmic feel, the following year.

In sum, I always considered "Nobody's Hero" as a "noble failure"—a *heroic* failure. (I stated at the outset of this book that you should never tell anyone about your plans or your failures—but there's one of mine, no charge. And a good example of why you *shouldn't*—people who might like that song will think I'm knocking it—and maybe *them*. It's still a good song, just not what I had hoped it would be.)

To show this is not me being hypercritical, two other songs from that same *Counterparts* album, "Animate" and "Cold Fire," still please me in both the lyrics and drumming. "Animate" has fun with Carl Jung's notion of the *anima*, the feminine aspect of the masculine soul, while "Cold Fire" presents a conversation between a smart female and a dumb male. (You only hope people catch things like that, of course.)

I said, "If love has these conditions, I don't understand the songs you love"
She said, "This is not a love song—this isn't fantasy land."

The use of dialogue was inspired by Paul Simon, who used that device to great effect, while the title and chorus imagery came from a PBS documentary about phosphorescence and such called, yes, "Cold Fire." (Strangely I can find no record of that program, but I watched it in a hotel room on a night off after a long bicycle ride, and was inspired to make a note of those words.) That idea in turn was an important element in the world of *Clockwork Angels* and *Clockwork Lives*.

As for the drum parts, perhaps they remain more satisfying because I was just playing "me," rather than trying to emulate someone else (the sublime Manu Katché in "Nobody's Hero").

One aspect of the lyrical statement that stands out to me now is the first half of the second chorus—examples of "private heroism," of living by *principles*.

[Chorus 2]
Hero—is the voice of reason
Against the howling mob
Hero—is the pride of purpose
In the unrewarding job

Hero—not the champion player
Who plays the perfect game
Hero—not the glamor boy
Who loves to sell his name
Everybody's buying, nobody's hero

In both choruses, the actual heroes *do good* in the world, and are worthy of unquestioning admiration. The others, the actors and players, are those with the Gift, who do something powerful that we can't do ourselves, like sports or performing. Art and athletics can indeed be admirable, and even inspiring, but are not necessarily *heroic*. Yet we elevate those mortals, and others, to demigods. Some are celebrated for mere unadorned (unearned) *celebrity*: famous for being famous. John Cleese chimes in on such a shallow state of popular culture:

> I truly believe that the worst aspect of the whole celebrity merry-go-round is the belief that your life becomes more meaningful because you have touched the hem of Simon Cowell's garment, or that true wisdom involves knowing the name of Steven Seagal's nanny's dog.

Cleese followed his lengthy rant on celebrity and selfie-seekers with a statement of relief: "I feel a lot better for that." So do I.

After a few hours on the Loneliest Road in America, those are the kind of thoughts, songs, and stories that play in a rider's head.

The day's temperatures had varied widely, from downright cold over the Tioga Pass (9,943 feet) to the low eighties across Nevada. I had been careful to check the forecast there, because if it had been hotter, like over one hundred, as July could often be in the high desert, I would have planned differently—stayed to the higher elevations. This was a perfect day for an all-day desert crossing—eventually adding up to almost exactly 500 miles. Not one of those miles was on a freeway or major road, and only the early part around Yosemite troubled us with any traffic—the rest was free and easy cruising.

After checking in at the Jailhouse (still "cheap and worth it," and perfectly adequate for bums like us), we walked over to the old Hotel Nevada, from 1929. A row of sparkling Harleys angled out from the curb, and I guess if there ever was a clichéd biker destination on a Friday night in summer, a casino in small-town Nevada would be it. Like Dave told me one time about why he gave up riding his Harley around Nashville, "Seemed like everybody just wanted to ride from one bar to another."

For accommodations I preferred the open walkways of a place like the Jailhouse, but inside the Hotel Nevada's once-stately lobby was the inevitable casino and a decent restaurant. Since my first visit to Ely it had seemed like the place to go for dinner, and sometimes breakfast. Its "historical Western atmosphere" was legitimate, yet contrasted in a pleasingly bizarre way with the casino's surreal, garish blinking and beeping. The restaurant walls were decorated with black-and-white photos from olden times, the mining history of Ely, and the people-watching was often intriguing, too.

Personally, I have always appreciated those small Southern Nevada towns like Ely, Austin, and Tonopah—they feel so quiet and peaceful, especially at night. Like an earlier definition of the "proper" size, they were "big enough to have motels and restaurants, but small enough to get into and out of quickly." A simple distinction like these towns' distance from an interstate gave them a different, more characterful atmosphere than the offramp-type of settlements.

Once again I had left us with over 300 miles on the show day, heading for the MGM Grand in Vegas. Oh, and a "mystery road" to start off with, too. It was a decent gravel road through Railroad Valley, all sagebrush and irrigated ranching country, dark cattle and distant ranch buildings framed by dark ranges of low peaks. We came out to pavement on Nevada State Route 375, better known as the Extraterrestrial Highway. Its location near the fabled Area 51 had made it famous among "believers," and the tiny town of Rachel (population about 50) caters to them with the Little A'Le'Inn. ("Alien," see.) Brutus and I passed that way in 1997, just a few years after the "craze" started, in 1989. Like the enduring mystery of what happened in Roswell, New Mexico, in 1948—and indeed, *associated* with that same mystery, because legend has it the dead aliens and the spaceship from the UFO crash in Roswell were taken to Area 51—the story grew and endured despite a complete lack of evidence beyond hearsay. (Oh wait— like religion.)

Early Morning Nevada
PHOTO BY MICHAEL MOSBACH

I have long admired the deep levels in the slogan for *The X-Files*, "I want to believe." Through my youth I shared that urge: I was fascinated with books about the paranormal, alien visitations, spiritual beings, everything that was "magical."

The UFO Museum in Roswell is a fitting symbol for eventual disillusionment. I passed that way on my *Ghost Rider* travels in 1999 and stopped to visit, my mind not only open but *eager*. I looked among the exhibits and read the displays of newspaper stories, and as I turned to go, I thought, "There isn't a *shred* of real evidence here."

I was disappointed, but at the same time I found I had a new opinion. Like Christopher Hitchens, "What can be asserted without evidence can be dismissed without evidence."

In the mid-'90s the crew of the movie *Independence Day* did some filming in the Rachel area, and later built a sizeable time capsule

"Population: Human Yes–Aliens?"

outside the Little A'Le'Inn—a stone block as big as a washing machine with a bronze plaque. We stopped there for breakfast, just as Brutus and I had done almost twenty years before, and I added a new coffee mug to my collection.

A couple of guys came in who must have recognized our bikes outside, because they headed straight for me. When I saw their cell-phones come out to start taking photographs, no doubt to ask for a "selfie" with me, I was immediately jolted into a "different reality," an uncomfortable one. Michael noticed it, too, our eyes met, and I told him, "I'm getting out of here."

Even as I stood by the bike and pulled my helmet on, I saw them coming out, brandishing their handheld devices in my direction. (Talk about "alien visitations"!) I quickly mounted and rode up the highway a little to wait for Michael and Greg.

I felt . . . anxiety, yes, as always in such situations, but "disappointed" is a better word. A few sanctuaries on the American road where I had always counted on (and received) anonymity were, for example, national park visitor centers, roadside rest areas, and small-town diners. On this tour, every one of those sanctuaries had been breached at least once. Sometimes innocent and kind of amusing, like at a diner in Michigan ("Ronnie's Lunch Box, Good Down Home Cookin'"), where we had stopped one rainy morning after "a hundred miles before breakfast." Putting on my gear and waiting outside while Michael paid the bill, he came out and told me a local cop had leaned over and said, "Where you guys playing tonight?" Recognized the bikes, obviously.

Greg told me later that at the Little A'Le'Inn he had followed me outside, just behind my pursuers. Knowing me, he performed a kindness, as he wrote to describe it: "I stopped them and told them it wasn't going to improve your day to be spotted and slowed down, and that they might have a better day knowing they did the cool thing. They were okay with that."

And still, I appreciated that for almost twenty years of touring by motorcycle I had nearly always stayed under the radar that way. The reality was that our increasing celebrity in recent years, through a documentary, a few very public award presentations, and media like that *Rolling Stone* cover, had raised our profile. And, *mea culpa*, people knew from my many touring stories that I traveled on a red BMW GS motorcycle.

Extraterrestrial Highway
PHOTO BY MICHAEL MOSBACH

But I also tried to remember it was the last time I would be "exposed" like that—standing out because I was traveling near a city where the band was performing. So, deal with it.

(Incidentally, this location is where the book's cover shot was taken.)

At the east end of the Extraterrestrial Highway you pass through an expanse of Joshua trees and distant brown mountains up and over the Coyote Summit at 5,604 feet. At the site of the ghost town of Crystal Springs a grove of cottonwoods shades a gravel parking area. When I passed that way a few times in the '90s it was always full of RVs with giant satellite dishes and telescopes pointed to the sky—presumably searching for evidence of "reverse-engineered" UFOs and such—but this time it was empty. Perhaps over time that conspiracy craze has . . . lost steam.

Meanwhile, Greg's bike had a flat tire. When he went to ride away from the Little A'Le'Inn to catch up with us, he discovered his rear tire was flat and would prove to be unrepairable. Damaged by some debris on the gravel road, we guessed. Michael circled back to get the news, and later I asked Greg to describe for me what happened.

> After five minutes or so a tall fifty-something man who was sitting at the counter turned around and said he could probably give me a ride to the next town. He and his wife finished eating and met me outside, where they mentioned they were actually going to Las Vegas to pick up their daughter from college, and could just give me a lift all the way there. I was super thankful for their kindness, and accepted.
>
> He had a sweet GMC pickup and was willing to drive it into a depression to get the tailgate closer to the ground. Another fellow who was around (and gave me a full can of fix-a-flat for free) helped us lift the bike into the trailer, where the friendly ATV-owning, Church of Latter-Day Saints worshipping man—and his cool, wine-loving, frosted blond chill mama—whipped out some tie downs so we could tie my bitch down. Bam! We hit the road.
>
> They wouldn't accept a dime for gas or the inconvenience, even after driving me to *two* bike shops. The first shop wouldn't repair a tire, and the second said they would—but ended up not doing so because the tire was beyond hope.
>
> But back to the kind Mormon couple—they were cool and intelligent, with a smart, well-educated daughter. I made sure not to reveal my agnosticism, for fear of tension, or me being cast out of the vehicle. We didn't exchange info and that was okay. It was a beautiful thing and that was the end of that.

Meanwhile, Michael and I carried on to find gas at the highway leading south to Interstate 15. By then the temperature was 100 degrees, and with the heat back in the Southwest, I would have to start planning around that factor.

It seems to me that for some reason we *always* have a good show in Vegas, and that MGM Grand Arena must be the best-run venue in America. (Because who knows how to put on shows better than Vegas?)

Good place for a journal note summing up the musical side of things:

Last run of shows so tight and powerful, it seemed to me. Each leg different (second distinguished mostly by *pain*). So confident now in *knowing* the songs inside out that can concentrate more on power, groove, and even refining new details.

"Jake" ["Jacob's Ladder"] a good example of that.

In this run trouble with end of "Monkey Business"—always a small miracle when it *does* work. Starts going awry, and again, blame myself. "Fixed" it one night when I heard it out of sync—added a beat.

Didn't work the next night.

Finally mention it before soundcheck one day—find out, "Oh, it's not you—it's Lerxst!"

Finally we got it right.

Grand Canyon
PHOTO BY MICHAEL MOSBACH

The next day would be the "Last Ride," although I honestly wasn't thinking of it that way. I was just looking at the Most Excellent Thing I could do that day, which was to visit Grand Canyon National Park, get a good riding shot in front of the canyon's majesty—then meet up with a crew to do a video shoot with a drone. (As you do.)

That night Papa John parked us in Williams, Arizona, "Gateway to the Grand Canyon," and Michael and I made an early start in that direction. On a summer Sunday, I knew it would be busy, but I hoped we could get in and out before the largest crowds appeared.

As with Crater Lake, I had visited Grand Canyon many times, but never managed to capture a *riding* photo there. Strange, because both attractions were *massive*, and easy enough to photograph statically—just hard to get a passing motorcycle in front of the most evocative views. The scenic overlooks are no good for that, making any ride-by obviously fake, and between them the view is often obscured by trees. And the problem with *big* vistas, like the western national parks featured, is that a single "representative" photograph is that much more difficult to frame. Whether in Glacier, Yosemite, Bryce Canyon, or Death Valley, I try to find that *one* image that captures a sense

Bubba at Desert View
PHOTO BY MICHAEL MOSBACH

of the place—preferably with a motorcycle in it! On this flying visit to Grand Canyon National Park I was determined to set up a shot combining that majestic scenery and a moving motorcycle. For my purposes, that is how art is made.

After we escaped the crowded visitor center (passport stamp in my journal), the scenic roadway along the South Rim was not unbearably busy. With the enormous canyon to our left often blocked by dense conifers, I kept watching for a clear shot from an elevated place on the right—where my designated photographer Michael could stand and spray me (remembering his "spray and pray" approach) as I rode by. I found just the place near the Desert View overlook and pointed Michael to a clearing high on the roadside. After he clambered up there, I did a couple of slow passes. Then we paused at Desert View itself, so I could continue Michael's education in American history and geography—his *favorite* subjects.

The stone Watchtower at Desert View was designed by a wonderful architect named Mary Colter—what great work she did around there, and what a story she is. Rare enough that she was a female architect in the early twentieth century, she is also credited with pioneering the graceful synthesis of Spanish and Native American styles. Even her Lookout Studio on the South Rim is a little masterpiece, and the nearby Hopi House is breathtaking. I stood inside a faux ruin near the Watchtower and explained to a *fascinated* Michael that Desert View is one of the few overlooks where you can actually see the Colorado River at the bottom of the Canyon. I could tell he was *profoundly* impressed . . .

Desert View Overlook
PHOTO BY MICHAEL MOSBACH

From there we hooked around to the south, then back to Interstate 40. Riding west for a while, we turned off to seek out that day's mystery road. But alas, this one did *not* exist—we were stopped by a barbed-wire gate across the gravel road with a No Trespassing sign. It was one of those desolate places where a landowner has been able to appropriate a formerly public road, I guess. It happens. And you always have to remember that people in the West have guns.

We turned around to head back to pavement and loop around the long way toward Seligman, Arizona (used to think it was Seligman, but no—Seligman), to meet the film crew.

Sebastien worked on our crew controlling the moving trusses in the lightshow and was also a longtime drone pilot. For years I had seen him hovering them around empty arenas during soundchecks. A while back I chanced to view an online clip shot by a drone above Burning Man, the breathtaking footage set to electronic dance music. That inspired me to want to capture motorcycling that way, and early in the tour I talked to Sebastien about the idea. I thought the spacious landscapes of northwestern Arizona would be ideal, and we arranged to meet on July 26, a day off between shows in Vegas and Phoenix.

My first idea for a backdrop for the drone shoot had been an area west of Prescott, Arizona, where I remembered a remote paved two-lane through saguaro cactus desert, in an area fetchingly named the Vulture Mountains. However, the forecast was for 105 degrees around there—too hot for the drone, said Sebastien.

I was glad to hear that, for that kind of heat is too hot for a motorcyclist, too—though we have often borne it. I looked a little farther north, to a higher elevation—Arizona's well-preserved stretch of Old Route 66, at around 5,000 feet, and a forecast "only" in the nineties.

The previous day I had looked at the map of the region and chose Seligman as a rendezvous point. There Michael and I could meet up with Sebastien and his wife, Cynthia, and Miller, our documentarian, in a rented SUV driven by Kevin.

I described to Sebastien what I hoped to capture—some long, high aerial shots of the two of us riding, on both pavement and gravel. I had noted a junction like that a little way back, where a gravel road crossed Old 66 on the way into Seligman, but thought we might find something better farther west. Kevin and company set off in their big SUV to scout, while I sent Michael inside the Roadkill Café ("You Kill It We Grill It") for the strawberry milkshake I suddenly desperately needed. Perhaps because it was over 90 degrees, and the day had already been long and hard. I wanted to be both energized and patient for this upcoming shoot. No sense compromising its possibilities for the lack of energy or patience.

Michael and I followed the SUV about fifteen miles west of Seligman into the open country of grasses, sage, and scattered mesquite. They parked at the junction of a good long stretch of 66's paved two-lane running east and west and a gravel lane heading south toward the railroad tracks. (Burlington Northern and Santa Fe these days, formerly the more musical Atchison, Topeka, and Santa Fe.) When Sebastien got the drone airborne, Michael and I did a few "formation" rides in each direction on the gravel, with long dust trails behind us, then on 66. Sebastien piloted the drone and controlled the camera, while Miller shot footage of the entire activity, and Cynthia took stills.

By the next day Miller had put together a surprisingly impressive edit of the "making of" footage, tastefully shown over the music of the hauntingly original Icelandic band Sigur Rós. After a day off to work on his drone footage, Sebastien presented us with a cut of the aerial shots, and it was *magnificent*. At the time of planning the shoot I didn't know what I would use the film for, but felt it was worth making that *opportunity*, at least. Later I thought it would make the basis for a great "book trailer," with music from our own "catalog" and me reading from the eventual book. Such a blend of images, sound textures, and words can create powerful alchemy.

Bringing the drone in at the end, Sebastien didn't want to try landing on the highway, for fear of traffic. He also worried that the long grass at the roadside would tip over the delicate drone. So Kevin stepped up to perform the careful operation of grabbing it from the air. With four spinning rotors coming at him, the catch required much concentration and decisiveness—but ex-military and retired firefighter Kevin was up to the job.

We applauded politely . . .

By late afternoon I decided we would not press on another eighty miles to Prescott—we would stay right there in Seligman, at the Historic Route 66 Motel. Take it easy on ourselves—though we would still log 377 miles that day, in hundred-degree heat, and spend the next two hours working with Sebastien and crew with the drone.

PHOTO BY CYNTHIA LEVESQUE

Kevin Makes the Catch
PHOTO BY MICHAEL MOSBACH

PHOTO BY MICHAEL MOSBACH

And what a perfect location for the tour's last overnight stay—the classic American motel. A line of rooms facing the highway, park in front of your door, sit outside and watch the traffic pass, walk across the road to dinner—no-frills-and-who-needs-'em.

One humble "frill" this traveler does appreciate is when housekeepers take the time to fold the tissues and facecloths a little bit fancy—not some swan origami, but just a spreading fan-fold, say,

Sense a Theme?

or the tidy little point on the toilet paper. It gives a plain room just that touch of "hominess," of care having been taken. That raises a good rule of Roadcraft: Appreciate your housekeeper. Whether that means your mom, your spouse, your roommate, or a hardworking cleaner in a hotel (it has occurred to me that no professions are more familiar with the sordidness of humans than police officers and hotel maids)—even, or especially, if your housekeeper is *yourself*. Appreciate them, reward them. If it's a paid professional cleaning up after you, leave them a nice piece of paper with a dead president—even if it's not folded all fancy.

At that time, after one night in a modest motel, Mr. Lincoln was a generous denomination. Every night after dinner I would hold out my palm and say to Michael, "Gimme fi' dolla!" He would chime in, "Make you holla," and hand it over.

That first ride to Tulsa three months before had started with Old 66 in California, then a long stretch of Interstate 40 through Arizona and New Mexico. "I-40 to R40," I called it then. But the legendary road that really bookended the entire tour was Route 66—which ends, happily enough, not far from my home. Along the way we encountered it again in Oklahoma, Missouri, and Illinois—at its other end, Chicago.

In late afternoon I sat on a white plastic chair in front of my room with the usual journal, camera, and plastic cup of The Macallan on ice. I looked out past our parked motorcycles (on their sidestands because gravel) at the occasional traffic on Route 66, behind to the Santa Fe railroad and long freight trains at intervals, and behind that to Interstate 40 and its whining semis. The story of the modern Southwest right there, really.

The overloaded old van and trailer on the highway behind the motorcycles reminded me of a modern-day version of the Joads in *The Grapes of Wrath*. They fled the Oklahoma Dust Bowl with all the possessions they could carry on their old car and struggled west on this same Mother Road in the 1930s. The train reminded me of the great Bob Dylan title, "It Takes a Lot to Laugh, It Takes a Train to Cry."

That association may have been a subconscious *cri de coeur* from my feet. They didn't bother me so much on the bike, but as soon as I pulled off my boots and socks they started to itch madly, unbearably, setting my nerves on edge. A dermatologist once asked me which was worse, pain or itching. I said pain, but she shook her head, "No—people will scratch an itch until it *bleeds*, right? They'd rather have the pain than the itch." So I was sitting there scrubbing my feet into the gravel, replacing the itching with pain, when I saw a bicyclist come to a stop at the roadside.

Migrants on the Mother Road, Train Behind

During our video shoot Michael and I had noticed him, a touring cyclist with panniers front and rear, grinding his solitary way across the high desert on the shoulder of 66. While making our motorcycle maneuvers for the drone, slow runs in each direction and a lot of turning around (Michael kept pulling up too early for the long shots I wanted, and I had to shout a line from some forgotten movie, "*Nobody calls 'cut' on my set!*"), we saw the hunched-over rider a few times. Having done a lot of long-distance bicycling myself, I knew what it felt like.

After we had checked into the motel I mentioned that cyclist to Michael, who has traveled pretty widely in Southeast Asia. He thought the little flag behind the guy's saddle was South Korean. In the slow desert twilight we saw the rider pull up in front of the motel and put his feet down. Michael went over to talk to him and on a whim I called out, "Get him a room!"

It looked like he carried camping gear, but I thought he would surely appreciate a shower and a bed—and with room prices at about $65, it was not a big gesture.

Having dined at the Roadkill Café on an earlier visit, we decided to

Corfu 1991–Munich to Istanbul
PHOTO BY GAY BURGIEL

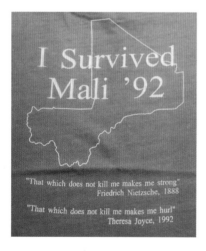

I Survived
Mali '92

"That which does not kill me makes me strong"
Friedrich Nietzsche, 1888

"That which does not kill me makes me hurl"
Theresa Joyce, 1992

Souvenir of Mali, Senegal,
The Gambia, 1992
PHOTO BY HERB MASTERS

try Lilo's across the road (no judgment—just for a change) and invited our new friend to join us. His name was Mine, "Me-neh," for Minekazu Ito (he presented us with his card). He was a twenty-nine-year-old high-school teacher from Nagoya (whose city flag Michael had mistaken for the South Korean), bicycling from Los Angeles to New York.

Despite telling us he had studied English (yes, he pronounced it "Ingrish") at a school in Japan for three months, he struggled. I was surprised to learn that Michael spoke a fair amount of Japanese—at least enough to amaze Mine. (He had lived there for about two years back in his modeling days—hard to imagine now, as I love to remind him. As he reaches his mid-forties, sometimes when we're having one of our half-serious, half-mock arguments, I will look into his eyes—or *at* them, as if at the crow's feet—and sneer, "You need to get some *work* done." Crushes him deliciously.)

Over the years Michael had been back to Japan frequently enough to retain a smattering of vocabulary—though perhaps not at the most *refined* level. That was evident one time when Mine giggled at something Michael said, and choked out, "Dirty word."

We helped Mine order his meal—beer, potato soup, and a big

FAR AND WIDE

T-bone steak. I asked him about his route and advised him to make a few detours, if he could—to see places like Grand Canyon and Monument Valley. I told him Williams wasn't too much farther east, and there he could park his bike for a day and take the train up to Grand Canyon. "On a long ride, a day off the bike can do you a lot of good. And you probably need to do laundry, right?"

Mine laughed at that traveler's reality, then shook his head and said, "I can't believe you two are being *nice* to me." He said he had not expected that from "Americans." An older friend of Mine's from Nagoya had done the bicycle crossing a few years ago, which inspired Mine's journey, and perhaps the friend had warned him of unpleasant people.

Too bad—and glad we could redress that a little bit.

All the while I had been introduced to Mine only as "Bubba," and when he asked us what we did, I told him we traveled around writing and photographing motorcycle stories. (True enough!)

After dinner, outside the restaurant—dark now, with colorful neon lighting up the few businesses along Old 66 in Seligman—Mine held up his camera toward me and said, "Photograph of Bubba?" I smiled and posed for him: it will be a little sweeter twist if Mine discovers the background to the story of our encounter.

And he will also learn that he is the only stranger whose camera I have willingly posed for—in about forty years!

We rode out at 6:00 the next morning—once again "rise and ride" into a hot day, get in some distance in the cooler hours, and stop for breakfast later. With the previous day's mileage shortened by staying in Seligman rather than Prescott, we were farther from Phoenix now and would have to make up that distance. So once again we had over 300 miles to cover on a show day. We started with "a hundred miles before breakfast," which I think always gives a good start to a long day, and stopped near Prescott.

Sunrise 66
PHOTO BY MICHAEL MOSBACH

From there we headed east on little backroads into the high pine forests around Strawberry and Payson. Amid the conifers of the Tonto National Forest and an elevation around 5,000 feet, we could be cool and comfortable for a while. Many people think of Arizona and picture cactus desert, but the state has a wide variety of landscapes and winding roads. As we traveled south and descended, the vegetation thinned to scattered cactus and desert scrub over raw peaks and ridges of the Superstition Mountains. Appearing out of that backdrop, the shining blue expanse of Theodore Roosevelt Lake opened before us like a mirage. At about 2,000 feet now, the temperature rose into the nineties.

Apache Trail, Arizona

The dam that forms that lake on the Salt River was built a hundred years ago for irrigation, flood control, and hydroelectric power. It was actually dedicated by its namesake in 1911—a year before Arizona achieved statehood. At that time traffic crossed on top of the dam, but it became too narrow for modern vehicles to pass in both directions. A stunning bridge was completed in 1990, said to be one of the most beautiful in the country, its frame a simple, perfect arch cradling the horizontal roadway.

Best of all, Theodore Roosevelt Dam is where we joined one of our all-time favorite roads, the Apache Trail. After riding it four or five times now, I consider it one of the top motorcycling roads in the West—at least for our kind of riding.

The trail was originally a stagecoach route that followed a Native American footpath, then was further developed for the construction of the smaller dams downriver. From the Roosevelt Dam, the Apache Trail begins with twenty-two miles of unpaved, sometimes treacherous gravel. That part attracts little traffic, mainly recreational boaters getting to marinas on the lakes. The narrow gravel track winds up and down along the steep banks among saguaro cactus, prickly pear, and mesquite. The temperature was edging up to 100 by then, as it nearly always did when we got close to Phoenix.

After the twenty-two miles of dirt, you get twenty-two miles of twisty pavement. Yeehaw! That's the combination that makes the Apache Trail unique, and so perfect for riders like us. That paved section also offered an important photo opportunity for some more "technical" shots. We had a lot of scenic photographs (over 400 of my "three star" picks just from that last run), but not a lot of dynamic *riding* photographs. They take a whole different approach to set up and capture, and I made that the day's "focus," so to speak. That paved stretch of the Apache Trail was ideal, because its tight turns could be taken at dramatic lean angles but relatively sane speeds.

Phoenix is always hot—110 degrees that day—and its traffic is dense, often feeling like the "anti-destination league." So it was a relief to pull into the arena loading area and up to the bus, then haul my gear inside to its air-conditioning and change out of my heavy riding clothes.

Apache Trail, Arizona
PHOTO BY MICHAEL MOSBACH

Soundcheck, Phoenix
(Gump behind)

This time before I took off my boots and socks I asked Papa John to please find me a basin and some ice. Then I sat in the front lounge and kept my bare feet in that ice as long as I could stand, pulled them up to "thaw" for a minute, then dunked them back in. It helped—at least so I didn't feel an almost irresistible desire to go at them with a wire brush.

Soundcheck at 5, dinner at 6, warm-up at 7 for a 7:30 start. (That's a fine rhythmic line to say out loud.) Everybody knew we were "counting down" now, and everything felt just a little more urgent and heartfelt that night—for the band and the audience, I know, and probably for the rest of the Guys at Work, too.

After Phoenix we would have a couple of days off before the final two shows in the Los Angeles area. For me, that would mean heading home— the true Final Ride. I had hoped to have Papa John park us on the far side of the Angeles Crest Highway, then take that gorgeous route over the San Gabriel Mountains toward home. Originally built as a fire access road, the Angeles Crest climbs to elevations of 7,000 feet and more. Thus it is subject to avalanches and landslides—closed for years sometimes. As it was that summer. Fortunately I had mentioned my intentions to Greg when he was with us, and later he let us know that the Angeles Crest was closed.

Parking the bus elsewhere and riding through Los Angeles in morning traffic was not appealing, so I decided to do as I always did—go *around* it. If Papa John parked us in Pasadena, I could avoid traffic by riding west to Topanga Canyon, then over the Santa Monica Mountains to the ocean, and home on the Pacific Coast Highway. I would get there exhausted, in pain ("da feets!"), and knowing I still had two shows and three parties to get through, but at least the bike was safely parked—and me with it.

After 17,000 miles, I had the same feeling I have expressed before:

"When I am riding my motorcycle I am glad to be alive. When I stop riding my motorcycle I am glad to be alive."

A well-defined ending to the unspoken fears is always a great sense of *relief*, elevated this time by the happiness of being parked in my own garage. The hardships and dangers of the road were behind me—but there were still more challenges ahead before this journey was done.

Apache Trail
PHOTO BY MICHAEL MOSBACH

19

BUBBA CROSSES THE BACKLINE MERIDIAN

Before the next, and second-to-last, show at Irvine Meadows Amphitheater, down in Orange County, we had a rare two days off. But they too were pretty full.

The first night we held an end-of-tour party for the crew at an oceanfront hotel in Manhattan Beach. (Mention should be made of someone who was *very* busy through this time—our publicist Meghan Symsyk, who had to organize all this stuff.)

On past tours we have held golf parties (boo) and bowling parties (yay!), but for this one we thought it would be nicest just to have a "hang." A beautiful setting with plenty of food, plenty of drinks, and plenty of laughs—like when groups of us mugged together for the photo booth.

As usual at parties, all the fun people gathered on the smoking balcony. We looked out to the twilit ocean behind the pier, and down at one of the white trucks from our fleet—looking *very* out of place on the beachfront avenue.

Juli, a driver for several tours, along with her husband, Steve, parked her tractor there (not valet, we guessed) because she hadn't wanted to leave her dog alone in a motel room. The advantage of a sleeper cab is that she wouldn't need to *drive*, though the local authorities might not smile on a huge white semi parking there overnight.

The second night off we were invited to a dinner at the residence of the Canadian Consul General, James Villeneuve, and his family, in a genteel older part of Los Angeles called Hancock Park. Some of our local friends had been invited as well, including Jack Black and Matt Stone—a good friend to me since the dark days of *Ghost Rider*, he appeared for and with us at the Governor General's Awards a couple of years ago, plus he and partner Trey Parker created the animated opening to "Tom Sawyer" with the *South Park* characters as "L'il Rush." I was pleased to see the popular Canadian broadcaster George "Strombo" Stroumboulopoulos, for he is a fellow BMW GS rider. Strombo spends his off-season in Venice, California, and he and I have been trying to get together for a motorcycle ride. It would be fun to ride and talk together without cameras and microphones.

Amid lighted trees and gardens, elegantly dressed tables were placed on the lawn. Bartenders offered wine and other drinks, and a fine buffet dinner was served. It was an informal night of conversation and goodwill, and Mr. Villeneuve gave only a *short* speech. He presented us with a certificate from the mayor of Los Angeles, Eric Garcetti.

> On the occasion of the final show of their 40th anniversary tour, the City of Los Angeles welcomes Rush and celebrates their four decades of success and status as icons of rock 'n' roll.
>
> Transforming rock 'n' roll into an expression of art, Rush has captured the imaginations of fans around the world. From their beginnings in Toronto, Canada, to their world

tours, including 30 shows in Los Angeles, Rush has attracted legions of admirers.

Over the course of their career, Rush has achieved countless accolades, including 24 Gold, 14 Platinum, and 3 multi-Platinum albums, enshrinement in the Rock & Roll Hall of Fame, and—finally—the cover of *Rolling Stone*.

The City of Los Angeles duly recognizes Geddy Lee, Alex Lifeson, and Neil Peart for their extraordinary charitable contributions to many causes close to their hearts. These gifts continue to improve the lives of people in the United States, Canada, and around the world.

As Mayor of the City of Los Angeles, I am pleased to congratulate Rush on their 40-year artistic legacy and thank them for their contributions to the lives of others and to the vibrant musical culture of Los Angeles.

That night was also Geddy's sixty-second birthday (still almost a whole year younger than me!), which we also celebrate as the official anniversary of when I joined the band in 1974, so it was nice to share it with our wives and friends.

And a Mountie.

Avoiding any *hint* of puerility about a young woman in a Mountie uniform, let's just say her name is Nancy Howell, and she is from

PHOTO BY DAN PASQUINI

Newfoundland—which always earns extra points. Probably before she was born, we began a tour in St. John's in 1987, with pre-production rehearsals and the first show. I was able to explore around the St. John's area pretty widely by bicycle, and in the years since I have toured there twice by motorcycle, all around the island ("*Fogo, Twillingate, Moreton's Harbour, all around the circle*," goes the Newfoundlander anthem) and across to Labrador. Fabulous place, wonderful people—and so many great *writers*!

The next night's show at Irvine was outdoors, one of only

a handful of amphitheaters on this tour. One reason was because the R40 production used a front screen called an Austrian curtain. It was lowered before the show and during intermission at the front of the stage, and films were projected on it. Outdoors, it would be like a giant mainsail, forty feet high and over sixty feet wide, and the worry was that a sudden gust of wind might send it billowing over the audience and hurt somebody. Instead, the same films were projected onto the rear screen, but it wasn't the same—wasn't "ideal."

Performing outdoors had compensations, though, at least for me. It was never completely dark when we hit the stage, which likewise diminished the "drama,"

Bubba Deep Inside

but I kind of liked it. For a while I could see more of the audience, and that was entertaining. While I'm performing I always feel like *I* am the audience—watching them.

When I'm not too busy, that is . . .

This photo catches my eye because I am playing traditional grip (left stick "cradled," as opposed to self-explanatory matched grip), which I use in only a few brief parts of the show. Intros like "The Camera Eye" and "Jacob's Ladder" require more delicate sticking than is displayed here, so I must be playing the rudimental snare part of my solo—one of my favorite, more "interior" passages. Also, for me, the most time-honored—patterns and techniques I learned before I even had drums, practicing on a pad or a pillow. (And perfected while tapping quietly and waiting for Aerosmith to finish their soundchecks!)

After the Irvine show I did my usual "runner," though not to the bus, but to my own Aston Martin Vanquish. I had asked Papa John to bring the bus to the venue that afternoon so I could do my unpacking —considerable, after three months of basically living aboard—then said goodbye and offered sincere thanks for all his help.

(One funny memory we carried away to share: in Salt Lake City I told Papa John that before the next show, in Calgary, I would want to do an oil change. I asked him to talk to Dave about how to "set up" for it, and he called Dave with a worried tone and said, "I don't know if I'm qualified to change the oil on a BMW motorcycle." He thought I expected *him* to do it! Dave had a good laugh, then told Papa John he only had to put out a couple of rubber mats for me to lie on as I worked, and the drain pan for the old oil—I would take care of the rest.)

At the car I had a dry T-shirt ready to change into, and a towel on the seat, and was quickly ready to go. As I followed behind the police escort and the SUV carrying the other Guys at Work, my body heat steamed up the windows. I cracked them open and turned on the demister. (I just figured out why the English call it that, while we Canadians call it the defroster. Icechuckers!)

Los Angeles Forum
PHOTO BY PAUL HEBERT

Which brings us right back to where we began—when we began as we meant to go on. (And did we ever!)

The Los Angeles Forum, August 1, 2015, the final show of the tour and, as far as this Bubba can tell, the final show of our career.

(When we discussed with manager Ray where to end the tour, we considered Toronto, where the band started; Cleveland, where a "buzz" first happened for Rush in the U.S. [thank you Donna Halper]; and even Pittsburgh, where we had played our first show together in August 1974. Unfortunately, none of those cities were possible logistically, so we settled on the historic Los Angeles Forum, where we had played so many times and had such positive memories.)

Revisiting that historic building not only reminded me of our own previous appearances there over many years, but of the many other rock concerts that had made that venue famous, and infamous.

For example, I think of the stories and legends about the six-night stand Led Zeppelin did there in 1977. One night the Beach Boys' drummer Dennis Wilson and the Who's Keith Moon were hanging with John Bonham, there and later at the Hyatt House ("Riot House") on Sunset Boulevard. During the show Keith came onstage during Bonzo's famously long solo in "Moby-Dick" and banged away drunkenly on the big timpani. The after-show tales from that time and place might stand as the height of rock decadence, sex and drugs and Bonzo riding a Harley down the hotel hallway. But the "height of rock decadence" was actually more like rock bottom.

One hates to dwell too much on tragedy, but alas, it is always there. In fact, it could be said that the triumph of surviving into my own seventh decade is exactly measured by the piling up of tragedy along the way. "The cost of living is heartbreak" sounds true, and was so in different ways for those three drummers, who all died young. Their fates stand as cautionary tales for anyone—but especially for one who shared the profession and the lifestyle (if not to such extremes), and survived only because of a lucky genetic Gift of will. When no one else in the world is saying "no" to you, you need the strength and discipline to say it to yourself.

Keith Moon, the hero of my teenage years, died in London in 1978, at age thirty-two, from an overdose of anti-alcoholism drugs. By that time he was already more or less broken, physically and psychologically, after years of massive substance abuse.

Dennis Wilson was the only member of the Beach Boys who actually surfed and raced sports cars. In those ways and more, he was his brother Brian's muse—though Dennis seldom played drums on their records (Hal Blaine did), which must have rankled deep inside. Other things certainly burned at him, perhaps not least his abusive father, and his life was a downward spiral of character issues and helpless overindulgence.

In December 1983, at age thirty-nine, broke and broken, he had been drinking hard and diving into a California marina to retrieve objects he had years ago thrown off his sailing yacht, *Harmony*—long lost to creditors. One time he didn't come back up.

Dennis Wilson came to fascinate me as a *character* rather than a drummer, though I had been galvanized (and probably inspired) by his big-screen appearance on *The T.A.M.I. Show* back in 1964. Shaking his "bushy, bushy blond hairdo" and making faces as he played, Dennis certainly inspired a young Keith Moon. Both of their lives have been documented in worthy biographies, and they make sad reading. From what one can sense about Dennis Wilson and Keith Moon, and from hearing others speak about them, you see similar psychological patterns. Both of them were exceedingly lovable and well loved, yet damned by the sense of unworthiness that scarred them. Trying too hard to earn it, they became exasperating, then unbearable, then gone. Ultimately they both seemed to fit that great Saul Bellow title *More Die of Heartbreak*.

John Bonham, pioneer of the "baseball bats and diving boots" style—heavy but with sublime groove—influenced pretty well every rock drummer of my generation. That will likely be true as long as there is such a thing as rock drumming. However, like numerous other "rock casualties" and many, many unfortunate non-celebrities,

My Bonsai Dennis
(alas, he *too* has died!
Didn't survive the move
back home after five months
at friend Craiggie's house in
Pasadena during the tour)

Strumming for Lerxst
PHOTO BY CRAIG M. RENWICK

he just overdid it one night—as who has not?—and was unlucky. Also just thirty-two years old, after a night of heavy drinking at Jimmy Page's house in September 1980, his body tried to eject an overdose of vodka. He choked on it and died.

But enough tragedy—that time and place just called up a few sad songs, that's all.

"Now let us be of good cheer, for lo, the end is always near!"

(Wasn't sure if I made that up—it sounds like the King James Bible or Shakespeare—but apparently I did. Fine—it's good advice.)

Near the end of that show, I was inspired to do something I had only done four times before—the first time in Santiago, Chile (see "The Power of Magical Thinking" in *Far and Near*), and since then in Toronto, Montreal, and London. Those last three were all "hometowns" of a sort, and now for the past fifteen years Los Angeles was, too. Not to mention a certain . . . historical significance . . . to the time and place. I wanted to photograph that audience.

Yes, here Bubba is playing guitar with drumsticks. Drums, orchestra chimes, violin, guitar—that night I was a multi-instrumentalist, as well as a photographer. The first shot I took, of the entire Forum audience, appears on the dedication page. The timing of that impromptu "photo op" was a significant moment in the show for me throughout the tour.

One day during pre-tour rehearsals we were goofing around, riffing on our *oldest* songs—the truly "prehistoric" ones from before I joined, that were never recorded. Just for fun we decided to end the night with a few bars of one called "Garden Road." It had been in the band's repertoire before I joined, and we had played it on the first tour, but it didn't make the cut for *Fly by Night*. That snippet would also be a humorous nod to the reverse chronology of the show that took us back to the first album—now we went back even *farther*.

Trouble was, after the furious burnout ending of "Working Man," the thing always felt *done* to me. I would get up and walk away—only to sense a certain "expectancy," and turn around to see the other two waiting and laughing. Thinking, "Oops," I would jump back up on the riser and count in the finale.

That happened a couple of times in rehearsals, and again in one of the early shows. The other guys were amused by that lapse (Alex said, "I *love* when you do that!"), so I was inspired to make it into a "thing."

Thinking, Checking Nails
PHOTOS BY JOHN ARROWSMITH

Smoking, Hiding
PHOTOS BY JOHN ARROWSMITH

Each night in that spot I would do a little act—each time something different. Pretend to file and polish my nails, read a book, thumb out a text (while holding up a hand to the other guys with a "just a sec" expression), take a nap on my folded hands, talk on an imaginary phone, have a smoke, or jump down to hide behind the subwoofer behind me.

In Vancouver I saw a magazine in my hotel room with a cover photo of Canadian musician Buffy St. Marie, and it gave me a new idea for the bit. Because (oh, this takes some explaining) one time back in the '70s the three of us had been sitting around somewhere, and Alex launched into a tale.

"That reminds me of when I was living with Buffy St. Marie in Kapuskasing . . ."

It was said in apparent seriousness, as if he believed it himself. And it's not like we were in some psychedelic state—at most having shared a little of the ceremonial herb, nothing that should cause utter *hallucinations*. Geddy and I just looked at him, truly puzzled. We were sure Alex didn't even *know* Buffy St. Marie, and had never been to Kapuskasing.

Then all three of us started laughing—two of us perhaps a little nervously. From time to time over the years, naturally, Buffy St. Marie and Kapuskasing would be mentioned, and laughed about.

(What a store of shared jokes we have built up over the decades. We can simply quote one line from a Mel Brooks, Steve Martin, or David Lynch movie, an episode of *SCTV*, or a forty-year-old out-of-mind utterance, and convey volumes. The previous November, when the three of us gathered in Toronto for drinks and dinner, and to discuss this tour, within five minutes Geddy said, "It's so nice to be around people who get my jokes!")

That afternoon in Vancouver I asked dear Lydia in the production office if she could make that cover photo into a mask for me, and she did, with cardboard and a stick. At that moment in the show I held it up in front of my face, and somehow it was even funnier knowing that only the three of us in all the world would get that joke.

At the Forum show, during my "improv moment," after photographing the audience, I turned my camera toward Alex and then Geddy. Playing up the "act," and the moment, I mimed that I was waiting for nice poses and big smiles. They did not disappoint—Alex waving and smiling with his foot on the wah-wah ready for "Garden Road," Geddy strolling over, fingers ready on the frets, to give me a big wave for the camera.

Naturally the audience loved all this, and roared their delight all the while.

And wonderful that it happened only that once, on that night.

Even then, I had one more little surprise in mind—if I had the nerve to carry it out.

In forty-one years I had never ventured onto the stage in front of my drums. The simplest way to explain that reluctance is a feeling that it was not my "territory." Before soundcheck I wandered freely around the front of the riser, visiting with the Guys at Work, including various crew members. But during the show I lived and worked behind the drums and behind the cymbals. At the end I stood up behind my throne (not stool!) and waved my thanks and goodnights from there. I thought of the line across the stage beside my riser, called the "backline"—where the amps (of whatever description that tour, from clothes dryers to automats to chicken rotisseries to R40's constantly devolving mountains of prop amps) were placed—as the border, the Backline Meridian, which I did not cross.

Early in the tour, when we were planning the DVD shoot for Toronto, our directors of staging and filming Dale and Allan had asked if I would go out front and take a bow with

PHOTO BY CRAIG M. RENWICK

Surprise!
PHOTO BY CRAIG M. RENWICK

the guys. They wanted me to do it to provide "continuity" with the after-show film we had shot before the tour, which showed the three of us walking offstage together.

I shook my head and gave a dramatic shudder, "No, no—I couldn't do that. Impossible."

Before the Forum show Allan asked again if I would consider doing it, for the same reason. Once again I shook my head and said no. "Couldn't possibly."

Yet in my own heart and mind, I *did* want to do it—breach that Backline Meridian this one time. Not for Allan's and Dale's reasons, but for my own—it would be a beautiful thing to do. If I didn't mention it to anyone, then I could try to "let it happen" when the very ending came—see if I felt like it, if it seemed right, if I was *brave* enough.

I told myself, like Lady Macbeth, "But screw your courage to the sticking-place."

Whatever that meant, exactly, I would try to be brave and cross that line. But no commitment, to myself or others.

After the final beat and stick-toss of "Garden Road," I put my sticks down on the right floor tom one last time, jumped down, and ran out behind Alex. I tapped him on the shoulder and waved him over to stage left, then ran across to Geddy and tapped his shoulder. He stopped talking to the audience and looked around briefly, eyes wide. He turned back to the mic and said, "Well—this is a surprise!"

Not least to *me*—but now I am glad I found out where the sticking-place was, or found the courage, or whatever.

It was just the right thing to do—the perfect closing statement.

Love and gratitude and respect and pride and good vibrations. That's what it's all about.

All the journeys
Of this great adventure
It didn't always feel that way
I wouldn't trade them
Because I made them
The best I could
And that's enough to say

——

"Headlong Flight," 2012

PHOTO BY JOHN ARROWSMITH

THE GARDEN

The other day I was looking up something in the lyrics for *Clockwork Angels*. (I can happily say that if those are the last lyrics I ever write, I remain modestly but proudly content.)

For the first time in a few years, I noticed the little prose introductions I wrote for each song, and was struck by the one that introduced "The Garden," in the voice of our hero, Owen Hardy.

Long ago I read a story from another timeline about a character named Candide. He also survived a harrowing series of misadventures and tragedies, then settled on a farm near Constantinople. Listening to a philosophical rant, Candide replied, "That is all very well, but now we must tend our garden."

I have now arrived at that point in my own story. There is a metaphorical garden in the acts and attitudes of a person's life, and the treasures of that garden are love and respect. I have come to realize that the gathering of love and respect—from others and for myself—has been the real quest of my life.

"Now we must tend our garden."

The treasure of a life is a measure of love and respect
The way you live, the gifts that you give
In the fullness of time
It's the only return that you expect